TEACHING YEAR THREE

Edited by Lucy Hall

Published by Scholastic Ltd.
Villiers House
Clarendon Avenue
Leamington Spa
Warwickshire CV32 5PR
Text © 1999 Nick Phillips; David Waugh; Peter Clarke; Terry Jennings; Paul Noble;
Margaret Mackintosh; Dorothy Tipton; Gillian Robinson; Pauline Boorman; Richard Ager;
Lynn Newton; Douglas Newton; Geoffrey Teece
© 1999 Scholastic Ltd.
34567890   12345678

Authors
Nick Phillips, David Waugh, Peter Clarke, Terry Jennings, Paul Noble,
Margaret Mackintosh, Dorothy Tipton, Gillian Robinson, Pauline Boorman, Richard Ager,
Lynn Newton, Douglas Newton, Geoffrey Teece

Series Editor
Lucy Hall

Editor
Helen Skelton

Series Designer
Lynne Joesbury

Designer
Sarah Rock

Illustrations
Maggie Downer

Cover photograph
Fiona Pragoff

Designed using Adobe Pagemaker

British Library Cataloguing-in-Publication Data
A catalogue record for this book is available from the British Library

ISBN 0 590 53821 7

The publishers acknowledge and thank the following for the use of copyright material:
National Curriculum 2000 © The Queen's Printer and Controller of HMSO. Reproduced under the terms of HMSO Guidance Note 8. © Qualifications and Curriculum Authority. Reproduced under the terms of Guidance Note 8. National Literacy and Numeracy Documents © Crown Copyright. Reproduced under the terms of HMSO Guidance Note 8. Early Learning Goals © Qualifications and Curriculum Authority.

Contents

4 **Preface**

5 **Your Class** Nick Phillips

16 **Curriculum and Classroom Planning** Nick Phillips

23 **English** David Waugh

41 **Mathematics** Peter Clarke

72 **Science** Terry Jennings

91 **History** Paul Noble

99 **Geography** Margaret Mackintosh

108 **Music** Dorothy Tipton

118 **Art and Design** Gillian Robinson

129 **Physical Education** Pauline Boorman

141 **Information and Communication Technology** Richard Ager

145 **Design and Technology** Lynn and Douglas Newton

153 **Religious Education** Geoffrey Teece

Preface

Primary school teachers don't say, as secondary teachers would, 'I teach history'. They say 'I teach year 4s' or 'I teach a reception class'. Why, then, have all the books for primary teachers been wholly subject-orientated? It seems that primary teachers are supposed to buy about 13 different books and read through them all to extract the relevant bits.

It was about 20 years ago that the thought occurred to me that it would make teachers' lives much easier if all the information about teaching their year group was provided in *one* book. Since then I have been waiting for someone to do it. But no-one did. So, finally, fourteen different authors, Scholastic and I have put together the seven *Primary Teacher Yearbooks.*

I should like to thank all the authors. They faced a difficult task in tailoring their writing to a common format and structuring their guidance, about what to teach and what to expect from children, so that it correlated with the seven different stages of the primary school. They have all been extremely patient.

Particular thanks are due to Paul Noble, who not only wrote 13 chapters in the series, but was also deeply involved in the development of the project from the very beginning. His practical, knowledgeable advice and cheerful imperturbability kept the whole project stuck together.

We all hope that you will find your Yearbook useful and that it meets your needs – whichever class you teach.

Lucy Hall, Series Editor

Your Class

Getting started

Planning your classroom

There are many ways to organize a classroom – the essential point is that it *should* be organized and not left to chance. As a teacher of Year 3 children, you will need to be sensitive to their needs in the transition from being an 'infant' to a 'junior'. This will be particularly important during the early part of the school year.

Your classroom should be no less warm and welcoming than a Year 2 one. Just as the children's needs will be changing, so too should the organization of the classroom.
Here is a checklist.

1 Make sure you know what the school expects from you. Check all relevant documentation and discuss your ideas with a senior member of staff.

2 Spend time planning. Consider the space available; list the furniture and equipment. Record your ideas.

3 Draw an outline plan of the room (to scale, ideally); show fixtures, power points, and so on.

4 Photocopy the plan several times – and file the master in a safe place.

On the copies of the plan, develop your ideas until you have a design that you feel comfortable with and that is practical. Consider where the 'gathering' area and class library will be; whether you will need a role-play area; how large any practical area should be and which is the best place for the computer(s).

Make sure that the general teaching space is of a sufficient size and organized appropriately to allow for your Literacy and Numeracy Hour work. Consider:

- how many groups you should have;
- how large these groups might be;
- how they can best be arranged in the room;
- how the children will be organized: friendship groups/mixed ability or ability groups for different activities;
- whether you will have a desk;
- whether the children can see the board.

Much of this will reflect your teaching style and the strategies you intend to employ.

Resources

Organize and store your resources with care. Label the areas, storage trays, racks and cupboards. Only have available the materials and equipment that the children will be using. Put other items away until required. Avoid clutter. Piles of unwanted, unused materials will be confusing for the children, take up valuable space and detract from displays.

Establish a classroom which encourages independence and responsibility. Develop a sense of ownership and pride so that the children feel that it is their space. These are important principles and the foundation for the future.

Display

When planning the layout, consider the purpose of display. Do not rely on fixed wall boards alone. Establish areas in your room by using the backs of cupboards or movable furniture to display children's work or create centres of interest.

Interactive displays are particularly important for Year 3 children. Include helpful captions and information which encourage them to explore further. Many children will be happy to contribute to displays themselves by bringing in items from home.

The key points for display are that written work should be on unlined paper and that work should rarely be displayed unmounted. Care should be used in selecting backing materials. Children's work should be named, and displays titled.

If you are not confident about displaying children's work, plan it on paper before you start. Ask a colleague for advice and do not be afraid to copy ideas from other teachers. Finally, remember that displays should work for children, not children for displays.

The children

Year 3 can be quite a shock for some children. Expectations, routines, the organization and you as their teacher will all be new to them at the same time. If they are moving to a junior school from an infant school, the other children in the class may also be unfamiliar.

Children need security. This will come from you through sound organization, understood routines and a sensitive approach. Establish a positive behaviour charter with the class and a recognized reward and punishment system which they can respect. Talk to the children about what you expect. Explain:

- how the classroom is organized;
- how they will be working;
- why they are sitting where they are;
- where all the resources are stored;
- how class equipment should be used;
- how they should attract your attention when they need help;
- the times when they will be unable to have your attention;
- where finished work should be put.

A thoughtfully planned classroom, appropriate resources, and a structure that is both supportive and challenging should be equally reassuring for both parents and children and help with the transition.

Social and emotional development

General behaviour

Uncertainty and a new environment will affect children of this age in different ways. Your response to any situation will need to take into account how all the changes may be affecting the child as well as whether the behaviour is typical. Once you have established relationships and made assessments of the children, management will be easier. Do seek advice from teachers who have been involved with the children before and discuss any concerns you may have with their parents.

Concentration, motivation and responsibility

Levels of concentration and motivation vary significantly at this age for a variety of reasons. Look carefully at the time available to you during the week and timetable your days to allow for reasonable periods of work but plenty of changes during the day. Consider these points.

- Have at least three periods of physical education each week on different days.
- Include drama on a different day from PE.
- Try to use the morning sessions for your language- and mathematics-based activities when the children's concentration will be better.
- Introduce a quiet period of reading after lunch to encourage the children to settle back into a working mode.
- During any extended periods of work, change around the groups, the activities and your focus.

Keep the children actively involved, with periods of stimulation and opportunities for reflection. It is all about maintaining a balance, planning carefully and using your antennae to control each session.

Year 3 children need to be given responsibilities. Have library monitors, children responsible for the register, messages or helping you set up for an art lesson. Change the jobs around at regular times and do not forget to praise and reward their efforts.

Other responsibilities will include homework matters and remembering appropriate kit for games or swimming lessons. For some topic activities, have the children working in different groups looking at a particular aspect. Nominate a group leader who will be responsible for organizing the group's response and presentation to the rest of the class. Encourage independence with responsibilities, important skills that can be developed in the future.

Friendships

You may find that only a minority of the children know each other when they arrive in your classroom on the first day. Alternatively, if you are teaching in a primary school, firm friendships will already have been established. Both situations will present different challenges for you.

If the children are a new class, it will take time for them to trust each other and develop relationships. You will need to be aware of individuals or groups excluded from the main thrust of the classroom and school life. Again, use those antennae in class and when on duty at playtime. Elements of the school PSHE programme should address many of the issues you will want to explore. Encourage and develop community spirit with a whole-class awareness of the needs of others. When things break down, step in and reason with the children. Involving the 'victim' with the child or group who may have caused concern, can be an effective strategy.

An established class moving up from Year 2 will come with records, a history, and will have made an impression on colleagues. But be careful to judge for yourself rather than relying on pre-conceived ideas. Children can change and will respond to different teachers in different ways. If you have concerns, ask for guidance. Find out what information you can at an early stage. Be aware of 'positive' and 'negative' friendships. Take care where you place children or allow them to sit. You may have to manage the class so that certain children are kept apart for their own benefit and to ensure that other children can learn without unnecessary disturbance.

Children with special needs

Disruptive children

A child may be disruptive for a number of reasons. Try not to be caught out. Make sure you have gathered as much information about the children as possible before you start. This should include reading reports and records and talking to colleagues who have been involved with the class. However, avoid labelling children as disruptive (see previous paragraph) until you have had some experience with them. The special educational needs co-ordinator (SENCO) will have a wealth of information to share with you about any children with statements or any that he/she has been involved with. Use this to your advantage and be prepared.

Having established the ground rules with the class, stick to them. Strategies for responding to inappropriate behaviour need to be sensitive and fair. You may decide to agree a warning system and sanctions where minor misdemeanours result in a loss of privilege or breaktime. More serious incidents will require the involvement of more senior staff, parents or carers and the child. All children should be treated equally but some will be more demanding. When challenged, follow the systems that are in place and are understood by the children and never be afraid to seek advice.

Able children

Very able children will be just as challenging but in a different way. As with all levels of ability, differentiation in planning is the key to ensuring that they are equally involved and that work is appropriate. (This is addressed more fully in the Curriculum Planning chapter.) However, the same principles apply here as in responding to the disruptive pupil. Do your homework. Make sure you have the background information you need and try to develop a relationship that involves the parents. At this stage in the primary school, a little extra homework or follow-up activity will be as reassuring for the parents as it will be beneficial to the child.

Mobile children

Children of travelling or other mobile families have the same entitlement at school as do children of the settled population. Schools have a responsibility to provide for mobile children, however short their stay may be.

Roadside travellers are usually highly mobile and often educationally disadvantaged. The whole process of their introduction to the class needs to be handled with great sensitivity. Your headteacher will have made contact with the proper authorities and support will be available to you and to the children. If you are to have travellers' children in your class:

● make sure you have basic information about them, for example, their names, how old they

are, where they are staying, if there is any friction between their family and the family of any other child in your class;
- be prepared for them; have their place ready, name their tray and books;
- talk to the class before the new child arrives, just as you would about any new pupil;
- liaise closely with the support agencies and ask for help, advice and guidance.

For children of families in the forces, the same principles apply. The school may have a long-standing relationship with any one of the services. If this is the case, it is likely that a number of service children will already be in the school and supportive, effective networks will be established. If so, use them. Establish what the children's needs are and organize their learning to best meet these. Always look at the positive and build on the strengths. Make their time in your class, however short, a happy and worthwhile period.

Children with learning difficulties

Records and general information about any child in your class with learning difficulties should be made available to you before you take over the class. Study the background notes and arrange to meet with the school's SENCO. Make sure you:
- are aware of any children with learning difficulties;
- know exactly what these are;
- have an idea of the level they are working at;
- know what their planned programmes and targets are;
- are aware of all support available;
- know about any involvement with external agencies.

This year will be crucial for these children and it is essential for their future that all support available is utilised for their benefit and that you monitor their progress carefully.

Whatever the child's difficulty:
- plan for his/her learning;
- set achievable targets which are regularly reviewed and assessed;
- liaise closely with the SENCO, outside agencies and the child's parents;
- ensure that the child is, and feels, integrated as a valued member of the class.

Celebrate successes and achievements, however small they may appear compared with some other children. Look for opportunities to promote the child within the class group and be sensitive to needs at stressful times when there are class or school assessments.

Physically disabled children and children with health problems

If you are teaching in a primary school, it is probable that any child in your class with a physical disability or significant health problem will already have a track record with the school. Practices should have been established and you will need to familiarize yourself with these.

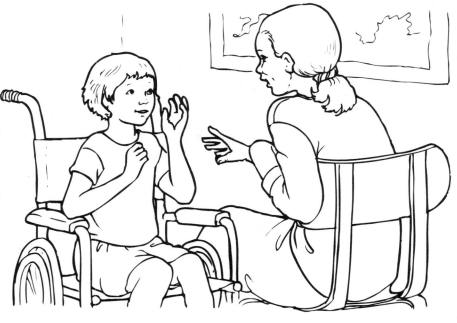

If the child is new to the school, your headteacher will have been involved in making an assessment of the child's needs and the suitability of the premises. There should have been support from the local authority, governors and representatives of all involved with the child and family.

Find out background information about the child. Seek out the parents before they come looking for you. Spend time talking openly to the child about his/her needs and how he/she would like your support. Establish a good relationship and maintain close links with the home. Finally, remember to take appropriate precautions and make special provision for any children in your class with disabilities or health problems when arranging visits or special events.

Home-school

It is common for parents of Year 3 children to be anxious about the transition from Key Stage 1 to 2, especially if this has involved a change in school. You need to be aware of this and reassure them. If possible, meet with the parents before you take over the class. Use the opportunity to introduce yourself, to find out about their children and to start to develop trust between you. Then, at an early stage in the term, invite them in so that you can talk to them about the way you organize and manage their children's learning. They will appreciate knowing:

- how you manage the class;
- what the topics for the year will be;
- how they should be involved with homework;
- about any trips or visits you are planning;
- details of tests that may be taking place during the year;
- how they can help;
- what to do if there is a problem and they need to contact you.

Keep notes of what you say and keep a record of who attends so that you can send an account of the meeting to those parents who did not come.

Be visible and available for parents at regular times before and after school. You will often prevent a minor problem from developing if you can deal with it at an early stage.

Parents of children in Year 3 may not be as evident around school as they were when their children were of infant age. With the transition from Key Stage 1 to 2, good and effective communication between you and the parents will be essential. If you have not had an opportunity to meet with parents before you take over the class, write to them and introduce yourself. They will be interested to know something of your background and special interests, as well as the learning their children will be involved in during the year.

Meetings with parents

When there are evening or after-school meetings with parents, ensure that they are given a reasonable amount of notice and are aware of the appointment time and period of time available to them. Before the meeting, decide where you will talk with parents and where they will wait before seeing you (out of earshot of the previous parents). Decide whether they should look through their child's work before the consultation.

Before the meeting, make time for children to sort through and organize their tray or drawer and any folders. It is surprising what finds its way to the bottom of a drawer!

Whatever the stage of the day or evening, imagine that each appointment is the first of the day. Be well organized. Parents will be unimpressed if you spend part of the consultation rummaging through papers, or telling them what a hard day you have had. Appear fresh, alert and professional, even if you are not feeling at your best. Know the main points you need to make. Keep the discussions crisp and relevant and at the end of the conversation sum up and note anything that has been agreed.

Writing reports

Whatever the arrangements are at your school for compiling reports, be well prepared. Check when the 'hand-in' date for the report is and work backwards, blocking in time so that you have a schedule, for example, three reports a night for four nights a week over a three-week period. Agree a time scale with anyone else who has to write on the reports. Gather all the information you will need on which to base your reports. If possible, persuade a literate friend to check your completed reports. At the least, check your spelling and punctuation very carefully. You don't want to be the subject of one of those 'and his teacher can't even spell' stories.

Reports should provide a summary of significant achievements, some details of areas where children have experienced difficulties, together with an indication of what they should focus on in the future. Comments about their behaviour or attitude should not come as a surprise to parents. Avoid bland statements. Be specific, to ensure that what you say is of value. Remember, other teachers who have your children after you have to live by what you say. Be as accurate as you can with the statements you make. Find something positive to say – even about the child who seems to have no redeeming feature!

Children in care

There may be children in your class who do not live with their natural parents but are cared for in a residential or foster home. School can have a strong and beneficial influence on such children. Your classroom will be one environment where the 'looked-after' child will have largely the same experiences as other children of a similar age.

Your school should be informed by a social worker which adults share parental responsibility, the relevant parts of the care plan, and the child's particular needs that will require your attention in school. Make contact with the carers and, during the course of the child's time in your class, include them as you would any parent. Liaise closely with them on a regular basis and follow up any concerns you may have. Keep yourself informed, seek support and advice from the school's SENCO and be particularly vigilant of the child's well being and any noticeable changes in mood or behaviour. If possible, you or your headteacher should attend the meetings about the child which are held regularly with carers and social workers.

Parents in the classroom

Parents helping in the classroom can be an invaluable resource. They can also cause you sleepless nights and anxious moments!

You may be fortunate enough to inherit a group of skilled and trained parents from the teacher who had your children the previous year. If this is not the case, and especially if the parents are new to the school, you will be responsible for establishing the ground rules and for the training.

Find out about the school's policy on parent helpers and any set procedures. There will probably be police enquiry forms to complete and the school may have a prepared information sheet for volunteers. If you are able to accept offers of help, plan and prepare for them carefully. Establish if parents have any special skills, decide how they can best help and then discuss the details with them. Ensure that they are aware of school procedures for evacuation of the premises, access to the staffroom, school office, and so on. Talk to them about policies of confidentiality and what they should do if they are concerned about a child or if they are approached by another parent. Make sure the children are aware that you have parent helpers coming in and what it is they will be doing.

When the parent helpers arrive, make sure that they feel welcome and that they know what is expected of them. Be reassuring and do not forget to thank them at the end of the session.

Remember that how you treat them will influence their view of how you respond to the children.

Dealing with problem parents

Not all parents will agree with school policies or practices. While major disputes will be directed at the headteacher, you may be the first person parents focus their attention on. Remain outwardly calm and always be polite. Never raise your voice, even if a parent is shouting and screaming! Try to manoeuvre them away from children or other interested parties, and call on a colleague for assistance. Listen to what they have to say. Take notes. (This can have a calming effect and may be helpful later.) Assure them that you are interested and that you are taking what they have to say seriously.

Explain your position or the school's policy but avoid an argument. Advise them of correct procedures for complaints and ask them to put any complaints which they do have into writing.

When faced with aggressive parents, you may not be able to calm them. Seek help immediately; again try to lead them away from children and, if necessary, call the local police for assistance. Individuals can be totally unreasonable. Often their grievance will not be directly school-related, but you can be seen as a soft target. The children's safety and your own is your first responsibility.

Changes at home

Year 3 children will normally be affected by the birth of a new brother or sister and demonstrate this in a number of ways. They can become attention-seeking, revert to infantile ways, be emotional and generally confused. Work with the parents so that they are aware of any changes and can respond accordingly at home. Support the children at school, talk with them, lend them books from the school library which deal with the subject and allow them to work through the process.

Other changes in their home circumstances, such as parents' separation or divorce, a parent in prison or the death of a relative, will have a dramatic effect. A change in character will be the first symptom, for example the outgoing, confident child who becomes withdrawn, the friendly, popular pupil who is suddenly falling out with friends, or the happy child who is moody and difficult in class.

Your relationship with the child is crucial. If you do notice a change in behaviour or attitude, seek the child out at an appropriate time. Gently encourage him/her to talk to you. Let the child know what you have noticed and reassure him/her that you are concerned and want to help. Check whether a letter has come in to the school office. Talk to the headteacher and, if you do have an opportunity to see the parents on the playground, let them know that you are concerned. You may decide that you need to make more formal contact with the parents by telephone or by writing to them, inviting them to come and see you.

The important point is to establish what the problem is so that you can guide and support the child and modify your response accordingly.

Health education
Substance abuse

Regrettably, substance abuse is a growing problem in a number of schools. Teachers must be aware of this and your local health authority staff or advisory service should have raised the issue. Year 3 children are vulnerable to substance abuse. They can be easily influenced by peer group pressure and by older children in their neighbourhood. You need to know what the symptoms of substance abuse are. Seek out background literature, talk to the school nurse and look for helpful INSET courses.

If you ever have the slightest suspicion that a child is involved in substance abuse, go straight to your headteacher.

Sex education

The governors are responsible for the school's policy on sex education. Normally different aspects will be allocated to different year groups in Key Stage 2. Make sure you are aware of the policy and discuss its implementation into your teaching programme with the headteacher. Discuss who else will be involved, the school nurse, perhaps, or another member of staff from the opposite sex to yours.

Inform the parents by letter, or at a special meeting, of the planned programme. Explain to the children what the programme is; why it is important and how the sessions will be arranged.

This is not an easy subject and some children will find it embarrassing. However, it is extremely important for the child's future health and safety and you should deal with it sensitively and thoroughly.

Citizenship and moral development
Racial prejudice/multicultural issues

While the organization and administration of the school will shape and influence its ethos, your attitude, your class routines, your relationships and your appreciation and tolerance will be equally influential.

Take a positive stance. Encourage respect between individuals by helping them to understand cultural diversity. It is important that your children learn to recognize the equality, value and dignity of all cultures. Ensure that they have opportunities to learn and develop informed attitudes. Encourage tolerance but do not be tolerant of any racial prejudice. Emphasize that such behaviour is totally unacceptable and that you will respond immediately to instances of racial prejudice and support the victim.

Bullying

Your school will have established procedures and practices that all staff and children should be aware of. This is not a topic to leave until there is an incident. It should form part of your regular PSHE work. Encourage your children to be a 'telling' class. One idea that can work is to have a 'telling book' which is confidential between you and the child. Often children will be more comfortable writing about their fears, problems or a particular incident than discussing it.

Serious incidents, or repeated difficulties involving the same individual or group, should always be reported. It will often be helpful to bring such matters to the attention of the whole staff as the problem will inevitably not be limited to the classroom situation.

Parents should always be contacted about any incident or concern at an early stage. Ideally, they should have heard the school's side of any dispute before their child arrives home. Offer them an opportunity to meet with you and the headteacher. Take the initiative when you can and record details of the incident, your response and the times of any telephone calls you have made. Be over-cautious rather than caught out by a situation that develops at a later stage.

Gender issues

Your conduct and attitude will influence how the children regard and value each other now and in the future. Gender is not an organizing principle or a classroom management strategy. Unless you are involved in a particularly sensitive element of sex education, never segregate the boys from the girls. Your role is to promote equality by changing the stereotypical ideas about boys and girls that many children come to school with.

Ensure that both boys and girls receive broad-based education with opportunities to follow up specific interests and activities that may not conform with tradition. Addressing this issue needs to be part of a whole-school policy and should include a considered approach not only to the curriculum but to assemblies, classroom practices, games and even playtimes.

Respect for property

This is another whole-school issue. Respect for others and other people's property will form part of the ethos of any good school. This should percolate down to the way children regard their belongings and the school's resources. It is essential that they develop a sense of ownership and responsibility for school and class equipment. Lead by example. Provide the class with the best that you can and organize the resources with care. Draw the children's attention to anything that is new and establish strict controls for checking and maintaining class equipment.

Stranger danger

Some of the children in your class will be coming to school unaccompanied. They will also be at a stage when this independence is exciting and adventurous. In addition, there may be an increasing amount of time outside school hours when they are not directly supervised by an adult. Children are vulnerable but at this stage in their development they need to be made aware of their responsibilities for themselves. Invite the police liaison officer in to talk to the children on a termly basis. Warn the class before holiday periods, and of any potential threats, but at the same time avoid over-reacting and causing undue concern. Being aware is an essential part of their growing independence. Ignorance and apathy are potentially as threatening as any perpetrator.

The Year 3 year

New years, new classes, new teachers all present different anxieties, challenges and uncertainties. Year 3 marks an important step from being an infant to the world of the junior. Some children will take time to adjust to this transition, especially if this has involved a change of school. Your style will inevitably change as the year progresses, and as the children gain confidence and become more familiar with you and their new surroundings.

The learning that you inspire, the skills and attitudes you teach, encourage and develop are fundamental. Enjoy the children's company, engage their interest and earn their respect. Together you can build on their infant experiences and establish firm foundations for their future junior years.

Curriculum and Classroom Planning

If you have the opportunity, spend time in the classroom you are to 'inherit' prior to any move. It is a little like buying a house. You need to establish what is being left, exactly what will be taken and how you should go about getting hold of equipment you will need.

If you are new to the school, you may be entitled to a 'start up' sum. If you are moving classrooms, prepare a needs list with supporting information and tackle your headteacher. You may not be fortunate immediately, but your needs may be included in future planning.

Assess the materials and resources you have. Dispose of tatty, inappropriate materials. Store equipment you will not be using. Present the children with good quality, well-cared-for resources. If you do, the chances are that they will present you with good work.

Library resources

Familiarize yourself with the school's library policy. Find out if there are set times for your class and how the resources should be used. Arrange to withdraw some of the books you will need for planned topic work. If the children have moved from an infant school or perhaps another floor, they will need to be shown how to make the best use of the library and how the system works. Assume little knowledge. You may find it helpful to organize a library 'treasure hunt' with groups of children having to find out specific information and locate materials. Library skills will need to be taught, reinforced and practised regularly.

Check the class library and make sure you are familiar with what it contains. Weed out any out-of-date information books and mend or discard torn or tattered books. Arrange with the school library service or local children's library, well in advance, to borrow collections of books to complement the work you are planning through the year.

Audio visual resources

Make sure that all your slides, video tapes and audio tapes are clearly labelled. Avoid being caught fumbling with the controls for the television or video. Always set up equipment in advance. Practise beforehand and make sure that everything works and that the tape is set to start at the right point. The slide that keeps making an unwelcome return or the carousel that refuses to move on will destroy the impact of the lesson.

If you intend to watch a live broadcast it is a good idea to check well in advance that there have not been any programme changes and that the TV is available at the time you want.

Information technology

Get to know the hardware and software that is available for your Year 3s and how it can support their learning.

Plan for the place and use of information technology. Do not leave it to chance. Look for opportunities across the curriculum and decide how you are going to ensure that all the children in your class have similar experiences and spend an equal amount of time using the equipment. A tick-list record by the computer, perhaps? (The children most anxious to spend time on the computer are likely to be those who least need practice.)

Display

Before you purchase or look for any display materials, read through the school's policy. Try to plan ahead, identifying what your needs will be for the term or even the year. You may have to order your display resources. If this is the case, place orders well in advance. Keep a running list of your needs. Slightly more expensive backing paper will last longer, should be able to be used more than once and will not fade. Invest in border strips and limit yourself to a range of colours that complement each other.

Collect your own set of drapes and artefacts. Visit jumble sales, car boot stalls and markets. Local fabric outlets may offer you discount prices, or free remnants if they know they are helping a school.

Plan where the displays will go in the classroom. Ensure that you include a range of subjects. Art for art's sake is fun, but should not cover every board. Try to include work from each child.

People

Do not forget to plan how you will make use of any personnel available to you. This may include a classroom assistant, support staff, parents, governors or contacts from outside the school such

as the school nurse or police liaison officer.

If you are fortunate enough to have a classroom assistant, use his/her time carefully. You may decide that while the majority of the classroom assistant's hours should be spent supporting the children, there will be administrative tasks such as photocopying, filing or covering boards which he/she can do to free valuable time for you.

Organize a book for all regular helpers with their tasks clearly identified. People like to know what is expected. Preparation will save time for you in the end.

Visits

Plan these well in advance for the year. Be careful that the visits do not make an unreasonable demand on limited finances or involve too much travelling time. Have a good mix of local, inexpensive visits as well as trips further afield. It is a good idea to find an opportunity to talk to the parents early in the school year about visits. If you are arranging a longer trip or residential week, offer a 'pay as they learn' scheme so that parents can send in small amounts towards the cost on a weekly basis. (The school can then use any interest gained towards the cost of the trip.)

Always follow school procedures. Notify parents by letter with a consent slip. Check to see if you need insurance and that any transport arrangements satisfy local and school agreements.

Use your local environment for art work, statistical counts, creative writing stimulus, history and geography. Children enjoy escaping from the confines of the classroom and periodic ventures outside can have a stimulating and positive effect on their work.

Requirements of various curriculum areas

Your school will be used to adapting to change and adopting new practices. Its policies and schemes of work should reflect legislation and will be an important reference for you to base your planning on. Seek advice from senior staff if you have any doubts or difficulties with planning. Use the National Curriculum orders and the strategy documents for the Literacy and Numeracy Hours together with any local education authority and school documentation.

Time

DfEE recommendations

The DfEE's recommended minimum time for Key Stage 2 children is 23.5 hours a week. This does not include breaks, lunch time or the daily act of worship. When deciding on the percentage allocations for curriculum subjects, you will need to take account of Literacy and Numeracy times, the National Curriculum for science and ICT and the need to provide a broad and balanced curriculum in the other subjects, the school's curriculum and any established special priorities. For a typical Year 3 class the breakdown may look like that shown in the table below.

	Eng.	Maths	Sci.	Tech.	Hist.	Geog.	Art	Music	PE	RE	PSHE
Hrs pw	6	4.5	3	2	1	1	2	1	2	1	0.5
%	25	19	13	8	4	4	8	4	8	4	2

This allows for a broad, balanced approach. However, do not attempt to cover all subject areas each week. Think in terms of blocks of time over a longer period so that you can do justice to a topic or activity.

Timetable

To begin with, mark on all the 'immovable feasts' such as:

- assemblies;
- hall, PE, games times;
- set time when another teacher takes your class;
- agreed times when other commitments are set.

Next, include your block times for the Literacy and Numeracy Hours. Your school may have established a general policy for this. Think carefully about appropriate times for the different subjects. Last period on a Friday afternoon is not when children or you will be at your most receptive for introducing a new maths concept. Also, think how one session leads on to the next. A morning of art, swimming and physical education followed by an afternoon of music and religious education could not be considered as a reasonable or effective balance and would cause difficulties for other days.

Long-/medium-/short-term planning

There is no single approach to planning or any common understanding of what each stage should include, although the National Literacy termly and weekly examples are a helpful guide. Your school will have developed a system that works for the children and meets their needs.

Long-term plans

Long-term planning may be included in a school's curriculum framework and in schemes of work for individual subjects. These will be quite specific and should form the core from which you take your plans.

You may be fortunate enough to be a member of a team for planning. This can provide you with opportunities to reflect together on past practices and activities as well as to plan for the future. You can use each others' strengths, support each other and help with resource issues. Being a member of a team for planning will be particularly helpful for newly qualified teachers.

Medium-term plans

Your medium-term planning might include an overview sheet for the half term that shows what you will be covering, subject by subject. This can be helpful for anyone looking at intended coverage and can be shared with parents.

You will then need to break this planning down and add some more details. A half-termly grid is a helpful tool.

If you use the grid, highlight what you have covered at the end of each week. This then gives you an immediate record, is visually reassuring, is informative, and is very useful to any supply teacher who takes over your class.

Class:.................... *Teacher:*...................... *Date:*................

English	History – topic	PE
Mathematics	Geography – topic	RE/PSHE
	Art	Music
Science	Technology	Help

Short-term plans

Short-term planning may be for a fortnight or just for the week. A sheet like this allows you to include as much information as you need to deliver the curriculum. You can show the assessments you intend to make and any evaluations that will help you to inform what you need to do in the future. A fortnightly plan might look like the following chart.

Week beginning . . . .*Group/Year group* . . . .

NC ref	Learning intentions	Activities	Resources	Groupings	Evaluation

Your daily plans will be drawn from the fortnightly or weekly sheets. Again, the Literacy initiative offers a planning pro-forma which can be adopted. Normally, it is up to you to devise a format that deals with how you organize the class or groups. In many respects these plans will be a memory jogger.

Class, group and individual teaching

You will need to be able to teach your children using a combination of approaches. The essential point to consider is 'fitness for purpose'. Be clear about the learning intentions. Use your professional judgement to determine which strategy will best encourage and engage your children in learning.

Class teaching

The requirements for class teaching in the Literacy and Numeracy Hours has given renewed importance to teaching the class as a whole. It involves a high level of control. You need to provide instructions, pace the lesson so that attention does not wander and assess responses so that you can move the children on. Explanations need to be given in a logical, coherent manner.

If thoughtfully planned and approached, whole-class teaching will often prove to be both personally and professionally very satisfying and rewarding.

Group teaching

Teaching children in groups is an equally important strategy. It allows for resources to be shared and provides planned opportunities for children to interact together and with you. Focusing your teaching on selected groups while others work with an assistant or on independent tasks is an effective approach.

Group activities can, however, be counter-productive if you have too many groups, too many different activities at the same time, or if the criteria for grouping has not been carefully thought through.

Individual teaching

To teach every child in the class individually would be extremely difficult, if not impossible. Interaction with the child can be superficial and the real amount of teaching time the child experiences will be minimal. However, there will be times when it is appropriate to focus on and support an individual pupil. Children of all abilities, but particularly those with special educational needs, will benefit from one-to-one teaching. It is up to you as the class teacher to decide if, while being best for the child, it is manageable. Can the other children in the class work independently and meaningfully without your immediate attention?

Conclusion

Whatever your method of organization, strategy or style of delivery, 'fitness for purpose' is your guiding consideration.
- Teach your class using a variety of methods, including the whole class, in smaller groups of various compositions and individually.
- Remember that no single exclusive method is ever appropriate.
- Ensure that you have a manageable number of groups and learning activities provided at any one time.
- Use your time effectively to instruct, question, explain, listen and assess.

Differentiation by task/outcome

Whatever the age group you are responsible for, you should be aware of what to expect from each individual pupil. This will involve not only getting to know the child, but careful planning and evaluation. The evaluations you make at the end of any activity or assessment should then be used to form your future plans.

When you plan an activity for the whole class, their response or follow-up work may be 'open ended' with all the children working to their own level. An example of this would be a piece of creative writing on a set subject. Children will probably spend the same amount of time but write different amounts and produce a range of results. You will need to know the children to decide if the work they produce is at an appropriate level for them.

With other activities, you may decide that, while your introduction will be for the whole class, it is more appropriate for the children still to operate in ability groups. Your expectations for each group will be different. The more able will have extension activities, special needs children will need to be considered and you have to decide which group or groups you will be focusing on.

Ensure that the activity is thoughtfully planned and that you are meeting the needs of all the children in the class through a differentiated approach that best fits your learning intentions.

Recording and presentation

Familiarize yourself with the school's policy that outlines how work should be recorded and presented. Check this against examples of work from the previous year so that you can compare practice with policy.

When you first meet the children, agree a statement with them that sets the standards for the year. The main points will need to be taken from the school's policy or from a proposed sheet that you have drawn up. This might include details of how work should be dated, titled and laid out, which writing implements are appropriate and so on. The children should understand what is expected. There is little point having a policy that they are unaware of.

While the processes that the children have worked through are important, the presentation of the final product will say as much about their level of attainment as it will about you as their teacher. Use it to motivate and to build for the future.

Homework

Establish what the school's policy is and plan accordingly. If the school does not have a set approach, discuss the matter with any colleagues who are teaching the same age group as you.

If you are going to set homework, set sensible ground rules. Explain to the parents as well as the children what they can expect, why it is important and what the procedures for distribution, collection and marking will be. Ensure that any work you set is meaningful, challenging and something the children can do in the home environment. Types of homework for Year 3 children might include:

- finishing off a piece of work from class;
- special handwriting practice;
- spellings or multiplication tables to learn for a test;
- a personal study as part of a class topic.

Assessment

You will need to get to know your school's procedures for assessment. This is not an easy area, particularly if you are relatively inexperienced. With Year 3 children, you will have the Key Stage 1 SATs and teacher assessment as a sound basis. Keep on top of assessment by maintaining helpful formative sheets for each child, as well as other records. Although you are no longer required to keep assessment sheets on the non-core subjects, it makes sense to keep a record of any significant achievements or problems. Keep all information up to date. You never know when you will be challenged by a parent, inspector or even by a colleague!

At appropriate stages in any topic, include assessment opportunities in your planning for identified children. Organize this on a regular basis so that it is manageable. This information will be invaluable for end-of-year reports and consultation times with parents.

Towards the end of the summer term, on the basis of the SATs information and your own judgements, predict the final level of attainment you would expect each child to achieve at the end of the Key Stage. This should be annually reviewed and can provide useful, additional information.

English
including Literacy Hour

By the time children enter Year 3, there will already be a wide diversity in their linguistic abilities. There may, for example, be some children who have mastered many of the key skills in reading and read independently and for pleasure, and there may be others who struggle to read even the simplest sentences. So central is English to the curriculum as a whole, that the Year 3 teacher has a vital role in ensuring that children develop the literacy and oracy skills which will provide them with access to all areas of learning.

The task is potentially complex and you may have to work closely with learning support teachers to determine what provision is necessary for those children whose language skills are limited. You may also need to discuss with colleagues from Year 4 or even Year 5 classes strategies and materials which will further extend those children whose linguistic abilities are more advanced. For children whose reading skills are less advanced, you will need to find materials which are at the appropriate reading level, but which allow for their increasing maturity of outlook.

What should they be able to do?

Year 3 children should, according to the National Curriculum, be able to show confidence in speaking and listening, especially in those topics which interest them. They should be showing awareness of the needs of listeners by supplying relevant detail when talking and should be speaking clearly and with a growing vocabulary. Their responses to other people should usually be appropriate and be based upon careful listening, and they should be beginning to be aware that in some situations a more formal vocabulary and tone of voice is used. They may also have experienced and feel confident about speaking to large audiences, perhaps in assemblies or school productions.

In reading, most children should be able to read simple texts with understanding and general accuracy and they should be able to express opinions about what they have read. Their experience of reading matter should be varied and should include stories, poems and non-fiction. They should also be able to employ different strategies to read unfamiliar words and to derive meaning from texts. These should include phonics, graphics and syntactic and contextual clues.

In writing, children should be able to communicate meaning in narrative and non-narrative forms and use appropriate and interesting vocabulary. They should show some awareness of the reader and develop ideas in sentences with some use of capital letters and full stops. By the end of the year, they should be beginning to use speech marks. They will usually be able to spell simple, monosyllabic words correctly and should be able to make phonetically plausible attempts at spelling simple polysyllabic words. Handwriting should be accurately formed and of a consistent size.

By the time they reach Year 3, children should be at a stage where they have begun to realize that literacy and oracy are two-way processes which demand that the producer (the speaker or writer) is aware of the needs of the receiver (the listener or reader).

Some will have begun to write for pleasure for real audiences and to read with some independence. Others, while they may have achieved some proficiency, may be reluctant writers and readers and may lack confidence in speaking to others even within the classroom environment.

Key areas

The key elements of English are speaking and listening, reading, and writing.

You will need to look carefully at the records which are passed on to you by Year 2 teachers in order to assess the extent to which you will have to differentiate when planning English work for your class. While there may well be a great deal of whole-class teaching, including the Literacy Hour, you will need to think about the activities in which children will subsequently be engaged. You should match these carefully to children's abilities and yet ensure that the activities are challenging and that they reinforce previous learning and foster development of skills and understanding. Be wary of activities which are simply time-fillers designed to enable you to hear readers or work with groups. Activities may demand independent work by children, but you should always identify clear learning objectives.

Children should already have become familiar with some aspects of information technology and you should look out for opportunities to extend this knowledge and to encourage them to make use of the computer whenever appropriate.

Key area: Speaking

Provide children with lots of opportunities to explore and develop their ideas through discussion with classmates. You might plan lessons with a built-in time for discussion followed by some recording of ideas. The discussion may be by the whole class at first in order to stimulate ideas, and it could then be followed by group work, with children noting conclusions before reporting back to the whole class. By engaging children's interest orally from the outset, you will be more likely to find that they have some ideas to use when it comes to the time for writing.

In class discussions it is important to emphasize the etiquette for conversation in the classroom. You can insist that children raise their hands and wait to be asked to speak by you or by whoever is chairing the discussion. Alternatively, you might like to establish another convention. This could be an item recognized by all the class as entitling its holder to speak. Children will mostly be keen to contribute their own thoughts, but some will be reluctant to do so, especially if they

have to compete with others who call out in order to gain attention. (Controls of speech may be criticized as artificial, but they are a feature of adult meetings too, where conventions are essential if order is to be maintained and if everyone who wishes to contribute is able to do so.)

It may be a good idea to talk with children about the rules which they would like to see for discussions. This could be the first language activity of the school year and might lead to children recording their own or their group's list of rules for talk before comparing them with those created by other groups and synthesising them all into a class list. In this way, children can be given some ownership of the rules and may be more likely to obey them. In addition, the list provides a handy reference point when discussions break down because everyone tries to talk at once!

Give your class plenty of opportunities to consider ways of improving and developing their speaking. Attention should be given to clarity and presentation when children talk to larger groups, but this should not lead to the inhibiting of expression. It is more productive to talk in a general way about the qualities in speech which make it enjoyable or interesting for listeners, rather than to single out individuals and comment negatively on their efforts.

Key area: Listening

Although many children in Year 3 may be able to listen carefully to discussions before making their own contributions, some will find this difficult. Using visual aids to stimulate interest and sustain attention is important here and, when children are making short presentations to the class, you might suggest that they could incorporate such aids. One way to do this, while making the children feel mature, is to ask them before presenting an assembly, for example, what they think the younger children will need if they are to be able to listen and understand.

Regular use of question-and-answer sessions will help children to develop an ability to listen if they are encouraged to respond. A mixture of closed questions which demand short answers and which keep a discussion moving, and open questions which require deeper thought and reflection, should help. You will be able to observe the ways in which children listen, and gauge the extent to which they are able to respond to what they have heard, through class and group discussions.

Key area: Reading

In Year 3, children will need to develop further their ability to read texts fluently and accurately. They should be developing strategies which will enable them to gain greater independence in their reading, so that they are able to make informed attempts to decipher unfamiliar words.

You should provide them with a wide range of reading materials, and they should frequently be reading non-fiction, plays and poetry as well as fiction. Some children, who have had a reading diet restricted to stories, may have problems with non-fiction. They may expect text to read as a story and find it difficult to adopt the more studied approach which is demanded if they are to extract information from text books, charts, diagrams and information sheets.

You may need to spend time reinforcing the concept of alphabetical order as children begin to make greater use of reference books. It is important that the reference materials they encounter at this stage are attractive and stimulating.

For many children, Year 3 is the year in which they 'crack' the reading code. Some teachers refer to an almost audible 'click' as children suddenly realize that reading is something they can manage, and that they now have the ability to seek and find information as well as enjoy stories. Maintain the momentum by presenting them with a constant diet of accessible and interesting material. While progress through reading schemes may remain at the core of the reading programme, it is important that children experience a greater range and you should encourage them to sample books from a wide variety of genres.

It is vital that they hear books being read to them, as well as reading independently and in groups. Without the example which a skilled and experienced reader can provide, they are unlikely to acquire the ability to read with expression and understand how a piece of writing may be brought to life by variations in tone by the reader. Hearing you read may also enhance their listening skills.

Don't restrict your reading aloud to fiction, but include poetry and non-fiction, too. (The National Literacy Strategy details the range of genres with which Year 3 children should be familiar.) The selection of fiction should be varied (Year 3 children are very responsive to myths and legends) and you don't have to read a whole book in the traditional serial fashion. You can read extracts to stimulate interest and to increase their awareness of what is available.

Provide opportunities to discuss some of the literary devices which authors use to make their writing more interesting to readers. For example, a discussion of the adjectives used to describe a character could be followed by children considering how they would describe a friend or relative. In this way, you can encourage them to relate their reading to their writing.

There will still be a need to reinforce the mechanics of reading and this may be done in short class lessons as part of Literacy Hours which emphasize phonics, word recognition and ways of breaking up words into constituent parts. If you show children the functions of, for example, prefixes, they will increasingly be able to extrapolate from this and decipher new and unfamiliar words.

There will still be a need to hear readers individually, but this should not be the only method employed. Many children at Year 3 are capable of group reading with in turn, while others follow the text. This approach will allow you to discuss features of the text such as punctuation, use of adjectives, and style, while enabling children to read and listen to text at some length.

For some teachers, the most significant method of teaching reading has been to hear children reading aloud individually. While this is a valuable activity if done well, too often hard-pressed teachers, faced with large classes and pressure from parents to hear each child read regularly, have been unable to devote sufficient time or concentration to their pupils' reading needs. HMI (OFSTED, 1996) found that listening to individual pupils read was 'the principal strategy used by most teachers for teaching reading in Year 2', but reported that, 'In many cases ... this simply became an unproductive routine exercise of such short duration that very little teaching took place'. The inspectors went on to note that, 'The effective teaching of pupils in groups, and especially as a whole class, about specific aspects of reading was uncommon'. This chapter refers constantly to group and class teaching, not only because such teaching is a productive way of making use of limited teaching time and large classes, but also because it is an effective way of developing children's reading skills.

The Literacy Hour demands this guided approach to reading, so there will be a need to reassess approaches as it becomes the principal strategy for the teaching of reading. Given the likely changes to the teaching of reading, it is important that parents understand that their children will still be learning to read, even though they may be heard individually far less than may have previously been the case.

Key area: Writing

Children in Year 3 may have become reluctant writers, particularly if they have experienced difficulties in Year 2. They may perceive writing as arduous, and may find it hard to cope with spelling and punctuation. You will need to encourage them to express their ideas, as well as helping them to write with increasing accuracy.

Much early writing takes the form of listing and there is some benefit in maintaining this approach at Year 3 for some writing activities. Children might begin a writing task by making a list of key points and then expanding upon them. The list acts as an *aide memoire* which they can draw upon to sustain their writing.

In Year 3, you should increasingly give your class opportunities to write for real audiences other than you. Activities such as letter writing and writing for younger children should be encouraged, and children should always be told, before they begin writing, who the intended readership will be.

Punctuation

Many children will punctuate inconsistently and it is likely that you will have to revisit the concept of the sentence, emphasizing the need to make use of full stops and capital letters. Children may have begun to use commas, but they will probably not be aware of the many ways in which commas may be used to make their writing easier for the reader to understand.

Spelling

Spelling of words which are unfamiliar and are **not polysyllabic** causes problems for many children, so you should provide regular work on phonics and word recognition, as well as discussing with the class the functions of different parts of words. Children need to make generalisations about the ways in which words may be spelled, if they are to apply what they learn about the ways in which the words they are taught relate to other words which they come to use independently.

If you provide lists of words for children to learn for a spelling test, it is important that the words are discussed extensively and children are encouraged to think about other, similar words which include the same letter clusters. Give them strategies for learning spellings and do not assume that they will be able to learn a list independently simply by looking at the words for a long time. *Look-cover-write-check* or *look-say-cover-write-check* are good strategies for learning spellings. Encourage them to look closely at words and identify the 'difficult' parts so that they concentrate their efforts on learning those. Ensure that the children are able to spell all of the words in List 1 in the National Literacy Strategy.

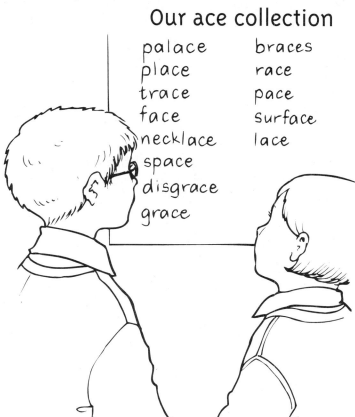

Our ace collection

palace · braces
place · race
trace · pace
face · surface
necklace · lace
space
disgrace
grace

Handwriting

This year they will need to develop their handwriting skills further, as they become increasingly well-coordinated and their fine motor skills develop.

Practical ideas

Literacy Hour

The teaching framework devised by the National Literacy Strategy is the foundation for the Literacy Hour. You must dedicate one hour a day to the teaching of reading and writing in a rhythmic transition from whole-class teaching to small-group work and back again.

During this hour, children should be engaged in work at:
- whole-text level, involving comprehension and composition;
- sentence level involving grammar and punctuation;
- word level involving vocabulary and spelling.

Those of the following activities which are particularly suitable for use in the Literacy Hour are marked with an ✅.

Speaking and listening

During their time in Year 3, children should develop an increased confidence in speaking to each other, to adults and to larger groups. The activities below incorporate these elements.

Rainbowing

After groups have been working on a topic, allocate each member of each group a number, letter or colour. Each then meets with all the others with the same number, letter or colour to share ideas and compare what each group did. Children are provided with a real audience for their speaking and will be able to listen and respond to a range of people. They will also be able to share ideas, insights and opinions.

Jigsawing

✅ Organize the class into groups and give each member of each group an aspect of the topic on which to become expert. The experts from each group meet to share ideas and then report back to their groups. Many of the benefits which are derived from rainbowing may be found here, but children will also have the opportunity to show their own expertise and to explore, develop and explain ideas.

Drama

● A variety of drama activities should be used in Year 3 and these should not be restricted to rehearsals for school or class productions. There should be opportunities for role play which is often well-developed at Key Stage 1 through the use of home corners, but which tends to be neglected at Key Stage 2.

● There may be a class shop which could be used as part of mathematical work, or there may be improvisation activities based upon work in religious education, geography and history.

● You might engage children in role play and improvisation as a prelude to writing. The drama work will help them to develop and internalize their thoughts so that they will have plenty of ideas when it comes to setting them down on paper.

Reading

In developing children's reading skills at this stage, it is important that you build upon the work which has been done already in Key Stage 1.

✅ Talk with the children regularly about the ways in which print is presented. Discuss features such as punctuation, capital letters and the use of illustrations which provide clues about the text. Focus on a big book or a piece of writing displayed on the board or with an overhead projector. Draw children's attention to different features and ask them to follow this by working with text to, for example, put in capital letters where appropriate.

Reading strategies

Work with the class and with groups to show different ways in which unfamiliar words may be approached: encourage children to read the whole sentence and then suggest which words might fit before looking closely at the structure of the one with which they are experiencing difficulty.

Alphabet

Display the alphabet prominently and make frequent reference to it. Teach the children how to sing it if they haven't already learned this.

Talk about how useful it is to know the alphabet. *Can you think of times when you need to know it?* (When using indexes, encyclopaedias, dictionaries, the library, thesauruses, telephone directories, the register, catalogues and so on.) You could have a chart on the wall for children to add to with headings such as: *Who used the alphabet? What for?* (Daniel's Mum: to find where the trainers were in the catalogue. Hannah: to find the Michael Bond stories in the library).

Pairs of children can play 'dictionary races'. Give them a list of words, two dictionaries and a timer. Ask them first to tell you what the key words at the top of each dictionary page are for. If they have forgotten, encourage them to work it out. Then they can have the race. *Who can find each word first? How long did it take? Did you get faster?*
Vary the difficulty of the word lists to match their ability.

It is helpful to have (ready in the computer) lists of words for alphabetical sorting which can be printed out as you need them. (Try to enlist a parent or another adult with good word-processing skills for this and other inputting tasks.) The lists can be varied from easy (where the initial letters are all different) to difficult (jumble adjacent words from a dictionary) and you can use words that you want the children to be able to spell. The children can number the words in alphabetical order and then perhaps write out the list as handwriting practice. Show them how to check their work by calling up the list on the computer, highlighting it and using the SORT command.

Children's literature

The environment in which the children work will affect their attitude to literacy and their ability to acquire a deeper understanding of it. If they are to produce interesting and well-constructed writing, they will need to experience a wide range of children's literature. Make them aware of the variety

of books which exists within the classroom and the school (and in libraries outside school), so that they are able to find texts which interest them. You should be familiar with the books yourself so you can discuss them with the children and help them to find those they will enjoy. The following methods may be used to broaden their knowledge of literature.

Book strategies

Display a range of books and poems prominently. Display some books open at exciting or interesting pages and encourage children to read these. Have interactive displays with things to respond to, questions to answer and so on.

Display extracts from books which are available in the classroom. Talk with the children about the extracts and use these to whet their appetites in the way that trailers for films and TV programmes do . If children enjoy a book, ask them if they would like to write a brief comment (on the computer perhaps) which can be added to the display.

☺ Rather than always reading a story from beginning to end, sometimes read extracts from several books and talk with the children about their content and the likely outcomes of the stories.

● Make use of commercially-recorded stories and poems and of video presentations to broaden children's knowledge of stories.

☺ Character quiz: to encourage children to think closely about the stories they read and hear, ask them to write statements about a character from a book in the class library. Display the statements and ask the rest of the class to try to identify the characters and the books.

● Invite other adults or older pupils into the classroom to read with children.

☺ Use play versions of familiar stories for the children to read together. Some versions (for example, the *Take Part* series, Ward Lock Educational) have parts written for different reading ages so they can be used by mixed-ability groups.

☺ Record stories, plays and poems on to audio tape and provide tape recorders and headphones so that children may listen to these while following the text.

You could ask parents or other adults to contribute to such recordings, as a change of voice is welcomed by children. (Look for different accents and timbres.) Some of the children in the class might record favourite stories for other children to listen to.

Poetry

☺ Help the children to learn poems and rhymes by heart. An emphasis on the rhymes within a poem should make this easier for children, as will discussion about the sequence of events in a poem.

● Set up a class anthology book on the computer and suggest that children can enter favourite poems, extracts from stories or jokes. At the end of the year, they can edit the material and use a DTP programme to present it attractively before it is printed out. Each child can design a cover for a personal copy of the anthology.

☺ Discuss rhyme with the children and ask them to suggest possible rhymes for the initial rhyming word in couplets when reading poetry aloud to them. This will help them to develop their phonic knowledge and to consider different ways in which the same sounds may be written down. More able children may be interested in looking at rhyming dictionaries which provide ideas for rhymes.

Rhymes and syllables

☺ Look at one poem or one type of poem and involve the children in looking at rhymes and at syllables to see how the lines scan. They could learn about syllables through clapping their own and other people's names (three claps for three syllables in Ryan Giggs, four for four syllables in David Jason – see also the Music chapter, page 108). Follow-up activities could include completing rhymes in poems in which the second rhyming word in some couplets has been removed, or trying to write alternative words for well-known songs so that these scan and fit the tunes.

Phonic skills

● Phonic knowledge is a key element in reading and children need extensive knowledge of the sounds which letters usually make if they are to be able to tackle unfamiliar words without difficulty and so develop as independent readers. Phonic skills may be developed through formal teaching of sounds of individual letters, blends and digraphs. The

THRASS programme is particularly helpful in showing the many different graphemes which can be used to represent the 44 phonemes in the English language. (*Teaching Handwriting, Reading and Spelling Skills* A Davies and D Ritchie.) Explain to your class that it is not always possible to make use of phonic knowledge when deciphering a word because of the many irregularities in English.

☑ Words such as *one*, *two* and *once*, which appear regularly in children's early reading and in the first list of high frequency words in the National Literacy Strategy, may have to be taught separately as exceptions. However, the vast majority of English words have some phonic regularity, particularly in initial sounds, and it is these which provide most help to readers. Suggest to children that they look at the initial sound of a word before and after reading beyond it. They can then make use of other strategies, such as grammatical knowledge and contextual understanding, in combination with sound/symbol correspondence.

☑ Show children how we can make use of phonic knowledge as well as of a range of other methods. Activities could include an exploration of graphemes and their phonemes and could lead to children making collections of words with common sounds or letter strings.

☑ Constantly relate the formal teaching of sounds to words which contain them. Taught in isolation, sounds can be meaningless to children. However, when they are able to relate the sounds to familiar words, they can appreciate the importance of phonic knowledge.

Sound/symbol games
Involve children in games and other activities which highlight sound/symbol correspondence.

I-spy
I-spy is a particularly useful game. Play it orally, but also use letters written on the board or on cards to illustrate the sounds which begin words. Gradually develop the game to include initial blends when appropriate, for example, *I-spy with my little eye something beginning with 'sh'*.

Matching
The children can match cards which have pictures to others which have letters or initial blends. At first you may find it necessary to cut the cards so the pairs fit each other and children can check the match but, as their skills develop, they can do without this.

They can play with you, in pairs, or individually. This activity may be particularly helpful for those children whose phonic skills are not yet well developed.

Alphabet Bingo
Children have cards with different letters on them and these are used instead of numbers to play bingo. The game may be played using names of letters, sounds or both. Develop the game to include capital letters, blends and words. For example, in **Sounds Bingo** give children cards with a range of blends and digraphs written in boxes on them. Read out the phonemes. The children cover up a square if they recognize its sound. The first child to cover all of the boxes in a line or the whole card is the winner. The cards can then be checked by asking children to sound the blends and digraphs they have covered.

Sight vocabulary
☑ As children's reading skills develop, they will build up a sight vocabulary of words which they recognize easily and which they do not need to decode in order to read. The National Literacy Strategy lists the 'sight recognition words' that children should know by this stage and this provides a useful checklist. Some may have a limited sight vocabulary even though they have begun to develop decoding strategies. Their sight vocabularies might include familiar words from the environment such as *bus stop*, *fish and chips* and *school*. This vocabulary may be built upon

through extensive use of environmental print as well as through class, group and individual teaching.

● Some teachers take children on 'word walks' encouraging them to look at signs and symbols in the environment. Photographs and slides can also be used to show the proliferation of words and symbols which exist all around us.

◉ Use the children's sight vocabulary as a starting point for some phonics work, with children discussing and being shown the functions of different letters or clusters of letters within the words.

● The labelling of drawers, cupboards and other parts of the classroom will also help children to develop their sight vocabularies. Talk about the labels and draw children's attention to them. Alternatively, or additionally, a display may be created with key features labelled. Involve the children in the labelling – they can use the computer to produce attractive labels and make use of the spellchecker to ensure accurate spelling.

◉ The use of flash cards with a group is a useful starting point for developing word recognition. However, it is important to discuss the structure of the words so that children look beyond the length of the words or their first letters to recognize them. Where it is available, the *Breakthrough to Literacy*

scheme can be useful here, since it provides common words printed on card which may be used to build sentences using the sentence-maker holders.

Developing knowledge about language

Many children will already have quite a sophisticated knowledge about language. For example, they will be aware of the ways in which plurals are made and the use of prefixes and suffixes to qualify or alter the meanings of root words. They will often make mistakes by applying this knowledge incorrectly where, for instance, plurals are irregular, referring to *sheeps* or *mans* rather than *sheep* or *men*.

◉ In order to develop graphic knowledge, build upon the children's oral abilities and show how words may be written down and the roles of different parts of words. Group reading and direct class teaching help here since you can create opportunities to discuss words in detail. For example, you might take a word such as *returned* and break it up into *re-turn-ed*. You could talk about the three parts of the word, their sounds and spellings and their meanings.

◉ Encourage the children to make collections of root words and then show them how these may be

changed to modify meanings. For example, children might start with a word such as *like* and then talk about how it changes its meaning as prefixes and suffixes are added to create *unlike, dislike, likely, unlikely, likeable, likeness* and so on.

✪ Focus a Literacy Hour on plurals. Ask children to rewrite sentences, converting singulars to plurals and plurals to singulars. *Is there anything else we have to change? What about the verbs – do they still sound right? Do we always add 's' to make a plural? What is the plural of 'man'? Let's start a list of words that have unusual plurals. You'll find some in these sentences. Can you think of any more?*

✪ On another occasion, include words which don't change in the plural and make a collection of them. Lists which the children themselves build over a period of time mean far more to them than ready-made lists.

● If you are giving children lists of spellings to learn, it is important to discuss the words and show the children how to form plurals and how to modify meaning using prefixes and suffixes. Reinforce this with games in which children turn over word cards and try to match root words with their modified forms. For example, *lucky* and *unlucky*, *appear* and *disappear*, and *read* and *re-read*.

✪ A game based upon opposites could also be used with the matching of root words and their antonyms. For example, *happy/sad, good/bad, tall/short*. (The most able children can prepare their own cards.)

✪ This can be further reinforced through group reading when you should draw children's attention to such words. You could base Literacy Hour work upon finding antonyms in dictionaries and in selected passages. Encourage children to use the term 'antonym'.

Grammatical knowledge

Grammatical knowledge can be developed through a range of activities:
✪ Use cloze exercises, in which some words in a sentence or passage are replaced by lines or spaces, to encourage children to consider possibilities. When you devise and use such exercises keep the following points in mind.
▌ Children need sufficient complete text to allow them to 'get into' the passage; the first sentence in a paragraph should have no omissions.
▌ The words omitted may be selected randomly

by removing every *n*th word (don't take out more than one in every ten words at this stage).
▌ Alternatively, the words omitted might all be the same part of speech, for example, some or all of the verbs might be removed.
▌ Encourage children to discuss possibilities and make it clear that there is not necessarily only one correct word to fill each space.

✪ Sentence building (perhaps using *Breakthrough to Literacy* materials) enables children to consider sentence structure and to think about the roles of each word, phrase and clause.

✪ You could give the children incomplete sentences as starting points for building sentences. Again, encourage them to realize that there are many possible ways of filling the spaces.

Reading aloud to children

Practise reading aloud and making use of different techniques such as the use of accents, expression and change of pace to make the text 'come alive'. Reading aloud to children is not only a pleasant experience and a form of entertainment, it also provides excellent opportunities for teaching and learning.
▌ It fosters listening skills and develops children's abilities to question and answer.
▌ It enables them to experience literature which would normally be beyond their reading capacities, but which can be accessible when read by an experienced reader.
▌ You can introduce them to more sophisticated uses of language and subjects which they would not otherwise have read about. They will also increase their knowledge of language and of literary devices, enabling them to read and write more adventurous material.
▌ Many children are preoccupied with decoding when they read. Listening to stories and poems being read aloud enables them to give their attention to the content of the text and to respond to changes in tone and pace.
▌ Children need extensive experience of hearing good readers reading aloud to them if they are to develop an understanding of the common patterns of language which are featured in English literature. Through this, you can help the children to understand the importance of word order. You can also familiarize them with sentence structures which are more complex than those beginning with the subject followed by a verb which feature strongly in early reading and writing.

If good use is made of these possibilities, children should be able to apply what they have learned to their independent reading too.

Extending and developing reading

● Activities which might be related to responding to stories and poems could include:

▶ children talking and/or writing about a character whom they particularly liked or disliked;

▶ hot-seating, in which children are asked to answer questions from the class or group as if they were a character from the story or poem;

▶ groups of children dramatizing the stories which they have read or heard;

▶ dramatizing stories using simple puppets – this device often helps those children who would usually be reticent about performing in front of others;

▶ writing letters in role as one of the characters from a story – this could form part of Literacy Hour work following class discussion and a whole-class attempt at this;

▶ writing alternative endings for stories;

▶ writing synopses of stories either in sentences or lists to show the sequence of events;

▶ writing a diary in role as one of the characters from a story.

Reference material

● Select dictionaries appropriate for your children, but ensure that there is always a large and more comprehensive version available for looking up words which do not feature in the children's dictionaries. There are many thesauruses available which are suitable for use in primary classrooms and children can become so absorbed in them that they go off at tangents looking up several words as their interest grows and they become familiar with the method of using them. It is important that children understand alphabetical order as early as possible, if they are to be able to use reference books successfully and without frustration.

◉ The provision of dictionaries and simple thesauruses as well as atlases, telephone directories, catalogues and other information books is important, but it is equally important for you to teach children to use these texts effectively. The Literacy Hour should provide many opportunities for whole-class work on locating information. You might, for example, reproduce a single page of a dictionary and display this as a focal point for a lesson on

dictionary layout and use. Encourage the children to suggest labels for different features and display these with the dictionary page.

◉ Make a class dictionary. This could be a general dictionary or one associated with a topic. Begin by writing words on the board and then discuss alphabetical order.

Children, working in pairs, might produce definitions and later compare their versions with those in a published dictionary. The class dictionary could be continually updated, particularly if words are written on cards which slot into a book with

double-card pages. Children could be given responsibility for maintaining the dictionary in alphabetical order and it could become a genuine reference point for the class.

◉ Build word banks for topics the class is studying. These may take the form of mini-dictionaries or might involve words being written on card and stored in alphabetical order or they could be posted alongside a relevant display.

◉ Fact or fiction? In this activity children use reference books to produce statements which may or may not be true. Others have to use books to check the veracity of the statements which could be displayed or placed in the fronts of different books. You might use a book of interesting or surprising facts and your own imagination to create some statements which will encourage children to use reference books. *(If you could jump as high as a flea can, you could jump over a double-decker bus.)* They will especially enjoy finding out that you have 'made a mistake'. This could form part of a series of Literacy Hour lessons designed to encourage close reading and develop information retrieval skills.

● Using simple databases on computers will help children to develop skills in recording and research. A database which records children's height, weight and so forth and which may be added to throughout the year can provide a good starting point.

Guided group reading

◉ Guided group reading, in which children take turns to read aloud, provides an opportunity to discuss the features of stories and may be used as an introduction to many of the directed activities related to texts (DARTS) described above.

◉ Guided group and shared class reading time is an important opportunity for developing children's language skills. Discussions about the vocabulary used by authors may centre around the adjectives or adverbs used or the ways in which an author uses words to build up a 'picture' of a character.

◉ The influence of reading and environmental print is evident in the misuse of apostrophes, which seem to appear in children's writing before they are taught about them. Given this influence, it may be useful to discuss in group reading sessions punctuation marks which arise in writing. Show examples which occur in reading books in order to demonstrate correct usage.

Non-fiction

Children may find it difficult to distinguish between fiction and non-fiction books and may expect to read text books in the same way as story books. The use of non-fiction books as part of shared and guided group reading can help children to understand the format of such books and should enable them to understand that a different approach is required when reading them. Talk about the books and look at features such as contents pages, captions, headings and indexes. Help the children to identify the different purposes of such texts and make a collection to put on display and to discuss as part of Literacy Hours.

Writing

Descriptive writing

The success of each of the following activities will depend upon your attitude to the task and the ages and abilities of the children in the class. It is often a good idea to show the children that you are a writer too, by producing something yourself before a lesson or even for a short time during one.

Acrostics

◉ Acrostics are created when the initial letters of each line of a description of a person or thing form the name of the subject which is to be written about.

> **S**ometimes I love it
> **C**an't wait to get there!
> **H**ate it sometimes
> **O**h, it's so boring!
> **O**pen the door —
> **L**et me out!

Children could write about spring, school, rain, my friend, sport or whatever they are interested in. This activity enables you to discuss initial sounds with the children and to reinforce their knowledge of onset and rime.

Rotating stories

This may begin as an oral activity and develop into a writing one. Children take turns to write a word, phrase, sentence or paragraph, passing the work around the group. Children can work in pairs so that every pair has at least one child who is able to write legibly and with some accuracy.

Letters

◉ In Year 3, children should increasingly see the need to write for real audiences. Letter-writing is an ideal activity, particularly when arrangements have been made for the children to receive replies. Letters can be sent to pen pals, classes in other schools, celebrities, museums, authors (write care of the publishers), industries, parents (letters home may stand a better chance of being delivered if the children have written them themselves) or even to you.

◉ As a way of introducing yourself to a new class you might produce a letter for each child describing your own interests, family and so on and asking about his/hers. The children then write back to you. As well as providing selected information, make sure

Secretarial aspects

● In Year 3, you will need to introduce and reinforce many of the more formal, secretarial aspects of writing such as punctuation and spelling. However, it is important that this is not done at the expense of children's enthusiasm and creativity. When you give them writing tasks, ask them to get their ideas down quickly and then begin to draft the ideas into a more refined form. At this stage, they should be aware of the need for legibility and accuracy because their writing will be read by someone else.

● Focus on one or two secretarial features in each writing lesson and discuss these with the children before, during and after the writing time. For example, you may ask them to pay particular attention to full stops and capital letters in one lesson, while in another the emphasis might be on accurate spelling of certain words. This is not to suggest that they should ignore other elements, but they may acquire skills and knowledge more readily if they are not overwhelmed by a feeling that they must get *everything* right every time they write.

that you include plenty of questions so that children can structure their replies around answering these. For example, you might write *My favourite football team is Barnsley. Do you have a favourite team?* or *I really enjoy line dancing. Do you have any special hobbies or interests?*

Food

Smarties, crisps and fruit make ideal stimuli for discussions about taste, texture and appearance of food. Carefully structured lessons in which children examine food closely and taste it can lead to thoughtful and interesting descriptive writing.

Breakthrough to Literacy

Breakthrough, though it has its critics, can facilitate early writing and may be used to help children to recognize words which they need to use frequently. It can be used imaginatively as an aid to topic work with the folders acting as word banks for children to draw upon when writing, using the *look-cover-write-check* approach. The word-building materials provide morphemes and graphemes which can easily be shown in the context of whole words so that children may see the function of letters, blends and digraphs.

Punctuation

◉ Teach punctuation in stages and take opportunities presented in children's reading to explain commas, exclamation marks and so on. Some class or group lessons may be used to discuss, for example, the use of capital letters and, while it is important to relate what is learned to children's writing, it may be helpful to provide some illustrative exercises in order to reinforce concepts.

The sentence

The most basic concept in punctuation is the sentence. However, although the sentence is at the heart of writing, young children, and even adults, do not necessarily speak in sentences or always pause at the ends of sentences when they do use them. We should, therefore, be careful not to give children the impression that written language is simply spoken language written down.

Appropriate use of the comma, colon, semi-colon and paragraph can only be taught when children have an understanding of the nature of a sentence. In the early stages of writing, children place full stops in many places. Sometimes full stops appear at the end of each line of writing. This may be because they are used to books in which sentences are short and contained within single lines. Publishers' 'easy to read' books tend to avoid line breaks within a sentence.

◙ One activity which may be used to develop and reinforce the concept of the sentence is to provide children with incomplete sentences and to ask them to use their imaginations to finish them. This can lead to a discussion of the nature of a sentence. You can ask them to join beginnings and endings of sentences, choosing from a list. This can lead to some interesting combinations and some discussion of what is possible and impossible, as well as what makes sense and what does not. For example:
The big, brown dog flew over the hill.
The little sparrow played football.
The children begged for a bone.

Commas

◙ Much of children's early writing is made up of lists. (The list may be a feature of preparation for writing for experienced writers, too.) Introduce commas when children begin to turn their lists into prose. You might ask them to write descriptions of members of the class using a series of adjectives separated by commas.

◙ At a later stage, the children could examine the use of commas in their reading books and could try to work out why they were used in particular places. You could help them to classify the different uses. For example, they might discover that commas can be used:
▶ to separate words in a list;
▶ to separate the name of a person being addressed in direct speech from the rest of the sentence;
▶ to separate an adverbial clause or phrase from the rest of a sentence;
▶ to separate clauses in a sentence.

◙ The story of the comma which saved a human life on page 133 of *Curriculum Bank Writing KS2*, D Waugh with N McGuinn (Scholastic), may be used to show how the insertion of a comma into text can change meaning dramatically.

Speech marks

◙ An old strategy for teaching speech marks is still a good one. Draw a picture/cartoon on the board with a speech bubble coming out of a character's mouth. Talk about comics and speech bubbles. *What are they for? Do we see them in books?* Then take the board

rubber and rub out most of the speech bubble just leaving enough of it to form two speech marks. Now erase the picture of the character and add *said the pirate*, or whatever is appropriate. Explain that this is how the same information is conveyed in books. The children can then choose a frame from a strip cartoon and write down the words in the speech bubbles with speech marks and attribution to the speakers.

Children are normally taught to write double speech marks (to avoid confusion with apostrophes) but they can look in books and see examples of the use of both double and single speech marks. Discuss this with them and explain that both are acceptable.

◙ Group reading sessions may be used to reinforce concepts in punctuation. For example, give each child a copy of the same book and ask the children to read in turn, changing the reader after each sentence or paragraph. They could be assigned different characters in a story and be asked to read dialogue without using words such as *said the ghost* or *asked Josie*. This helps to develop an understanding of the purpose of speech marks and their placement.

Word detectives!
Can you deduce the SPELLING RULE?

ban   banned   pat   patted
chat   chatted   rot   rotted
drip   dripped   rub   rubbed
drum   drummed   slam   slammed
grab   grabbed   slip   slipped
hop   hopped   stop   stopped
pad   padded   wag   wagged

Question marks

☑ Asking children to look at a list of sentences to identify those which require full stops and those which need question marks may help to reinforce the use of punctuation. A more creative way of developing their conception of the question and its punctuation is to provide them with answers and ask them to write their own questions.

Punctuation walk

Give children a short passage which is unpunctuated and ask them to read it aloud while they walk. Tell them to pause briefly when the text seems to need a short pause and a comma, and for longer when a full stop might be required. They could begin working individually and go on to discuss with partners the place where punctuation might be needed.

Identifying punctuation

☑ Present a passage on the board, a flip chart, or an overhead transparency with the punctuation omitted or covered. Children listen to the passage or read it aloud and then re-read it and try to decide what the hidden punctuation marks were.

Spelling

☑ There are few spelling rules which apply with regularity and which children at Year 3 can

understand. 'I before e except after c', for example, has so many exceptions and its application is so difficult to explain and understand, that it is probably inappropriate for Year 3 children to learn. However, you might teach them that, in English:

▶ *q* is always followed by *u*;
▶ words do not end with *v* and rarely with *i* or *u*;
▶ in the past tense, verbs usually have -*ed* added to them;
▶ when *ed* is added, any final consonant is often doubled.

☑ Encourage your class to discover some spelling rules or regularities for themselves by providing them with collections of appropriate words to sort and group (for example: hop/hopped, pat/patted, pull/pulled.) *Can you see a spelling rule? Can you find some words which break the rule?* This enables them to apply what they learn about the words they are taught to other words which they come across independently. They are also more likely to remember rules which they have worked out for themselves.

Games

☑ I-spy, rhyming games, tongue-twisters and work on alliteration all emphasize word relationships. Ask the children to create their own spoonerisms beginning with their names (for example, *Bason Jell* for *Jason Bell*). The children will probably begin to realize that some names are more difficult than others because of the presence of letter and sound combinations which do not feature in English.

Developing an interest in letters and words
● Children can create collages of letters, make pastry letters, use magnetic letters, create patterns using groups of letters, trace letters in sand or cut letters out of newspapers to make sentences (like ransom notes). One teacher encourages her Year 3 children to add to her list of what she calls *silly words* (those which are irregular) and to find others (regular) which she calls *easy words*. Children can make collections of foreign words seen in shops and on television and can be encouraged to look for deliberate misspellings on household products and businesses (Kwikfit, Weetabix, Betabuy).

● Write an interesting word on the board each day and discuss it with the children. They can be asked to contribute words, too. *Can you find a chance to use to-day's word correctly?* Encourage them to think of related words by choosing root words. For example, *signature* might lead to discussion of *sign*, *signal* and *significant*.

Handwriting
Different styles
◙ Make a collection of different styles of handwriting for a display. Show the children that different styles are appropriate at different times. For example, you might talk about using:
❯ printing for labels, titles and posters;
❯ a quick hand for making notes and lists;
❯ neat, well-presented writing for material which is to be read by others.

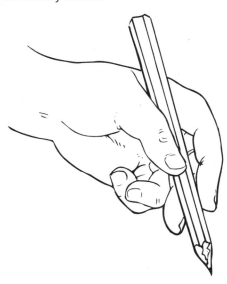

Samples
Make sure that children get plenty of practice at handwriting and keep samples of their writing throughout the year so that both they and their parents can see how they are progressing.

Checking for problems
● At this stage, pay attention to incorrect pencil grips which may lead to problems later if not corrected in Year 3. Children may remember the correct grip if you ask them to hold the pencil in the hand which they do not write with and then take it between the index finger and thumb of their preferred hand and turn the hand so that the pencil rests lightly on the joint of finger and thumb.

● Check that left-handed children have developed a comfortable writing position. The paper may be angled up to 45 degrees with the top right-hand side nearer to the child than the top left. Left-handed children may also hold pencils between 2.5 and 4cm from the tip to enable them to see their writing. They should be seated to the left of right-handed children to avoid collisions of arms.

Basic joins
◙ The National Literacy Strategy provides guidance on the basic joins which children should practise at Year 3.

Assessment

english

Year 3 is, then, a year in which children will increasingly come to understand the reciprocal nature of reading and writing and will begin to make increasing use of the devices they discover in their reading to enhance their writing. They should be developing into increasingly independent readers, but will still need plenty of direct teaching if they are to continue to make progress.

What do they know?

By the end of Year 3 children should know the following things:
- the function of full stops and capital letters in sentences;
- a wide range of graphemes, blends and digraphs;
- several key words by sight;
- how to use their phonic knowledge to make an attempt at an unfamiliar word;
- how to use a simple dictionary to look up spellings and definitions;
- how to learn spellings using a strategy such as *look-say-cover-write-check*;
- that they may be able to decode a word by breaking it into phonemes;
- that they may be able to work out what a word says by using context and reading ahead;
- that they should re-read their own writing to check for mistakes.

What can they do?

They should be able to:
- read aloud with increasing fluency;
- compare fact and fiction;
- be increasingly aware of audience in speaking and in writing;
- understand the difference between singular and plural;
- form letters correctly;
- use verb tenses with increasing accuracy;
- make use of punctuation marks when reading aloud to add intonation;
- make and use word banks;
- use the computer for writing.

What have they experienced?

They should have:
- read a range of different genres in both fiction and non-fiction;
- read independently and in groups;
- written in a variety of styles for real audiences;
- had opportunities to talk about their work in groups and to the whole class;
- developed a positive attitude to literacy;
- worked in a stimulating and 'literate' classroom;
- developed an increased awareness of the possibilities which are open to them as literate people.

Mathematics
including Numeracy Hour

The teaching and learning opportunities that you provide your children with in Year 3 build upon the mathematical foundations established in Key Stage 1. It is on this that all other mathematics (mathematical knowledge, skills and understanding) and applied mathematics (real-life, problem-solving investigations) are built in later primary years.

These experiences should allow children to continue to develop a firm understanding of mathematical concepts and make the necessary connections between:

- mathematical symbols: 'x' '÷' signs;
- mathematical language: *multiply, divide, quarter*;
- pictures:

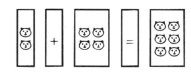

- concrete situations: *A quarter of our class can't swim. How many children in our class can swim?*

The teaching and learning objectives contained in this chapter show progression throughout Year 3. It is about 'what' mathematics to teach. So often children's learning is lead by the activity rather than the learning intention that underpins the activity.

What follows should enable you to identify what stage in their development most of the children have reached, and to decide how best to develop their work in the future. Children should be familiar and successful with the materials, language and activities for each learning objective before working on the next objective. Mathematics, however, is not a fixed, linear, hierarchical discipline: it is cumulative rather than sequential. Although the learning objectives presented in this chapter show a step-by-step sequence, they will be dependent upon the appropriate needs, strengths and abilities of individual children.

Language

When you ask children to talk about what they are doing and thinking in mathematics, they not only show you how much they understand, but they also clarify and develop their own understanding.

While still developing the vast range of skills, knowledge and understanding learned from previous learning objectives, children are being exposed to new mathematical concepts of ever-increasing difficulty. While you need to accept children's early mathematical vocabulary, you should help them to develop more formal mathematical language. For example, when learning about multiplication, children first use terms such as 'lots of', 'sets of', and 'groups of', however, when you are talking to them, you can use words such as 'times' and 'multiplied by'.

Ask questions that will help children to:

- make connections in mathematics: *If you know what $\frac{1}{2}$ of 12 is, what do you think $\frac{1}{4}$ of 12 equals? How does the solution to that problem help you to solve this question?*

- develop a greater understanding of the learning objective: *What have you learned from the investigation you have just undertaken?*
- make new discoveries in mathematics: *What have you done so far?*
- apply their mathematical knowledge to other contexts: *If you know that 3 x 6 = 18, what do you think the area of this rectangle with sides of 6cm and 3cm is?*

Estimation and approximation

Development of the ability to estimate and approximate should be a regular part of the mathematics programme in all classes. Provide children with opportunities that will enable them to estimate a rough answer to a problem, and approximate the range an answer is likely to occur within. This will help them to develop a 'feel' for numbers and assess whether an answer is reasonable or not. These skills also play an important role in their ability to measure with understanding.

As children develop, encourage them to estimate as close to the actual answer as possible in a variety of contexts, with a range of materials and units.

Linking concrete apparatus and mental mathematics

Children's first experiences of new mathematical concepts should, where appropriate, involve the use of concrete materials and real-life objects that are relevant and practical to their own experiences.

There does, however, come a time when they are ready to move away from manipulating concrete apparatus and begin to internalize their understanding.

Unfortunately, children don't give off a signal when this internalization has occurred and so it is difficult to know precisely when the need for concrete apparatus has passed. It is only through observation and questions and discussions that you can begin to ascertain whether they are ready to work without the apparatus. *You have just shown me that if you have 3 groups of blocks with 5 blocks in each group, you will have 15 blocks altogether. Let's see what happens when we add another group of 5. Can you tell me what 4 groups of 5 are?*

Practical experiences

Practical learning situations, ie where children use concrete apparatus in real-life problem-solving investigations, often require a considerable amount of time to organize. However, provided that practical work is properly structured, with clear learning objectives, and is followed up by appropriate questions and group discussions, it is time well spent.

For many children practical work provides the most effective means of understanding a particular mathematical concept. It enables children to think through the mathematics contained in the situation and develop a greater understanding of the learning objective.

The Numeracy Hour

During the Numeracy Hour, all the children should be working on mathematics at the same time for the whole period. The mathematics you do in Numeracy Hour will not be part of a general theme or integrated work but is focused on teaching specific mathematical concepts and methods with an emphasis on whole-class teaching.

You will be spending most of the time directly teaching and questioning the class. Children should spend approximately half of their time in a direct teaching relationship with you and the rest of the time working independently either in groups, pairs or individually.

Each lesson should follow this structure.

Oral work and mental calculations (about 5–10 minutes)
Aimed at:
● developing mental fluency in previously taught concepts/methods and developing children's oral skills (whole class).

Main teaching and pupil activities (about 30–40 minutes)
Aimed at:
● introducing children to new mathematical concepts/methods (whole class, group); or
● consolidating previously taught concepts/methods (whole class, group); and
● providing children with opportunities to practise, consolidate, use and apply taught mathematical concepts/methods (groups, pairs, individuals).

Plenary (about 10–15 minutes)
Aimed at:
● drawing together the main teaching points of the lesson (whole class).

Children's recording

When you introduce a new mathematics topic in Year 3 the emphasis should be on practical experiences and talking about mathematics. Do not expect children to write or copy copious amounts of mathematical calculations. However, when appropriate, Year 3 children should be able to record their results confidently using both their own methods of recording and more conventional ones.

What should they be able to do?

By the end of Year 3, children should have had appropriate and sufficient experiences to help them in the following key areas. The statement 'Children should' refers to the majority of children.

Using and applying mathematics

You need to provide children with opportunities to:
● use and apply mathematical knowledge, skills and understanding, that have been previously taught and practised and consolidated, in problem-solving situations;
● acquire knowledge, skills and understandings through 'real-life', meaningful, problem-solving investigations.
So often children enter Key Stage 2 experiencing real difficulties in solving mathematical problems. This may stem from a lack of mathematical knowledge or a failure to apply existing knowledge. However, these difficulties may also have nothing to do with children's mathematical understanding; rather it is often more to do with far more fundamental issues such as lack of confidence, an inability to persevere and failure to be motivated.

In Year 3, as in Key Stage 1, children should be given the opportunity to apply their mathematical knowledge, skills and understandings in an environment which both motivates them and promotes the self-confidence and perseverance they will need later in their primary school life to solve more sophisticated and challenging investigations.

Making and monitoring decisions to solve problems
Children should be able to:
● select and use materials and mathematics appropriate for a particular task;
● develop their own strategies for working through a problem;

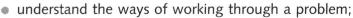

- understand the ways of working through a problem;
- begin to organize and plan their work;
- look for ways of overcoming problems;
- develop different mathematical approaches to a problem;
- begin to make decisions and to realize that results can vary according to the rule used;
- check results.

Developing mathematical language and forms of communication

Children should be able to:
- understand and use appropriate mathematical language;
- discuss mathematical work and begin to explain their thinking;
- use and interpret mathematical information and relate it to a range of situations;
- represent their work in a variety of mathematical forms.

Developing mathematical reasoning

Children should be able to:
- make and test predictions and statements about patterns and relationships;
- make a simple rule;
- understand a general statement;
- investigate statements and predictions by finding and trying out examples.

Key area: Number

Children should be given opportunities to develop both their own and standard methods of working; mentally, orally and in the written form; in a variety of contexts, using a range of practical resources. In order to ensure that the children receive a broad and balanced range of experiences, you need to provide them with activities that employ the following tools:
- concrete materials;
- mental mathematics;
- paper and pencil;
- information technology.

Numbers and the number system

Children should be able to:
- count forwards to 1000 and beyond;
- count backwards from 1000 and beyond;
- recognize, read, write and order numbers to 1000 and beyond;
- recognize written number names to 1000;
- know what each digit in a number represents and partition a number into hundreds, tens and units (HTU);
- say the number that is 1, 10 or 100 more or less than a given two- or three-digit number;
- use ordinal numbers;
- compare two familiar numbers saying which is more or less and giving a number which lies between them;
- begin to make sensible estimates and approximates of at least 200 objects;
- round a two-digit number to the nearest 10 and any three-digit number to the nearest 100.

Money

Children should be able to:
- recognize the value of all coins and of £5, £10, £20 and £50 notes;
- use all coins in simple contexts;

- use combinations of coins to make amounts up to £1;
- trade a number of 1p, 2p, 5p, 10p, 20p, 50p coins for £1;
- add and subtract amounts of money up to £1;
- use notes and coins in simple contexts, adding and subtracting up to £5.

Fractions and decimals

Children should be able to:
- recognize and use in context simple fractions such as halves, thirds, quarters, fifths and tenths;
- recognize the equivalence between two familiar fractions;
- compare two familiar fractions;
- recognize decimal notation in money and in metres and centimetres;
- recognize 0.5 as one half on a calculator.

Negative numbers

Children should be able to:
- recognize negative numbers in context.

Calculations

Patterns

Children should be able to:
- recognize patterns involving numbers to 1000;
- count forwards and backwards in 1s, 10s and 100s from any two- or three-digit number;
- count forwards and backwards in 2s, 3s, 4s and 5s from any small number to 100;
- copy, continue and devise patterns involving numbers to 1000;
- recognize odd and even numbers up to 100;
- explore and use the patterns in addition and subtraction facts to 10;
- explore and use the patterns in multiplication and related division facts including 2x, 5x, 10x;
- make generalisations about patterns;
- make predictions about patterns;
- record observations.

Addition

Children should be able to:
- understand that addition can be done in any order and applied to more than two numbers;
- understand and use the vocabulary associated with addition;
- understand all number pairs for 20;
- understand addition doubles for multiples of 10 to 100;
- understand and use addition facts to 20;
- use knowledge of number facts and place value to add a pair of numbers mentally;
- add three or more single-digit numbers mentally (totals up to 50);
- add three or more two-digit numbers using appropriate apparatus;
- add three or more three-digit numbers using appropriate apparatus;
- add numbers mentally where the units cross the tens boundary.

Subtraction

Children should be able to:
- understand and use vocabulary associated with subtraction;
- understand number patterns in subtraction facts to 10;
- understand and use subtraction facts to 20;
- use knowledge of number facts and place value to subtract a pair of numbers mentally;
- subtract a single-digit number from any two-digit number;
- subtract two two-digit numbers using appropriate apparatus;
- subtract two two-digit numbers mentally where the units cross the tens boundary.

Addition and subtraction

Children should be able to:
- understand further the relationship between addition and subtraction;
- further develop mental strategies for addition and subtraction;
- further develop paper and pencil methods for calculations;
- solve problems involving addition and subtraction.

Multiplication

Children should be able to:
- understand and use the vocabulary associated with multiplication;
- understand that multiplication can be done in any order;
- understand doubles of multiples of 10 to 100;
- recall 2x, 5x and 10x multiplication tables;
- begin to recall 3x and 4x multiplication tables;
- use knowledge of number facts and place value to multiply mentally by 2, 3, 4, 5, 10 or 100.

Division

Children should be able to:
- understand and use the vocabulary associated with division;
- develop an understanding of remainder;
- make sensible decisions about rounding up and down after division;
- understand halves of multiples of 10 to 100;
- recall division facts related to the 2x, 5x and 10x multiplication tables;
- develop an understanding of the division facts related to the 3x, 4x multiplication tables;
- use knowledge of number facts and place value to divide mentally by 2, 3, 4, 5, 10 or 100.

Multiplication and division

Children should be able to:

● understand further the relationship between multiplication and division;

● further develop mental strategies for multiplication and division;

● further develop paper and pencil methods for calculations;

● solve problems involving known multiplication and division facts;

● choose the appropriate operation when solving multiplication and division problems.

Solving numerical problems

Children should be able to:

● solve numerical problems involving known addition, subtraction, multiplication and division facts in the context of real-life, investigative problems involving:

❱ money;

❱ length;

❱ mass;

❱ volume and capacity;

❱ time.

Key area: Shape, space and measures

Children enter Year 3 with a practical understanding of their world gained through movement of themselves, interaction with others and of everyday things around them.

In this area, activities involving concrete apparatus provide opportunities for allowing children to develop their spatial and geometric skills, knowledge and understanding.

Understanding and using properties of shape

3-D solids

Children should be able to:

● understand and use appropriate vocabulary associated with 3-D solids;

● continue to recognize, name and describe the properties of 3-D solids including a pyramid, cone, prism and hemisphere;

● construct 3-D solids using various apparatus;

● sort known 3-D solids according to faces, edges and corners.

2-D shapes

Children should be able to:

● understand and use appropriate vocabulary associated with 2-D shapes;

● continue to recognize and name 2-D shapes including octagons and regular polygons;

● recognize and use appropriate vocabulary including sides, corners;

- describe the properties of 2-D shapes;
- make 2-D shapes with increasing care and accuracy;
- sort known 2-D shapes using a variety of criteria including length of sides, right-angled corners and lines of symmetry.

Symmetry

Children should be able to:
- understand and use appropriate vocabulary associated with symmetry;
- recognize and sketch a line of symmetry in a 2D shape or pattern.

Understanding and using properties of position and movement

Position

Children should be able to:
- understand and use appropriate vocabulary associated with position;
- find the position of an object on a grid using columns and rows;
- recognize directions N, S, E, W.

Movement

Children should be able to:
- understand and use appropriate vocabulary associated with movement;
- measure clockwise and anti-clockwise turns;
- develop their understanding of movement in a straight line (translations);
- recognize whole, half and quarter turns (rotations);
- combine rotations and translations.

Angle

Children should be able to:
- understand and use appropriate vocabulary associated with angle;
- recognize right angles in shapes and in the environment using an angle measurer or template;
- measure clockwise and anti-clockwise turns in terms of right angles, and relate them to the four points on the compass.

Understanding and using measures

Length

Children should be able to:
- understand and use appropriate vocabulary associated with length;
- recognize the centimetre (cm) and metre (m) lengths;
- estimate and measure to the nearest centimetre and metre;
- recognize the need for a standard unit larger than a metre;
- recognize the kilometre (km) length;
- choose and use appropriate measuring apparatus with increasing accuracy;
- record estimates and measurements;
- solve problems involving length.

Mass (weight)

(In the National Curriculum for mathematics the term 'weight' no longer appears, but has been replaced by the term 'mass'. 'Weight', the amount of pull something exerts, is properly measured in newtons; mass, the amount of substance, is measured in grams.)

Children should be able to:
- understand and use appropriate vocabulary associated with mass;
- recognize the gram (g) and kilogram (kg) measures;

- estimate and measure using grams and kilograms;
- choose and use appropriate measuring apparatus with increasing accuracy;
- record estimates and measurements;
- solve problems involving mass.

Volume and capacity

Volume is the measurement of space in a solid shape. Capacity is the amount of space something will hold.

Children should be able to:

- understand and use appropriate vocabulary associated with volume and capacity;
- recognize the litre (l) and millilitre (ml) measures;
- estimate and measure using litres and millilitres;
- choose and use appropriate measuring apparatus with increasing accuracy;
- record estimates and measurements;
- solve problems involving volume and capacity.

Area

Children should be able to:

- measure and compare area using direct comparison;
- measure and compare area using non-standard units.

Time

Children should be able to:

- understand and use appropriate vocabulary associated with time;
- continue to tell the time on the hour, half hour and quarter hour using digital and analogue clocks;
- tell the time using digital and analogue clocks to the nearest 5 minutes.

Key area: Handling data

In Year 3 children need to formulate questions and use simple statistical methods. They should be given opportunities to access and collect data through purposeful enquiries. The use of computers should be encouraged as a source of interesting data and as a tool for representing data.

Processing, representing and interpreting data

Children should be able to:

- collect, record, discuss and predict numerical data using:
  - bar charts;
  - tally charts;
  - lists and tables;
  - pictograms (with the symbol representing groups of units).

Practical ideas

Making a start

The first activities under each main heading are particularly suitable for introducing the concept.

Assessment

Most of the activities can be used for some form of assessment. However, activities that have the symbol ☺ beside them are particularly suitable for assessment purposes.

Numeracy Hour

All of the practical ideas which follow are suitable for using in the Numeracy Hour. If, for example, you were introducing children to the concept of negative numbers, then your work in the Numeracy Hour might follow this pattern.

Oral work and mental calculation (10 minutes)

▶ Count back from 50 to 0 chanting as a whole class and counting round the class.
▶ Count on and back in repeated steps (2, 3, 5, 10) to and from 100 as a whole class and counting round the class.
▶ Introduce the concept of negative numbers by asking *When we are counting back from any number to reach zero, what happens when we reach zero? Is it possible for us to count back any further?*

Main teaching and pupil activity (30 minutes)

▶ Discuss with the class the concept of negative numbers using familiar contexts such as temperature and calculator displays (see page 54).
▶ Introduce the concept of negative numbers using a number line (see page 54).
▶ Children complete a number line with missing positive and negative numbers (see page 55).

▶ Play Reach −1 with the children working in pairs (see page 55).

Plenary (10 minutes)

▶ Ask children to present and explain their work so you and the class can question them about it.
▶ Count back from 10 to −10 around the class.
▶ Count back from 10 to −10 chanting as a whole class with and without your help.

Number
Place value

☺ Count round the room within the range 0–1000 forwards and backwards. Start from any given number.

⬤ Display number posters for numbers within the range 0–1000 to familiarize the children with place value. On the number poster display the number, number name and place indicators.

Th H T U

4 2 3 1

four thousand two hundred and thirty one

Using 1–100 and 10–1000 charts and squares

☺ Ideas for using a 1–100 chart or 10–1000 chart.

⬤ Count forwards/backwards in ones, tens, hundreds.

10	20	30	40	**50**	60	70	80	90	100
110	120	130	140	1**50**	160	170	180	190	200
210	**2**20	**2**30	240	**250**	**2**60	270	**2**80	**2**90	300
310	320	330	340	3**50**	360	370	380	390	400

● Identify the pattern that occurs in the columns and rows (for example, a pattern of 50s in the tens column, a pattern of 200s in the hundreds row.

● Ask children to complete an incomplete 1–100 square or 10–1000 square. For example:

10	20		40	50	60	70		90	100
110	120	130		150	160	170	180	190	200
	220	230	240	250		270	280		300
310	320		340	350	360		380	390	400
	430						480		

Variation: Ask children to complete an incomplete 10–1000 square following another pattern, for example:

	110	210		410	510	610	710	810	
20		220	320	420	520		720	820	920
	130	230	330		530	630	730		
		240	340	440		640		840	940
	150		350				750		

● Cover up a number or numbers and ask the children to identify the covered number(s).

● Give children a 1–100 square or 10–1000 square on card that has been cut up to make a jigsaw and ask them to put it back together.

10	20	30	40	50	60	70	80	90	100
110	120	130	140	150	160	170	180	190	200
210	220	230	240	250	260	270	280	290	300
310	320	330	340	350	360	370	380	390	400
410	420	430	440	450	460	470	480	490	500
510	520	530	540	550	560	570	580	590	600

Variation: The children make their own 1–100 square or 10–100 square jigsaw.

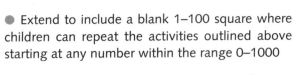

● Extend to include a blank 1–100 square where children can repeat the activities outlined above starting at any number within the range 0–1000

Using 0–100 and 0–1000 cards

✪ The children put a pack of jumbled 0–100 cards in order.

● Ask the children to pick out the cards:
❱ with 1 unit, 2 units and 3 units and put them in three separate piles;
❱ with 1 ten, 2 tens and 3 tens and put them in three separate piles.

● Remove a card from the pack and ask the children to find the missing card.

● Extend these activities by using a selection of cards within the 0–1000 range.

● Deal a jumbled set of 0–100 cards to the class, then ask two children to come out to the front and each to display one of their number cards (for example 46 and 67). Ask the remaining members of the class to stand up if they have a number which is in between 46 and 67. (They should hold up their cards so you can check them.) Repeat.

● Make the number 367 using 0–10 number cards. Discuss the values of the 3, the 6 and the 7. *What is the value of the 3 in 367? How many tens in 367?* Repeat using other three- and four-digit numbers.

● Using a selection of three- and four-digit number cards, ask the children to place them in order. For example:
475, 354, 243;
2646, 2534, 2756, 4657.

Tens and units

Use either Dienes apparatus (or similar Base-10 material) and interlocking cubes.
✪ Show 7 tens and 4 ones to the class. *How many cubes do I have altogether?* Ask a child to show 74 using the number cards and number name cards. Repeat using other numbers to 1000.

● Show 452 using the number cards. Ask a child to represent 452 using the Base-10 material. Repeat using other numbers to 1000.

✪ Ask children to compare the size of two numbers displayed using Base 10 material and number cards, for example 136 and 361. *Which number is larger/ smaller? How can you tell?* Try with numbers such as 401 and 104, 741 and 471.
Hint: An overhead projector is an excellent way to display Dienes apparatus to the whole class.

● Ask a child to make a tower of 27 interlocking cubes. Then ask another child to add 10 cubes to the tower to make a tower of 37 cubes. A third child adds another 10 cubes to the tower to make a tower of 47 cubes. *What does 27 and 10 make? What does 37 and 10 make?* Discuss the pattern with the children: 27, 37, 47 … 97

● Using Base 10 material, extend to include numbers within the range 0–1000, adding 100 each time.

Quick quiz

✪ Ask the children:
What is 1 more/less than (a given two-digit number)?
What is 10 more/less than (a given two-digit number)?
What is 100 more/less than (a given two-digit number)?
What is 1 more/less than (a given three-digit number?)
Extension: Ask for 10 and 100 more/less than three-digit numbers.
Variation: Display a number card or number name card and ask the same question.

✪ Ask the children to name two numbers in the

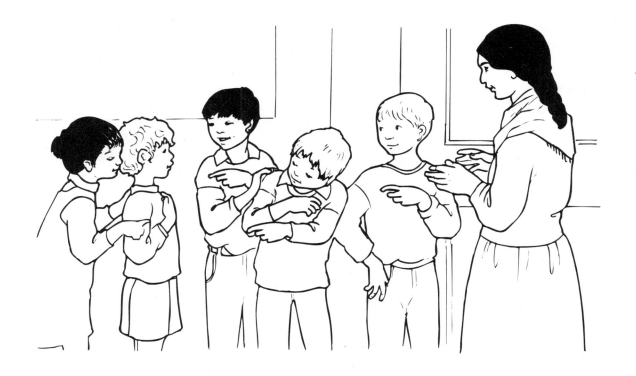

range 0–100. *Which number is greater? Can you think of a number that lies between these two numbers?*
Extension: include numbers in the range 0–1000

Multiples of 10

● Display cards showing the multiples of 10 up to 100. Remove a card and ask children to identify the missing number. Jumble the cards and ask the children to put them in the correct order.

Matching game 0–100

✪ Shuffle a selection of 0–100 number cards and corresponding number name cards together. Spread the cards face down on the table. Working in pairs, children play Pelmanism or Snap.
Extension: Use a selection of 0–1000 number cards and corresponding number name cards.

Ordinal numbers

Use a selection of ordinal cards.
● Randomly hand out cards to children and ask them to arrange themselves in order.

● Arrange a group of objects in a row on a table. *Which object is closest to the door? Put the 'first' card by it. Now put the other cards in the right places.*

✪ When children are lined up at the door, ask *Who is seventh in line? Who is third from the end of the line? What position is Jessica in the line?*

● During sports activities encourage children to identify their:
❱ position in the group;
❱ place in the game.

Estimation and approximation
(also see page 42)

● Encourage children to develop their estimation and approximation skills to about 200 by asking them questions such as:
How many dots are there on this page?
How many letters on this piece of newspaper?
How many cubes in this container?
How many toes in the class?
How many hours in a week?
How far is it from the classroom to the office?
What is 157 + 28?
What is half of 178?
What is 34 multiplied by 4?
Encourage children to explain how they arrived at their estimate. They should record their estimates and then find the difference between the estimate and the actual answer.

● Show children a number card in the range 0–99 and ask them to round it to the nearest 10 (for example, 64 rounded to the nearest 10 is 60; 65 is 70). Then show a number card in the range 0–999 and ask them to round it to the nearest 100 (for example, 272 rounded to the nearest 100 is 300). Finally, ask them to round a two-digit number to the nearest 10 and a three-digit number to the nearest 100 in their heads. Some children may need to use 0–100 or 10–1000 charts.

Money
Notes and coins
✪ Ask children to name and identify all the coins. Introduce the £5, £10, £20 and £50 notes. Discuss their design, size and colour. Then, presenting notes in turn, ask *What note is this?*

✪ Ask the children to make combinations of coins to make amounts up to £1 (for example, 50p, 20p, 5p, 2p, 2p = 79p). *Who can think of other ways to make 79p?*

● Ask the children to exchange a note for its equivalent value in smaller notes or coins.

● Encourage children to apply their knowledge of addition, subtraction, and multiplication number facts to solve calculations involving amounts of money up to £1, finding totals and giving change. For example, *In the post office Michael bought two stamps at 26p each and one stamp at 18p. How much did he spend altogether? How much change did he get from £1?*

● Encourage children to use notes and coins in simple contexts adding, subtracting, and multiplying up to £5. For example, *What is the total of £2.30 and £1.40?*
    If one banana costs 24p, how much do 3 bananas cost? Brian has £4.40. If it costs him £1.50 to go swimming, how much money will he have left?

Fractions
Revising halves and quarters
● Hold up an apple, then cut it in half. Say *This one apple has been cut into two parts. Each is the same size. Each is called a half.* Write '$\frac{1}{2}$' on the board.
    Hold up each half of the apple and cut it in half. Say *This half of the apple has been cut in half. Each of the four pieces is the same size. Each is called a quarter.* Write '$\frac{1}{4}$' on the board.
    If necessary repeat, using, for example an orange, string, paper, material, cake and so on.

● Discuss the concept of half and quarter in relation to measurements: $\frac{1}{2}$ a teaspoon of coffee, $\frac{1}{4}$ of an hour, $\frac{1}{2}$ a litre and so on. Use, for example, a clock and a litre measure.

● Count out eight cubes. Say *I am going to share these eight cubes equally into two halves. I am going to share them evenly between Freddy and Christina. How many cubes will each child have?* Then give out the cubes alternately one to each child. *Who was right? What is half of eight?* When you have been given the answer, write '$\frac{1}{2}$ of 8 = 4' on the board.
    Repeat using other objects such as buttons and marbles and then go on to numbers up to 20. Repeat the process to demonstrate $\frac{1}{4}$.

✪ Ask the children to divide a set of objects into halves and quarters and to write down the corresponding calculation.

Introducing thirds, fifths, tenths
● Introduce the children to the concept of thirds by:
❯ colouring one third of a grid

❯ dividing groups of objects into thirds

Repeat for fifths and tenths.

✪ Ask the children to divide a set of objects into thirds, fifths and tenths and to write down the corresponding calculation.
    (Make sure that the sets of objects are divisible without any remainders.)

Negative numbers
● Introduce the concept of negative numbers using a number line. Introduce the terms 'positive numbers' and 'negative numbers'.
    Discuss the fact that numbers go on forever in both directions, hence the arrows on the number line.

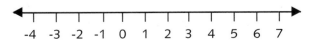

Ask children to complete a number line with missing positive and negative numbers.

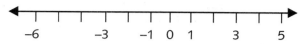

● Discuss with the children the concept of negative numbers in familiar contexts such as temperature and on a calculator display.

Play 'Reach −1'

● Give each child a number line similar to the one above and a counter. They place their counter on any number on the number line except 0 (for example, 2). Throw a dice calling either *add* or *subtract* before you call the number thrown (for example, *Add 4*). Children then have to move their counter along the corresponding number of spaces (landing, in this example, on the 6). Keep throwing the dice and calling out *add* or *subtract* until a child lands on −1.

Extension: After the game has been played several times ask children to place their counter on a negative number. Choose different numbers to be reached.

Methods of computation
Patterns

✪ Use a 1–100 chart to identify the patterns that occur in the columns and rows. Use a 1–1000 multiples of 10 chart to identify the patterns that occur in the columns and rows.

✪ Children count forwards and backwards in 1s, 10s and 100s from any two- or three-digit number.

✪ Children count forwards and backwards in 2s, 3s, 4s and 5s from any small number up to 100.

Odd and even

● Revise odd and even numbers. Ask the children to:

❱ put their hands on their head if they call out an even number when counting round the room;

❱ sort a pack of 0–100 or a random selection 0–1000 cards into odds and evens;

❱ identify odd and even numbers on a 0–100 chart;

❱ find numbers in the environment. *Are they odd or even?*

Patterns in the four rules

● Identify the patterns in addition and subtraction number facts to 10. *What do you notice about the first and second columns of numbers in the addition calculations? What do you notice about the first addition and the first subtraction – what things about them are the same?*

For example:

0 + 6 = 6	6 − 6 = 0
1 + 5 = 6	6 − 5 = 1
2 + 4 = 6	6 − 4 = 2
3 + 3 = 6	6 − 3 = 3
4 + 2 = 6	6 − 2 = 4
5 + 1 = 6	6 − 1 = 5
6 + 0 = 6	6 − 0 = 6

+	1	2	3	4
1	2	3	4	5
2	3	4	5	6
3	4	5	6	7
4	5	6	7	8

● Identify the patterns in 2x, 5x, 10x multiplication and related division facts.

For example:

1 x 2 = 2	2 ÷ 2 = 1
2 x 2 = 4	4 ÷ 2 = 2
3 x 2 = 6	6 ÷ 2 = 3
4 x 2 = 8	8 ÷ 2 = 4
5 x 2 = 10	10 ÷ 2 = 5
6 x 2 = 12	12 ÷ 2 = 6

Addition

Mental calculation strategies

● Children find crossing the 10s boundary difficult (for example, 45 + 27 =)

They need to be taught a range of mental strategies that will help them to solve these types of calculation easily. For example:

▶ start with the largest number first;
▶ count forward in repeated steps;
▶ know that 6 + 5 is the same as 5 + 6;
▶ use two stages to add 9 (ie +10 – 1);
▶ use two stages to add 11 (ie +10 + 1);
▶ know doubles, such as 6 + 6;
▶ know near doubles, based on doubles already known: 6 + 7 is one more than 6 + 6;
▶ partition 6, 7, or 8 into '5 and something' for example:

```
      8   +    7
  (5 + 3)  +  (5 + 2)
  (5 + 5)  +  (3 + 2)
     10   +    5
            15
```

▶ partition into '10 and something', for example:

```
     15   +    14
 (10 + 10) +  (5 + 4)
     20   +    9
            29
```

▶ increase the largest number to the next multiple of 10 and add the remainder, for example:

```
      8   +    3
  (8 + 2)  +    1
     10   +    1
            11
```

▶ add three or four small numbers: put the largest number first and/or find pairs totalling 9, 10 or 11;
▶ use patterns of similar calculations;
▶ use the relationship between addition and subtraction;
▶ use knowledge of number facts and place value to add a pair of numbers mentally.

Using the strategies

● Children should be taught to solve the following type of addition calculations using the mental calculation strategies above:

▶ addition of a single digit to any three-digit number without crossing the 10s boundary (385 + 4 = ❑, 561 + ❑ = 569);
▶ addition of a two-digit number to a multiple of 100 (200 + 45 = ❑, 400 + ❑ = 435);
▶ addition of a two-digit number to a multiple of 10, without crossing 100 (40+21=❑, ❑ + ❑ = 56);
▶ addition of a pair of two-digit numbers, without crossing the 10s boundary or 100 (43 + 21 = ❑, ❑ + ❑ = 45);
▶ addition of number facts to 20 (13 + 6 = ❑, 16 + ❑ = 18);
▶ addition of 10 to any two- or three-digit number, including crossing the hundreds boundary (94 + 10 = ❑, 10 + ❑ = 106, ❑ + 10 = ❑, 246 + ❑ = 256);
▶ addition of a pair of multiples of 10, crossing 100 (40 + 80 = ❑, 90 + ❑ = 120);
▶ addition of a three-digit multiple of 10 to make the next higher multiple of 100 (440 + ❑ = 500, ❑ + ❑ = 200);
▶ addition of a multiple of 10 to a two-digit number, crossing 100 (42 + 70 = ❑, 55 + ❑ = 155);
▶ addition of a pair of multiples of 100, crossing 1000 (300 + 800 = ❑, 200 + ❑ = 900);
▶ addition of 100 to any three-digit number, without crossing 1000 (576 + 100 = ❑, ❑+❑ = 487);
▶ addition of a single-digit number to a two-digit number, crossing the 10s boundary (75 + 8 = ❑, ❑ + ❑ = 94);
▶ addition of any pair of two-digit numbers (63 + 29 = ❑, ❑ + ❑ = 86).

Paper and pencil

● Children should be taught to solve addition calculations using paper and pencil procedures to record, support and explain mental methods, building on established mental strategies. They should be encouraged to discuss and compare their methods.

● Teach children, when setting out work in columns, to put units under units, tens under tens and so on. The following paper and pencil procedure should be encouraged for the addition of:

▶ TU + TU not crossing the 10s boundary;
▶ TU + TU crossing the 10s boundary;
▶ HTU + TU not crossing the 10s boundary;
▶ HTU + TU crossing the 10s or 100s boundary or both.

Method: Put the most significant (largest, worth most) digit first.

56	36	62	68
+	+	+	+
23	28	53	75
70	50	110	130
9	14	5	13
79	64	115	143

Make 30

● Use a blank dice and write numbers between 11 and 19 on it. Throw the dice and call out the number on it, for example, 13. Say *Make 30*. The children write down the answer which, when added to 13, equals 30 (17).

Variation: Make other numbers. Use a dice with other numbers on it.

Addition facts

Use a grid showing two rows of ten boxes to demonstrate addition of number facts between 10 and 20 (for example, involving answers that cross the 10s boundary):

$$8 + 7 =$$
$$(8 + 2) + 5 =$$
$$10 + 5 =$$

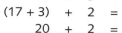

Number lines

Use number lines:

$$15 + 6 =$$

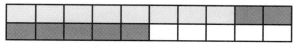

$$17 + 5 =$$
$$(17 + 3) + 2 =$$
$$20 + 2 =$$

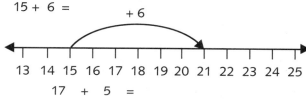

$$26 + 17 =$$
$$(26+10) + 7 =$$
$$36 + 7 =$$

Base 10 material

Use Base 10 material:

$$58 + 25 =$$

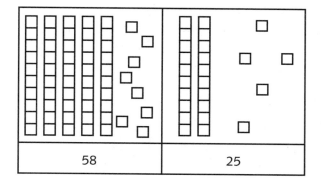

Add the 5 tens and 2 tens.
Add the 8 ones/units and 5 ones/units 70 + 13 =

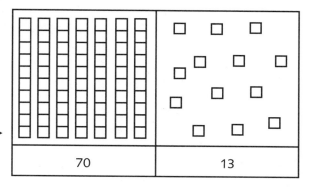

Exchange the 13 ones/units for 1 ten and 3 ones/units:

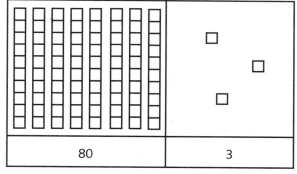

Subtraction
Mental strategies

● Teach the children a range of mental strategies that will help them to solve subtraction calculations easily. Some of these include the following:

▶ count backwards in repeated steps;

▶ if we know that 7 + 8 = 15, then we also know what 15 – 8 and 15 – 7 are, as all three calculations involve the same three numbers (7, 8, 15);

▶ find a small difference by counting up from the

smaller to the larger number (304 – 298 = 299, 300, 301, 302, 303, 304 = 6) or by *saying* 298 + 2 = 300, *knowing* 300 + 4 = 304, *thinking* 2 + 4 = 6;

▶ use two stages to subtract 9 (– 10 + 1);
▶ use two stages to subtract 11 (– 10 – 1);
▶ decrease the largest number to the next multiple of 10 and subtract the remainder:

$$
\begin{array}{rcl}
14 & - & 8 \\
(14-4) & - & 4 \\
10 & - & 4 = 6
\end{array}
$$

▶ use patterns of similar calculations;
▶ use the relationship between addition and subtraction;
▶ use knowledge of number facts and place value to subtract a pair of numbers mentally.

Using the strategies

● Children should be taught to solve the following subtraction calculations using the above-mentioned mental calculation strategies:

▶ subtraction of a single-digit number from any three-digit number without crossing the 10s boundary (376 – 4 = ❑, 465 – ❑ = 462);
▶ subtraction of a single-digit number from a multiple of 100 (500 – 5 = ❑, 800 – ❑ = 795);
▶ subtraction of a pair of two-digit numbers, without crossing the 10s boundary or 100 (73 – 41 = ❑, ❑ – ❑ = 85);
▶ subtraction number facts to 20 (13 – 6 = ❑, 16 – ❑ = 14);
▶ subtraction of 10 from any two- or three-digit number, including crossing the 100s boundary (64 – 10 = ❑, 56 – ❑ = 46, 302–10= ❑, 246 – ❑ = 236);
▶ subtraction of a pair of multiples of 10, crossing 100 (140 – 80 = ❑, 110 – ❑ = 60);
▶ subtraction of a multiple of 10 from a three-digit number, crossing 100 (112 – 70 = ❑, 114 – ❑ = 84);
▶ subtraction of a pair of multiples of 100, crossing 1000 (1300 – 800 = ❑, 1200 – ❑ = 900)
▶ subtraction of 100 from any three-digit number (539 – 100 = ❑, ❑ – 100 = 187);
▶ subtraction of a single-digit number from a 'teens' number, crossing the 10s boundary (15 – 7 = ❑, ❑ – ❑ = 14);
▶ subtraction of a single-digit number from a two-digit number, crossing the 10s boundary (65 – 7 = ❑, ❑ – ❑ = 44);
▶ finding the difference between a pair of numbers lying either side of a multiple of 100 from 100 to 1000 (705 – 697 = ❑, 1004 – 993 = ❑);
▶ subtraction of any pair of two-digit numbers (62 – 39 = ❑, ❑ – ❑ = 28.

Paper and pencil procedures

● Children should be taught to solve subtraction calculations using paper and pencil procedures to record, support and explain mental methods, building on established mental strategies. They should be encouraged to discuss and compare their methods.

● The following paper and pencil procedures should be encouraged for subtraction of TU – TU and HTU – TU.

74 – 36 =

Method 1: Counting on (complementary addition):

74		or	36 + 4 = 40
36 –			40 + 30 = 70
4	from 36 to 40		70 + 4 = 74
30	from 40 to 70		38
4	from 70 to 74		
38			

Method 2: Counting down through a multiple of 10:

$$
\begin{array}{ll}
74 & \\
\underline{36} \;- & \\
40 & (70 - 30) \\
-\;\; \underline{2} & (4 - 6) \\
38 &
\end{array}
$$

Method 3: Approximating by taking away the next higher multiple of 10:

$$
\begin{array}{ll}
74 & \\
\underline{36} \;- & \\
34 & (74 - 40) \\
+\;\; \underline{4} & (40 - 36) \\
38 &
\end{array}
$$

Method 4: Decomposition:

$$
\begin{array}{lcl}
74 & = & 70 + 4 \\
-\;\underline{36} & & 30 + 6 \\
& = & 60 + 14 \quad \text{adjusting from T to U} \\
& & \underline{30 + 6} \\
& & 30 + 8 \quad = \quad 38
\end{array}
$$

Dice

Throw a dice and call out the number of dots on it, for example, 3. Say *Subtract from 20*. The children write down the answer (17).

Variations: Subtract from other numbers; use a blank dice and put larger numbers on it, for example numbers 11–19.

Number lines

For example: 23 – 4 = 19

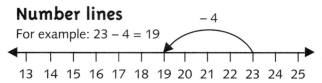

$$64 - 6 =$$
$$(64 - 4) - 2 =$$
$$60 - 2 = 58$$

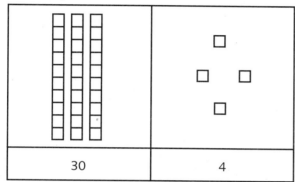

$$34 - 27 =$$
$$(34 - 20) - 7 =$$
$$14 - 7 = 7$$

Base 10 material

For example: 34 – 21

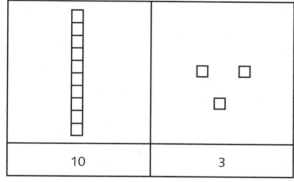

Relationship

Children need to understand and use the relationship of addition and subtraction. Make sure that they realize that knowing one of the relationships means that you also know the other three

$$36 + 27 = 63$$
$$27 + 36 = 63$$
$$63 - 36 = 27$$
$$63 - 27 = 36$$

Multiplication

● Count around the classroom in 2s, 3s, 4s, 5s and 10s. Use a number line or 1–100 chart if necessary.

● Reintroduce multiplication:

▶ Give one child a tower of four cubes;

▶ Ask *How many towers are there?* (1); *How many cubes are there in each tower?* (4);

▶ Write and say *1 x 4 = 4*;

▶ Give a second child another tower of four cubes.

▶ Ask *How many towers are there?* (2); *How many cubes are there in each tower?* (4);

▶ Write and say *2 x 4 = 8*;

▶ Continue this process until ten children are each holding a tower of four cubes;

▶ Recite with the class the 4x tables: *1 x 4 = 4, 2 x 4 = 8*;

▶ Repeat the same process as above for introducing the 3x multiplication facts (you could also use other appropriate apparatus, such as buttons, counters, children…).

● Revise the vocabulary associated with multiplication: *multiplication, multiply, times, groups of, lots of, sets of, product (3 times 4, 3 multiplied by 4, Multiply 3 by 4, Is 12 a multiple of 4?, 3 lots of 4, Product of 3 and 4)*.

● Give children opportunities to solve the following types of multiplication calculations:
3 x 4 = ❏, 12 = 3 x ❏; 3 x ❏ = 12, 12 = ❏ x 4; ❏ x 4 = 12, ❏ = 3 x 4.

Rule

● Teach children that multiplication can be carried out in any order (for example, 3 x 4 = 4 x 3).

Division

● Reintroduce division. Count out 32 cubes in front of the class. Say *We are going to share these 32 cubes evenly among eight children. How many do you think they will each get?* Choose the eight children and give one cube to each of them.

▶ Ask *How many cubes do each of you have?*;
▶ Say *32 shared among 8 is 4*;
▶ Write: 32 ÷ 8 = 4;
▶ Repeat using other examples.

● Repeat the process above to develop and reinforce understanding of the division facts related to the 2x, 3x, 4x, 5x and 10x multiplication tables.

● Identify the patterns in 2x, 3x, 4x, 5x and 10x multiplication and related division facts. For example:

1 x 2 = 2	2 ÷ 2 = 1
2 x 2 = 4	4 ÷ 2 = 2
3 x 2 = 6	6 ÷ 2 = 3
4 x 2 = 8	8 ÷ 2 = 4
5 x 2 = 10	10 ÷ 2 = 5
6 x 2 = 12	12 ÷ 2 = 6

● Revise the vocabulary associated with division: *division, divide, share, divided by* (Share 12 between 3, 12 divided by 3, Divide 12 by 3, *How many 3s in 12?, Is 3 a multiple of 12?*)

● Give children opportunities to solve the following types of division calculations:
12 ÷ 4 = ☐, ☐ = 12 ÷ 4; 12 ÷ ☐ = 3, 3 = 12 ÷ ☐; ☐ ÷ 4 = 3, 3 = ☐ ÷ 4.

Rule

● Teach children that division, unlike multiplication, **cannot** be carried out in any order (for example, 3 x 4 = 4 x 3 but 12 ÷ 3 ╪ 3 ÷ 12).

Consolidating the four rules

● Ask *How many ways can you make 26?* For example;

20 + 6 = ,	30 − 4 = ,
20 + 10 − 4 =,	(8 x 3) + 2 =.

Variation: Use any number to 100.

● Use flash cards with addition, subtraction, multiplication or division number facts to produce instant recall of number facts by the children in your class.

● Ask children to show examples of addition, subtraction, multiplication or division facts using real objects.

● Ask children to write and talk about examples of addition, subtraction, multiplication or division facts in real contexts. (For example, *I had 17 sweets. During the day I gave 3 to Gemma, 4 to Billy and 2 to Ruby. By the end of the day I had 8 sweets left.*)

● Have a wall chart displaying addition, subtraction, multiplication and division number facts.
For example: Subtraction number facts for 7

$$7 - 0 = 7$$
$$7 - 1 = 6$$
$$7 - 2 = 5$$
$$7 - 3 = 4$$
$$7 - 4 = 3$$
$$7 - 5 = 2$$
$$7 - 6 = 1$$
$$7 - 7 = 0$$

Bingo

Addition number facts to 20. Children write down any 16 numbers from 0 to 20 on a 4 x 4 grid (see at top of next column).

Give the children a number statement in one of the following ways:

▶ show them a number card, for example 13 + 6 =
▶ throw two or three dice, call out the numbers and ask the children to add them together;
▶ say an addition statement, for example, *six add fourteen equals*;
▶ in a problem-solving context, for example: *Sarah*

had 13p and was given another 5p by her brother. How much money did she have altogether? Children work out the answer and, if they have that

4	11	3	1
18	13	20	8
6	15	19	2
14	12	10	5

answer on their grid, cross out the number. Any four numbers crossed out together vertically, horizontally or diagonally, mean *Bingo!* Repeat until a child has crossed out all of his/her numbers on the chart. *Variations*: Play Subtraction Bingo/Multiplication Bingo/Division Bingo using other known subtraction/multiplication/division number facts.

Number of the day
○ Have a 'number of the day': throughout the day, when challenged, children have to give a number statement for a particular number using any operation or computational method they can.

Twenty questions
○ Give the children 20 quick-fire addition, subtraction, multiplication and division questions orally using a range of appropriate mathematical vocabulary. Ask them to write down only the answer. Repeat the next day. *Did you get them all finished? How many did you get correct today/yesterday?*

Beat the clock
○ Give the children a strip of paper containing 20 simple calculations. Ask them to complete it in a specified time (say, four minutes). Repeat the next day. *Did you get them all finished? How many did you get correct today/yesterday?*

Countdown
○ Work out a calculation involving known number facts and operations, for example, (3 x 4) + 5 – 2 = 15. Don't tell the children. Keep it to yourself! Write the numbers 2, 3, 4, 5 on the board. Tell the children that, using each of these numbers only once, in any order, and using some or all of the four operations they have to reach the total 15.

● The children can then make up their own and give them to each other.

● Ask the children to find alternative ways of reaching the total.

Solving number problems
Children should have experiences of applying their knowledge of number in a variety of contexts including:
▶ money;
▶ length;
▶ mass;
▶ volume and capacity;
▶ time.

Shape, space and measures
Properties of shape
3-D solids
● Show the children a cube. *Who can tell me what this is?* Revise its properties in relation to faces, edges and vertices, reminding children of what they have

previously learned. Repeat this for cuboid, cylinder, sphere, pyramid, cone, prism and hemisphere.

● The children identify cubes, cuboids, cylinders, spheres, pyramids, cones, prisms and hemispheres in pictures, drawings and in the environment. Make posters ('Our cone collection') on which children can stick appropriate pictures they have found and/or set up a display of real objects.

✪ Place a variety of 3-D solids in a feely bag. Ask individual children to choose a shape and describe it while it is still in the bag. The rest of the class have to try to identify the shape. The child then pulls the shape out to see if the class were correct and places the shape beside the appropriate label.

✪ Play *What am I?* Children describe the attributes of a shape/object and the class have to try and identify it.

● The children pull apart boxes of various shapes and reassemble them.
Variation: The children pull apart boxes of various shapes, trace around their net on to a sheet of card, cut around the net and assemble the shape.

● The children construct 3-D solids using various construction materials, including paper.

○ The children sort a collection of 3-D solids and everyday objects according to faces, edges and vertices.

2-D shapes

● Draw a square on the board or large sheet of paper. *Who can tell me what this is?* Revise with the children its properties in relation to sides and corners. Repeat this for regular and irregular squares, rectangles, triangles, circles, hexagons, pentagons, octagons and other polygons.

✪ The children identify regular and irregular squares, rectangles, triangles, circles, hexagons pentagons, octagons and other polygons in pictures, drawings and in the environment, and make posters and/or displays.

✪ The children sort a collection of 2-D shapes (regular and irregular) according to faces and corners.

Matching 2-D shape game
The children shuffle a variety of 2-D shape cards together – perhaps four each of regular and irregular squares, rectangles, triangles, circles, hexagons, pentagons and octagons – and spread them out face down on the table and play Pelmanism with them. *Variation:* Have one each of a regular square, rectangle, triangle, circle, hexagon, pentagon and octagon picture cards; one each of an irregular square, rectangle, triangle, circle, hexagon, pentagon and octagon picture cards; and two each of squares, rectangles, triangles, circles, hexagons pentagons, octagons and polygons label cards. The children match the picture cards with the label cards. (NB 'Irregular' squares are those shown standing on a point; 'irregular' circles are those shown as an oval.)

Symmetry

● Revise the concept of symmetry. Ask the children to make a symmetrical pattern. (They should fold a piece of paper in half, draw a shape around the fold, cut out the shape.) *Who can make a snowflake? Who can paint a symmetrical picture?* (Fold a piece of paper in half, draw a simple picture on one half with paint, fold the sheet in half again.)

● Discuss with the children:
◗ how the fold line divides the shape into two parts;
◗ how the two parts are the same – they are halves;
◗ that certain shapes have symmetry;
◗ that certain shapes are symmetrical;

▶ that the fold is called a line of symmetry.

✪ The children make their own symmetrical shapes/patterns.

✪ The children find examples of reflective symmetry in shapes and in the environment.

Position

● Discuss simple vocabulary to describe the position of an object, and encourage the children to use it:
▶ in relation to themselves;
▶ in relation to other subjects;
▶ in describing models, pictures and diagrams.
For example: *near, close, far, to the left, to the right, in front of, behind, beside, next, next to, above, across, along, after, back to back, before, top, bottom, centre, close, down, up, forward, further, from, here, high, low, in, inside, into, first, last, middle, on, onto, on top of, outside, past, right over, around, round, side by side, there, through, turn, under, over, underneath, upside down, clockwise, anticlockwise, grid, row, column, vertical, horizontal, diagonal, compass point, north (N), south (S), east (E), west (W).*

✪ The children draw a sketch of an object (a toy car, an open book on its end, a LEGO model) on the table in front of them.

Ask them to imagine they are standing behind/ to the left of/to the right of the model and to draw another picture from that position. When they have done so, they can go and stand in the suggested position and check their drawing.

'Copy my model'

The children work in pairs. Each child has the same number of LEGO bricks of the same colours and sizes. They sit back to back and one child puts pieces of LEGO together to make a model. When finished, he/she describes the model to the other child who has to try and copy it exactly without looking at it. They then show each other their models and discuss their similarities and differences. They swap roles and repeat.

ICT

Use a Roamer/Turtle/LOGO package to show position.

Co-ordinates

● Draw a 5 x 5 grid on the board or a large sheet of paper (as shown in the diagram on page 64). Discuss with the children the positions of the columns and the rows. Make sure they know that columns are vertical and rows horizontal. Put a mark in, say, co-ordinates 4, 3.

Tell the children the location of the mark (4,3). Explain to the children that to find a point using co–ordinates we look *along* the columns and then *up* the rows. They can remember this by saying to themselves *Along the hall then up the stairs.*

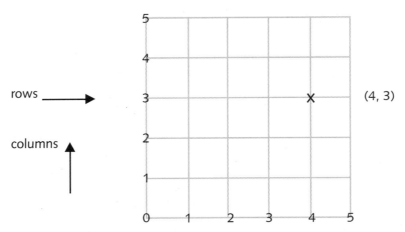

rows ⟶

columns ↑

(4, 3)

● Draw other marks on other locations on the grid. Ask individual children to name the location of the various marks.

✿ Give the children worksheets with various marks in a similar grid. Ask them to name the location of each of the marks.

Direction

● Ask children to point to various objects in the classroom. Tell them that they are pointing in the **direction** of the various objects.

● Show the class a direction compass. Explain that sometimes we need ways of explaining directions to other people or finding our way. Introduce the direction *North*.

Draw a compass on the board or a large sheet of paper. Write *North* on the compass. Introduce the other three directions, *South*, *East*, *West*, to the children. Explain that these are called the *points* of the compass.

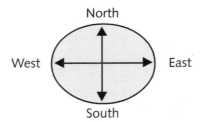

● Tell the children that they can remember in which order the points of the compass come if they go clockwise round the compass saying **N**ever **E**at **S**limy **W**orms to themselves. They could make up their own phrases.

✿ Using a directional compass find 'true' north and describe what you are doing. Then give pairs of children compasses and help them to do the same. When they can manage this, ask them to write down

objects in the classroom/playground that lie in each of the four directions from a given point.

ICT

Draw a large directional compass on a large sheet of paper and put it on the floor with a Roamer on it. Children have to move the Roamer towards various directions you give. For example, *Start at north, move the Roamer east, then south, then west and then north again*. Encourage the children to describe the direction in which the Roamer is turning and

travelling and to use vocabulary such as *clockwise* and *anti–clockwise* as well as the compass points.

Movement

● Use a clock face to revise clockwise and anti-clockwise.

● In PE, use the terms 'clockwise' and 'anti-clockwise' and ask the children to make straight and turning movements. Use a percussion instrument to signal changes in movement. The children work together in pairs to form sequences that involve straight and turning movements.

Translations

● Reintroduce translations (movement in a straight line) by asking the children to trace round a shape on to a sheet of paper. They then slide the shape along and draw around it again. They repeat this to make a sequence of shapes which they can colour to make a pattern.
Variation: The children can make similar pattern using two shapes.

● Look at fabric, wrapping papers, wallpaper and so on and find examples of translating patterns.

Rotations

● Reintroduce rotations (movement in whole, half and quarter turns) by asking the children to trace round a triangle. (Secure the triangle with a drawing pin to a piece of paper on top of a board.) The children draw around the triangle, rotate it a little, draw around it again and repeat.

● Once the children understand this process, ask them to draw round the triangle again using whole, half and quarter turns. Repeat using different shapes.

● Look at fabric, wrapping papers, wallpaper and so on and find examples of rotating patterns.

ICT
Use a Roamer/Turtle/LOGO package to draw various movement patterns.

Combinations
✪ The children combine translations and rotations to create their own patterns. These could be developed in art sessions and printed to create wrapping paper.

Angle
Right-angle tester
● Reintroduce the concept of a right angle. Give each child a sheet of paper. Ask them to fold the sheet of paper in half then in half again. Explain that the corner measures a 'square corner'.

Ask the children to draw a small square in the corner. *Who remembers what the square corner is called?* When they have remembered, or you have reminded them, about right angles, ask individual children to go around the room and using the tester show you a right angle (for example, blackboard corner, desk, book, door, bookcase and so on).

● Explain to the children that there are many other angles besides right angles. *Can you find angles which are not right angles?*

✪ Children continue to look for angles that are 'right angles' and those that are 'not right angles'. *Which of these are smaller than a right angle? Which are larger than a right angle?*

Measures
Length
Centimetres and metres
● Using a ruler reintroduce the centimetre (cm) length.

✪ Working in pairs, the children measure the length, height and distance of and between various objects and people in and around the classroom using a centimetre ruler. Encourage them to:
❯ find objects of varying lengths (*Find something about 14cm long*);

▶ estimate the length of objects before measuring them with the ruler;

▶ record both their estimates and the actual measurements.

Discuss with the children the:

▶ differences between their estimates and the actual measurements;

▶ concept of rounding measurements to the nearest centimetre.

● Discuss with the class the best way of measuring the length of the hall using a centimetre ruler. *How long do you think it will be?* Ask two children to measure. Discuss with the children the differences between their estimates and the actual measurements and the difficulty of measuring such a large distance with a centimetre ruler. *Is there another way to measure the hall?*

● Using a metre ruler, reintroduce the metre (m) length. Relate 100 centimetres to 1 metre.

✪ Once again, working in pairs, the children measure the length, height and distance of and between various objects and people in and around the classroom/school/playground using both centimetre and metre rules.

Encourage them to:

▶ find objects of varying lengths (*Find something about 2m and 25cm long*);

▶ estimate the length of objects before measuring them;

▶ record both their estimates and the actual measurements;

▶ use measuring apparatus with increasing accuracy.

Discuss with the children the:

▶ differences between their estimates and the actual measurements;

▶ concept of rounding measurements to the nearest metre.

● The children make lists of objects that are:

▶ less than a centimetre;

▶ exactly a centimetre;

▶ more than a centimetre but less than a metre;

▶ exactly a metre;

▶ more than a metre.

Kilometre

● Discuss with the class the best way of measuring the distance between the school and the nearest shops, where certain children live, the local police station, church and so on. Introduce the kilometre (km) length.

● Show the children atlases, road maps or any maps that show distances in kilometres. Ask the children to use these to find out the distances between various locations. *How far is it from our town to London?*

● By questioning them, make sure that children know that:

▶ 1 kilometre = 1000 metres;

▶ 1 metre = 100 centimetres.

Give them a wide variety of opportunities to solve problems involving length using the standard measures: centimetres, metres and kilometres.

Mass (weight)
Grams

● Reintroduce the standard measure, gram (g).

● Reintroduce the children to the 10g, 50g, 100g, 200g and 500g weights. Discuss and compare them.

● Using 100g weights and balances, ask the children to estimate, then measure, how many beads, scoops of rice/sand, marbles and so on it will take to balance 100g. They record their estimates and measurements. Repeat using other weights.

✪ Using 10g, 50g, and 100g weights, the children find items which weigh about the same. Encourage them to estimate first and to record both their estimates and the actual measurements.

✪ The children find individual items and weigh them. Encourage them to:

▶ use a variety of weights and combine them to ensure the most accurate measurement;

▶ estimate first;

▶ record both their estimates and the actual measurements.

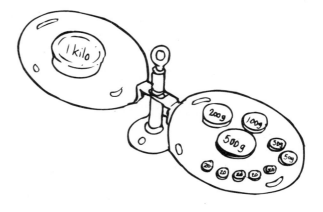

● Give children a wide variety of weighing apparatus (balances, scales, dial scales) to use.

Kilogram

● Discuss with the children the difficulty of measuring heavy items in grams. Reintroduce the standard measure, kilogram (kg).

● Show the children the kilogram weight. Using the kilogram mass and a balance, ask the children to estimate, then measure, how many books, scoops of rice/sand, marbles and so on it will take to balance a kilogram. They record their estimates and the measurements.

● The children use smaller weights to balance a kilogram. Challenge them to think of different combinations of gram weights that will equal a kilogram weight.

✪ Working in pairs, the children weigh various objects in and around the classroom using both grams and kilograms. Encourage them to:
▶ find objects of varying masses (*Find something that weighs about 1kg and 50g);*
▶ estimate the mass before weighing things;
▶ record both their estimates and the actual measurements;
▶ use measuring apparatus with increasing accuracy.
Discuss with the children the differences between their estimates and the actual measurements.

● The children make lists of objects that are:
▶ exactly or about 10g;
▶ exactly or about 50g;
▶ exactly or about 100g;
▶ exactly or about 500g;
▶ exactly or about kilogram;
▶ more than a kilogram.

Equivalence

Make sure that children know that 1 kilogram = 1000 grams. Give them plenty of opportunities to solve problems involving mass using the standard measures, gram and kilogram.

Capacity

Show the children a large container. Say *We are going to see how much water this container will hold. We are going to use this cup to measure. How many cups of water do you think the container will hold?* Record their estimates on the board. Measure the container using cups of water. Write the actual measurement on the board. Discuss the differences between the children's estimates and the actual measurement. Repeat using different measures such as a yoghurt pot, margarine container and so on.

Litre and half litre

● Discuss with the children the difficulty of using different-sized measures. *Would it be easier if everyone used the same measure?* Reintroduce the litre (l) standard measure and show the children a collection of litre containers. *Can you think of any other litre containers?*

● Show the children a collection of containers larger than a litre. *How many litres do you think this container will hold?* Record their estimates. Fill the litre measure and pour it into the container. Continue until the container is full. *How many litres were needed to fill the container?* Record the actual measurement. Discuss the differences between the children's estimates and the actual measurement. Repeat using other containers.

Would it be better if we had a smaller measure too? Introduce the half litre measure.

✪ Working in pairs the children estimate how many litre and half litre measures will be needed to fill various containers and then test. They record their estimates and the actual measurements.

● Encourage the children to find other containers that hold exactly or about one litre and exactly or about half a litre.

Millilitre

● Discuss with the children the problems of finding the capacity of containers that are smaller than a half litre and the need for a unit smaller than a half litre. Introduce the children to the standard measure, millilitre (ml). Show them a litre jug with millilitre calibrations. Explain that the markings on the side of the jug are measures in millilitres. Discuss the concept that there are 1000ml in one litre.

● Show the children a collection of containers smaller than a litre. *How many millilitres do you think this container will hold?* Record their estimates. Fill the container with water and pour the water into a calibrated litre jug. Examine the number of millilitres used to fill the container. Record the actual measurement. Discuss the differences between the children's estimates and the actual measurement. Repeat using other containers.

✪ Working in pairs the children estimate how many millilitres various containers hold. They record their estimates and the actual measurements.

● Children make a list of containers that hold exactly a litre, more than a litre, less than a litre.

Equivalence

Make sure that children know that 1 litre = 1000 millilitres. Give them plenty of opportunities to solve problems involving capacity using the standard measures, litre and millilitre.

Volume

● Using boxes and containers of various sizes the children estimate and count how many cubes/beads/counters/marbles will fit into them, and record their estimates and the actual measurements.

● Children make models using various materials, such as unifix, LEGO or wooden blocks, and count the number of blocks used. Then they make different models using the same number of blocks.

Area

● Introduce the children to the term 'area'. Ask them to find out which of two or more large flat spaces (table/desk/cupboard top) has the greatest area by covering them with various objects and counting them, for example, coins, cubes, sheets of A4 paper, sheets of newspaper, post cards, squares, playing cards and so on.

● Ask the children to estimate which of two or more flat areas has the greatest area by direct comparison. They check their answers by covering the areas with various objects and counting them.

Time

O'clock and half past

Show the children an analogue clock. Talk about clocks. Count the numbers. Talk about the hands on a clock. Revise 'o'clock' and half past. Give the children a worksheet on which they draw hands on clockfaces to show o'clock and half past times and write the time in words.

Quarter past and quarter to

● Show an analogue clock at 5 o'clock. Move the minute hand to the 3. *What time is it now?* Establish that it is quarter past 5. *The minute hand is a quarter way past the hour of 5.* Write the time on the board in both analogue (quarter past five, $\frac{1}{4}$ past 5) and digital (5:15) time. (Or challenge a child to do so.)

Explain to the children that there are 15 minutes in quarter of an hour, that is $\frac{1}{4} \times 60$. Ask individual children to demonstrate a variety of quarter past times.

● Repeat this process for quarter to.

Five-minute intervals

● Introduce the children to five-minute intervals on an analogue clock. Set the clock to 3 o'clock. Ask: *What time does the clock show?* Slowly move the big hand through five minutes counting: *one, two, three, four, five.* Say: *It is now pointing at one. It now shows five minutes past three. We say that it is five past three.* Write the time on the board in both analogue (five past three) and digital (3:05) time. Continue in the same way with five minute intervals up to half-past three.

Explain that quarter past is the same as fifteen minutes past, and half past is the same as thirty minutes past.

Explain that the big hand is now moving towards the next hour – four o'clock. That there are thirty minutes to go until the next hour. Slowly move the big hand another five minutes counting: *twenty-nine, twenty-eight, twenty-seven, twenty-six, twenty-five.* Say: *It is now pointing at seven. It now shows twenty-five minutes to four. We say that it is twenty-five to four.* Write the time on the board in both analogue (twenty-five to 4) and digital (3:35) time. Continue in five minute intervals up to 4 o'clock.

Practising time telling

☺ Using analogue and digital clocks: show the children times (o'clock, half past, quarter to, quarter past and to the nearest 5 minutes) and ask them to identify the time.

● Ask the children to show particular times on the clocks.

☺ Set the time on a clock hidden from the children, then give clues, for example, *The large hand is on the 5 and the small hand is just past the 7. What time is it?* The children can repeat this activity in pairs.

☺ The children make their own digital and analogue clocks and use them to show various times (o'clock,

half past four

$\frac{1}{2}$ past four

4.30

four thirty

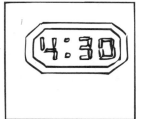

half past, quarter to, quarter past and to the nearest 5 minutes). They can take turns at testing each other's knowledge of times.

Time intervals

● Show the children the time on an analogue clock and write the time on the board. Show another time on the clock and write that time on the board. Discuss the time interval between the two times. Repeat with different times, and repeat using digital time.

● Give the children experience of working out time intervals using o'clock, half past, quarter to, quarter past and to the nearest 5 minutes.

Time matching game

✪ Working in pairs, the children shuffle together two different sets of time cards and play Pelmanism with them. (See illustration on page 69 for examples of time card sets.)
Variation: The children match three different sets of time cards.

● Give the children opportunities to solve problems involving time using o'clock, half past, quarter past, quarter to and 5 minute intervals.

Handling data

Collecting, representing and interpreting data

Block graph

● Draw a blank block graph on a large sheet of paper. Label the vertical axis 'Number of people'

and number it up to, say, 10. Label the horizontal axis 'Number of siblings' and draw and label five columns as 'none', 'one', 'two', 'three' and 'four or more'. See figure 2.

Teach the children the word 'siblings'. In turn, they colour in a square on the graph to show how many brothers and sisters they have. (You can do the same.) When the graph is completed ask questions that will enable the children to interpret it: *How many people are only children? Which number of siblings is the most/least common? Which number of siblings appears five times?*

● Use a graph where the intervals increase by more than one. *What shall we do with the odd numbers?* See figure 3.

● The children make their own block graphs (where the intervals increase by one or more) using other information, for example, favourite colour/food/pop group/TV programme and so on. Encourage them to collect their data using a tally (see below).

Pictograph

Draw a pictograph on a large sheet of paper. See figure 4.

Tally chart

Discuss tally charts with the children. Ask them to say how they come to school. For each mode of transportation make a tally to keep record of the number.

When the tally is complete, continue the activity as for the block graph activity – drawing pictures to record each of the travel methods. When the pictograph is complete ask questions that will enable

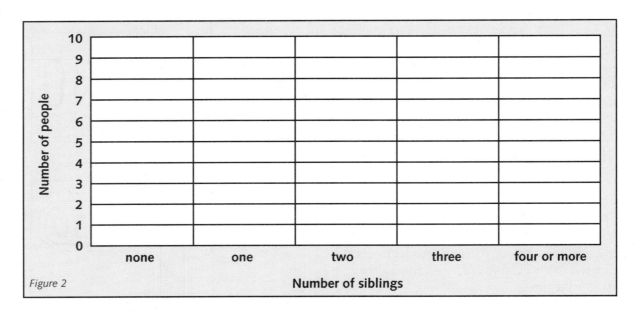

Figure 2

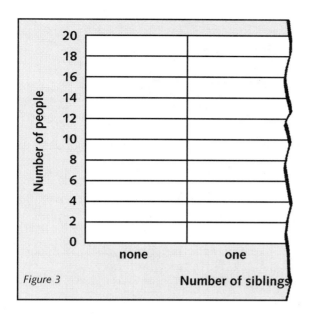

Figure 3

the children to interpret the graph: *How many children come to school by car? How do most children come to school? Which way of coming to school do four children use?*

● Repeat the activity, this time having the intervals increasing by more than one.

● The children make their own pictographs (where the intervals increase by one or more) using other information. For example, favourite colour/pet/drink/crisp flavour/pop group, hours of sunshine this week/number of children in school this week. They should use a tally to record their data.

● Ask children to interpret, discuss and make predictions from the data presented in different graphs, charts, lists and tables, for example, in a newspaper, a bus timetable, computer data.

ICT

◌ The children create block graphs and pictographs using a simple database package.

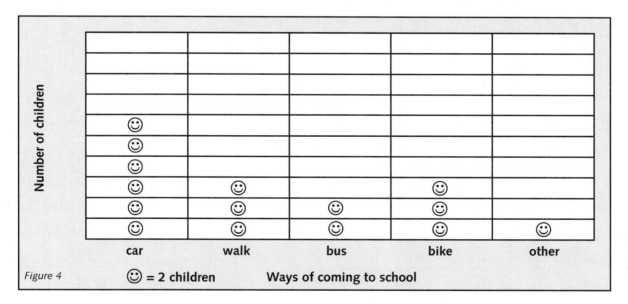

Figure 4   ☺ = 2 children   Ways of coming to school

Assessment

Children demonstrate the outcomes of their learning through speaking, writing, drawing and engaging in other activities.

A variety of assessment strategies is necessary if you are to have an understanding of where the children are in their learning and how best to further develop that understanding. Whatever assessment strategies you use, it is important to ensure that tasks are appropriate to the individual child and that they are directly related to the learning objectives. Remember that those activities marked with a ◌ in the practical ideas section are particularly suitable for assessment.

The levels of expectation suggested at the beginning of this chapter under the *What should they be able to do?* heading provide a comprehensive checklist for assessing your children's learning.

Science

Although the National Curriculum specifies what science must be taught at Key Stage 2, each school has to decide in which order it should be taught and make some choices.

There are 12 units of work to be taught over a 12-term period. It is not practical to deal here with every possible combination of units, so the following programme for Key Stage 2 an example. (Schools can devise their own combinations to suit their own needs – such as the number of classes in each year group or mixed year or KS classes.)

	Autumn term	Spring term	Summer term
YEAR 3	**Unit 6** *Materials and their properties* 1 Grouping and classifying materials	**Unit 11** *Physical processes* 3 Light and sound	**Unit 3** *Life processes and living things* 3 Green plants
YEAR 4	**Unit 7** *Materials and their properties* 2 Changing materials	**Unit 9** *Physical processes* 1 Electricity	**Unit 4** *Life processes and living things* 4 Variation and classification
YEAR 5	**Unit 8** *Materials and their properties* 3 Separating mixtures of materials	**Unit 12** *Physical processes* 4 The Earth and beyond	**Unit 5** *Life processes and living things* 5 Living things in their environment
YEAR 6	**Unit 10** *Physical processes* 2 Forces and motion	**Unit 1** *Life processes and living things* 1 Life processes	**Unit 2** *Life processes and living things* 2 Humans and other animals

This programme ensures that, in each year, every child will cover work within all three of the knowledge and understanding Attainment Targets.

Unit 6, *Grouping and classifying materials*, was chosen as a starting point for Year 3 because it provides a number of opportunities for simple introductory investigations. It also contains quite a large workload and may need the longer autumn term for its completion. Some units, such as Units 8, 10 and 12, are arguably more difficult to understand and so are included in years 5 or 6. Similarly, units which are easier for young children to understand, such as Unit 11, *Light and sound*, have been placed earlier in Key Stage 2.

Units 3, 4 and 5 also contain a heavy workload. They are about plant growth, variation and classification and living things in their environment, and ideally need to be undertaken in the summer term so that outdoor work can be carried out when appropriate.

What should they be able to do?

The Statutory Orders for science are set down in four sections. When we examine these, it is easy to be lulled into believing that three sections dealing with knowledge and understanding put the emphasis on the content of science rather than the process. This notion is soon dispelled by the realization that *Scientific Enquiry* (Sc1) is regarded as having roughly equal importance to the other three science sections combined. Although it offers no facts to be learned, Sc1 will only be achieved over a period of time, perhaps the whole of the primary school stage, or even longer. The aim is for children to develop an understanding of scientific phenomena through systematic and practical exploration and investigations.

The National Curriculum identifies three components within scientific investigations: Planning, Obtaining and presenting evidence, and Considering evidence and evaluating.

Planning

Young children have enquiring minds and are curious about everything around them. It comes naturally for them to try things out, to see how things work, to manipulate, to feel, to be curious, to ask questions and seek answers – exactly the attributes of a good scientist.

Planning includes asking questions and predicting. It is important to provide plenty of opportunities that promote discussion between the children and between you and the children. They should be encouraged to ask questions of the *Who? What? Where? When? Why? How many? How much? How far?* variety. By Year 3, the children should be given opportunities to identify questions that can be investigated and should be planning and carrying out their own

investigations with consideration about how to make them fair. Most of these investigations will be concerned with familiar, everyday experiences, but some will relate to contexts beyond their immediate experience.

Most Year 3 children should be able to explain what a prediction is and how it differs from a guess. With continued practice in carrying out appropriate investigations, activities and discussion, they will notice patterns in their recorded results and be able to make predictions that are based on their scientific knowledge and the data they have collected.

Obtaining and presenting evidence

In Year 3, children should be learning to carry out a fair test independently in certain more familiar contexts. They should be encouraged to use all their senses to measure and record accurately. They should be using suitable equipment to make observations that are adequate to the task and suggesting suitable ways of measuring these. They should be recording their predictions and actual results using tables and charts.

Considering evidence and evaluating

This includes the interpretation of the results of the investigation and evaluating the scientific evidence. Encourage the children to make comparisons, look for patterns and communicate their findings in a variety of ways. This gives them a great opportunity to share their thinking and to relate their understanding to scientific knowledge. In Year 3, most children's consideration of evidence will include presenting and interpreting charts, tables, pictograms, and simple bar charts and line graphs. They should be able to provide explanations of trends in data that relate to their knowledge of science in certain familiar contexts. They should also be able to suggest improvements to investigations, including ways of making an investigation fairer.

Knowledge and understanding

The three sections of the Programme of Study dealing with knowledge and understanding are: *Life processes and living things* (Sc2); *Materials and their properties* (Sc3); and *Physical processes* (Sc4). These are instantly recognizable as the biology, chemistry and physics of secondary school days.

What has replaced Sc0?

Sc0 has been incorporated into Sc1. This has consequences for investigative science and the process skills involved as well as subsequent planning and assessment. Children need to be taught, through science, how major scientific ideas contribute to technological change - impacting upon industry, business and medicine and improving the quality of life. They should be aware of the cultural significance of science and trace its worldwide development. Finally, they need to have the opportunity to learn to question and discuss science-based issues that may affect their own lives, the direction of society and the future of the world.

Practical ideas

Making a start

There are many ways of introducing the three units (3, 6 and 11) suggested for Year 3. The following are a few possibilities. Others are suggested in the Ideas Bank on page 88.

Materials all around

Make three different surveys of materials used in and around the school. In the first survey, the children write down all the materials they can touch without leaving their seats. In the second, they write down materials they can find around the classroom, and in the third things that they can see when standing in the playground. (The most likely materials they will find are plastic, metal, wood, rock, fabric, paper, rubber and glass.) Make a table to show the results of the three surveys. *Which material is the most/least common? Why is this?*

Grouping materials

Collect together a variety of materials, natural and man-made or synthetic. Include an example of a metal, plastic, wood, rock, paper, rubber, Plasticine, clay, pumice and possibly natural leather or sheep's wool. *What are these materials? Where do they come from? How they are made? How many ways can you think of to group the materials?* (The children might use colour, shape, texture, transparency, whether the materials float or sink, what they are used for, whether or not they are attracted by a magnet, and whether they are natural or man-made.) They can record their findings in the way you think most appropriate (including tables, charts, pie charts, block graphs or Venn diagrams).

Light

Make a collection of different light sources or collect and mount pictures of different light sources. Discuss how each is used. Find ways of grouping or classifying them. Discuss the differences between being in a room when it is light and when it is dark.

Sound

Collect together a variety of musical instruments, and pictures of musical instruments. Assemble these as a 'sound museum' on a table. Explore the ways in which the instruments make sounds and sort them into sets under the headings of *Scratching or Scraping, Tapping, Blowing, Plucking* and *Shaking*.

Green plants as organisms

Safety: Be careful to ask about any known allergies before letting children handle plants. Ensure that they wash their hands thoroughly afterwards.

● Go on a plant-spotting tour of the school grounds. Look for cultivated and wild plants. Look for any unusual places where plants are growing, such as on walls and the trunks of trees and between paving slabs. Try to find some of the smaller green plants, such as mosses, algae and ferns, as well as observing the larger ones, such as trees. (Explain that weeds are simply plants growing where they are not wanted.) Record observations by drawing or painting the plants. Use reference books to identify 'finds'.

● Examine a variety of common garden weeds, such as a grass plant, dandelion, common daisy, groundsel or shepherd's purse plant. Identify, and draw and label the roots, stems, leaves, buds and flowers of each plant. Examine the flowers of the plants with a hand lens. *Can you see the different parts of each flower? How are the plants similar? How are they different? Can you grow some of the seeds from the plant?*

Developing key areas
Materials and their properties

The word 'material' is often used to mean 'fabric'. However, the Concise Oxford Dictionary defines it as 'the matter from which a thing is made'. By this broad definition, which is that implied in *Materials and their Properties* (Sc3), everything in the universe, including all living organisms, is made up of materials.

Wood
Comparing wood

● Obtain small blocks or off-cuts of different kinds of wood (perhaps from a carpenter). Examine the different kinds of wood with a hand lens. Look at the different patterns or grain on them.

● Wet each block of wood with water. Describe what happens to the appearance of each of them.

● Try floating the blocks of wood in a bowl of water. *Which floats the best? Do any kinds of wood sink?* Weigh some of the blocks of wood before you float them. Leave them in the water overnight. Then wipe them dry and weigh them again. *Which kinds of wood have taken up the most water?*

● *Which block of wood is the hardest/softest?* Carefully knock a nail into each of the blocks. *Which block of wood does the nail go into most/least easily? Which wood is the easiest/most difficult to scratch with a nail?*

● Paint the blocks of wood with poster paint. *Which kind is the easiest/hardest to paint ? Why are some of the blocks hard to paint?*

● *If you had large pieces of the timber you used in these experiments, which kind would make the best workbench/boat? Which would be the best for carving?*

Paper
The strength of paper

Compare the strengths of different kinds of paper or tissues. *Is what the makers say about them true?* Use pieces of paper or tissue all the same size. Fix a square over the top of a tin using a rubber band. Stand a yoghurt pot in the centre of the piece of

paper. Put weights or marbles in the yoghurt pot, one at a time. *How many weights do you have to add before the yoghurt pot falls into the tin?* Try different papers. *Which is the strongest/weakest? Is a strong piece of paper or tissue always the best for everything?* (Strength is not always the most important factor. In the case of tissues, softness is also vital.)

Paper and water

Use paper of different kinds. Cut strips all the same size. Set up the experiment as shown. *Which kind*

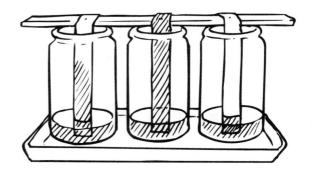

of paper absorbs or soaks up water the quickest? Leave the experiment overnight. *Are all the strips of paper wet right to the top the next day?* (You can tint the water with food dye.)

Science

Metals

Investigating metals

Make a collection of different kinds of metals. *Are they all shiny? Is it possible to make the dull ones shiny/the shiny ones dull? Which metals are easy/difficult to scratch? Which metals make a ringing sound when they are tapped? Which metals feel cold when you touch them? Do all of the metals conduct electricity?* (See page 79.) Present the results in the form of a table. Make a list or write a short written account of all the things they have found out about metals.

Using metals

Collect as many metal objects as you can. Suitable objects might include a nail, a paperclip, a drinks can, a coin, a key, a metal foil dish, a bell, a piece of wire, a 1 kg weight, scissors, a spoon, and a silver necklace. *Why do you think metal was used for each object? Could any other material have been used in its place?*

Shiny metals

● Collect samples of different kinds of metals. Clean them with emery cloth and shine them with metal polish. *Does the colour of the metal change?* Write down what each metal looked like before/after it was cleaned.

● Many metals go dull (tarnish) when they are left in the air, especially if the air is damp. Put some samples of metal that have been polished on a piece of wood in the open air. Examine them every day for a week or two. *What happens to each of the metals?*

● *Where can you see metals that are shiny and which do not tarnish easily? Can you find out what these metals are called?* (The two main metals of this kind are stainless steel and chromium. In the case of the latter, the object is usually made of steel and then coated with a thin layer of chromium to protect it. 'Tin' cans are actually made of steel coated with a thin layer of tin, which doesn't rust or tarnish and so protects the steel underneath.)

Why paint iron?

● Take two clean, shiny nails or screws, one made of steel and the other made of brass. Suspend them in a jar of cold water on threads hanging from a piece of wood . Leave them in the water for a few days. *What happens?*

● Repeat the experiment using two steel nails, one

of which has been painted with gloss paint. Hang both nails in a jar of cold water for a few days. *Can you see why iron often has to be painted?*

● Now leave two more clean steel nails on a windowsill outside. Give one of the nails a thin coating of oil or Vaseline. Look at the nails after a week or so. *What difference do you see?*

Magnetic materials

Safety: Tell children that dropping or heating magnets can make them lose their magnetic properties. Warn them that magnets must be kept away from watches, computers, disks and other electronic equipment.

● Make a collection of small items made of different materials, such as a pencil, a ruler, a crayon, a coin, a plastic cube, a small stone, a piece of paper, a rubber, a glass jar, a pair of scissors and a piece of cloth. *Are they attracted to a magnet?* Make a table to record the items tested, what each is made of, whether it was attracted to the magnet and, if so, whether the attraction was strong or weak. (All the materials attracted to a magnet are made of metal, but not all metals are attracted to a magnet.)

● Use a magnet to separate drinks cans made of aluminium from those made of steel, so that the former can be recycled.

● Find objects made of as many different metals as possible and test them with a magnet. For example, a silver necklace, aluminium foil, a steel nail, a brass screw, copper wire, a piece of lead, and a gold ring could be tested. Sort the objects into two groups: metals which respond to a magnet and those which do not. (Only cobalt, nickel, iron and steel and objects containing these metals are attracted by a magnet.)

Plastic
Useful plastic?
Make a collection of plastic items and also the same items made in other materials. Examine each item carefully and write down the properties of that object in a table. The table could have headings such as *Name of item, Transparent, Can be folded, Light in weight, Waterproof, Breakable, Long-lasting, Feels good, Looks nice.* What are the good points about plastic objects? What are the bad points about plastic objects?

Strength of plastic
Compare the strengths of plastic sheeting and polythene bags, plastic carrier bags and plastic wrapping materials. Cut strips about 30cm long and 3cm wide of each of the materials. Set up the experiment as shown. Place the weights in the yoghurt pot one at a time, until the strip finally breaks. Repeat with the other strips. *Which is the strongest/weakest plastic strip?*

Comparing plastics and metals
Make a collection of small pieces of metal and plastic of different kinds (for a fair experiment the pieces should be all the same size). Look at each of the materials in turn. Write down what colour each one is and say whether it is smooth or rough, dull or shiny. *Does the material feel warm or cold when you touch it?* Test each material to see if it is easy/difficult to scratch, whether it floats/sinks, whether it is/is not picked up by a magnet. Make a table of discoveries.

Fibres, threads and hair
Hard-wearing fabrics
Make a collection of some pieces of different fabrics, all the same size (pieces of old trousers, jeans, shorts, shirts, jackets and blouses are ideal but try to use pieces that are equally worn). A small block of wood, pieces of sandpaper all the same size and the same grade, drawing pins, a board and a hand lens will also be needed.

Use the drawing pins to fasten a piece of sandpaper to the board. Wrap one of the pieces of fabric round the wooden block. Examine it with the lens. Rub the fabric on the sandpaper once. Look at the fabric again. *Can you see any signs of wear?* Repeat, rubbing the material on the sandpaper five times, then ten times. Examine it after each series of rubs. Record what is observed.

Do the experiment again with other fabrics and a new piece of sandpaper for each one. For each experiment to be fair, each fabric must be rubbed the same way and pressed the same amount each time.

Which of the fabrics is the most/least hard wearing? Whereabouts on your clothes does most wear occur? Which type of fabric is suitable for work/party clothes?

(A less expensive modification of the experiment is to use a small block of wood with a small nail which has been knocked just through it to rub the different fabrics.)

Strong hair?
You will need to use scissors, sticky tape, a hook made from bent wire, a 30cm ruler, weights or small iron washers (all the same size), and (named) samples of long hair. *Who will volunteer to provide some hairs?*

Cut the hairs so that they are all the same length (say 40cm). Use sticky tape to fasten one end of a piece of hair to a shelf. Tie the other end to the hook. Measure the distance between the tape and the top of the hook. Now put a weight on the hook. Measure the distance again. Put another weight on the hook and measure again. *How much does the hair stretch? How many weights are needed to make the hair break?* Now compare with the other hairs. *Whose hair stretched the most? Whose hair was strongest?*

Comparing threads or fibres

Collect different kinds of fibres and threads. If possible, find out what each one is made of. Put a candle in the middle of a deep tray of sand. Light it and carefully heat a short length of each fibre or thread in the flame using a pair of tweezers. *Does the fibre or thread burn or melt? What does it smell like? What is left?* (You can judge whether your children can do this experiment themselves or whether you should do it.) Put the results in a table which might have the headings: 'Thread or fibre?' 'Does it melt or burn?' 'What kind of smell does it make?' 'What is left?' (This is a good opportunity to discuss the dangers of clothing catching fire and to talk about what to do if this happens.)

Insulators and conductors
Travelling heat

● Heat travels from hot spots to colder areas. Heat can travel through some materials more quickly than others. Find out which materials heat can travel through quickly.

Use a piece of card, a cork, a piece of fabric, something wooden, something plastic, a metal object, a piece of expanded polystyrene. First feel each object and decide whether it is hot, warm, cool or cold. Put the objects in a warm place, such as on a radiator or a sunny windowsill. After ten minutes touch each object carefully and decide if there is any change. Then put the same objects in a freezer for ten minutes. Quickly test how they feel. Put the results in a table.

● The materials that let heat or cold pass through them easily are good conductors of heat or cold. The materials that did not let heat or cold pass through them easily are good insulators of heat or cold. *Which materials are good conductors? Which materials are good insulators?* (Metals are good conductors, cork and polystyrene good insulators.)

Keeping cool, staying warm

We often try to stop heat moving about. Sometimes we use material to keep heat in, sometimes to keep heat out. The materials we choose are good thermal insulators.

● Find out which materials are best at keeping heat away from ice. Use some ice-cubes and six small identical containers. Quickly wrap each ice-cube in a different material (newspaper, writing paper, cling-film, aluminium foil and fabric could be used). Put each wrapped cube in its own container. Put an unwrapped cube in a container too. *Which ice-cube was the first to melt? Which ice-cube melted last? Which material was the best at keeping the heat away from the ice – therefore the best thermal insulator?*

● *Does a tea-cosy really work?* Devise a fair experiment to find out.

Conductors and insulators of electricity

Investigate which materials conduct (or carry) electricity and which do not.

Set up the circuit shown in the illustration. See that all the connections are tight. If a steel nail is now put between the crocodile clips, the bulb should light. The steel nail is a conductor (or 'carrier') of electricity. Now put a plastic ruler in the crocodile clips. *Does the bulb light now?* Materials which do not let electricity pass through them, so that the bulb does not light, are called insulators. Test some more things to see if they are conductors. Try to predict the result each time. Record the results in a

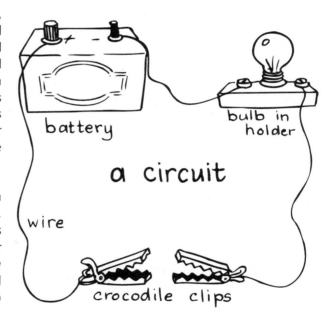

battery

bulb in holder

a circuit

wire

crocodile clips

table consisting of two columns, one headed 'Conductors' and the other 'Insulators'. (The insulators will be non-metals such as glass, wood, rubber, plastics and so on. Metal objects are conductors of electricity. It may be easier to leave this apparatus more or less permanently set up and fixed to a board which can be passed from desk to desk.)

Solids, liquids and gases

Materials can be grouped according to whether they are solids, liquids or gases. A solid has a definite shape, needs some help to move and is quite easy to control. A liquid has no definite shape, moves easily and is more difficult to control. A gas spreads out in all directions and is the most difficult to control.

● Make a collection of objects and pictures and sort them into the correct groups according to whether they are solids, liquids or gases. (The collection might include milk or water in a container, a newspaper, an air-filled balloon, a shoe, a bottle of engine oil, a picture of car exhaust fumes, a picture of rain drops, a brick.) *Which group has the fewest things in it?* (Usually the gases.) *Can you think of more things to add to that group?*

Rocks and soil
How hard are rocks?
Collect small pieces of rock. Carefully wash and dry them and examine each piece with a hand lens. *What colour is it? Is it rough or smooth to the touch? Is it made of grains or crystals? Is the rock or pebble made up of all the same materials? Will it soak up water? How hard or soft is each piece of rock?*

Test the hardness of the pieces of rock. *Can you scratch them?* Try a fingernail first. If that doesn't work, try a coin. Next (carefully) try the blade of a penknife or screwdriver. Finally, try a steel file. (It is best if the rock is in a vice. If it isn't, the children should be wearing thick gloves for the last two tests.)

Write about what you have done and arrange the rocks in a series of increasing hardness. *Which is the softest/hardest rock?*

What does frost do to rocks?
● Fill a small plastic bottle with water and screw the top on tightly. Leave it in the freezing compartment of the refrigerator or the deep freeze overnight. *What has happened to the bottle the next day? Why is this?* (The water expands when it freezes and splits the bottle.)

● Put a small piece of sandstone, chalk or limestone in a bowl of water overnight. Then place the piece of rock on a tin lid and freeze it overnight. *What has happened the next day?* Try this experiment with other kinds of rocks and building materials, including a small piece of concrete and a small piece of brick. *Which are most/least affected by frost?*

● *What will happen to rocks on a mountain when the water in the cracks freezes?* (The rocks splinter and fragment.) *Why, after a hard winter, do the roads and pavements often have large potholes in them?*

What does soil contain?
● Put a handful of garden soil in a clear plastic jar with straight sides and a lid. Pour in water until the jar is about three-quarters full. Put the lid on the jar and shake it hard. Then put the jar on a shelf or windowsill and look at it closely at intervals to see how the soil settles. *How long does it take for the water to clear? Can you see layers of different-sized particles in the jar? How many layers can you see? Which layer has the largest pieces in it? Which layer has the smallest pieces?* Measure the thickness of

each layer. *Are there any little pieces of humus and any dead plants or animals floating on the top of the water?*

● Do this test with samples of soil from other places. For comparisons to be fair, use the same size jar and the same amount of soil and water each time. Make drawings of the jars containing each of the soils. (If the soil sample contains a lot of clay, it may take several days for the water to clear. The largest and heaviest particles sink to the bottom of the jar very rapidly. The smaller and lighter particles sink much later.)

Sand and clay
Sand and clay both consist of tiny grains of rock, but in clay the pieces of rock are much smaller than they are in sand. One way to see the difference between a sandy soil and a clay soil is to rest two

funnels of the same size in the tops of two jars. Line each funnel with a piece of muslin or a piece from an old pair of tights.

Half fill one funnel with dry sand. Half fill the second funnel with dry, powdered clay. Fill up the funnels with water. Watch what happens. *What does this test tell you about a sandy soil and a clay soil? Which would be harder to dig, a clay soil or a sandy soil?* (Water runs through the sand much faster than through the clay, and the clay also retains some of the water. A clay soil is harder to dig because the water it absorbs makes it heavy and, unlike a sandy soil, it also sticks to the spade.)

Light and sound

Light

Sources of light

List sources of light. These will include the sun, flames such as candles and fires, electric lights and television sets. Certain animals, including glow-worms, fireflies and some deep-sea fish, also produce light through chemical reactions.

Paint large pictures of things that are sources of light. (Make these pictures into a large wall display, or display a collection of things which can produce light.)

Light and sight

What do we see when our eyes are closed? Why? (Stress the fact that we can only see when light enters our eyes. Our eyes do not, as many children seem to think, send out rays which enable us to see.)

Rays of light

Observe sunlight shining through a gap between partially closed curtains, or a light from a projector shining through dust or smoke. *It is possible to see that the rays of light travel in straight lines. What if someone stands in front of the light?* (The light rays are blocked. They do not bend round the obstruction.)

How does light travel?

● Give each child a length of cardboard tube. Set up a table lamp in the middle of the room. The class spreads out around the room, some high up and

some low down. Each person in turn looks at the lamp through the tube, while the others observe the direction in which the tube is pointing. *Which way must you point the tube to see the light? How does the light go from the lamp to your eyes? (In straight lines.)*

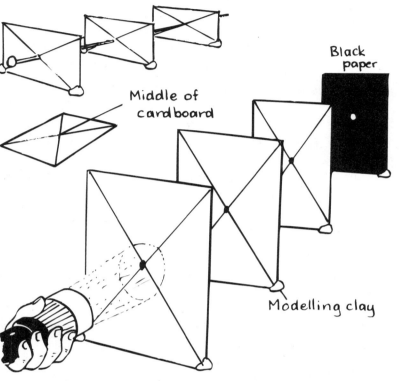

Black paper

Middle of cardboard

Modelling clay

● Use three pieces of card all the same size (postcards or index cards are ideal). Draw diagonal lines across each card to find the centre and then make a neat round hole in the middle of each card with a pencil or punch. A volunteer holds one of the cards at arm's length. *What do you see?* Now move the card slowly towards the eye. *What do you see?*

● Stand all three cards in a row, supported by lumps of Plasticine or Blu-Tack. Push a knitting needle through the holes to make sure that all three cards are in a straight line. Place a fourth, unperforated card in line with the other three. Shine a torch through the holes. *Where does the spot of light fall?* Move one of the perforated cards a little way to one side. *What happens to the spot of light? Are light rays able to bend round corners?*

Reflected light

Work in a darkened room. A volunteer sits at the front holding a large book in the normal reading position but about 45cm in front of his or her eyes. Shine a torch on to the back of the book. *Can you see to read the book?* Ask the rest of the class:

Where do I need to point the torch so that X can see to read? (The object is to show that some of the light needs to be reflected from the book into the reader's eyes to enable him or her to read.)

Shadow theatre

Make a shadow theatre. Draw and cut out figures on card. Tape or glue the characters on to short sticks or pencils. Set up a beam of light from a projector onto a screen (or a torch can be used in a darkened room). *How are the shadows formed?* (Light travels in straight lines and the rays do not bend around the cut-out figures or any other object.)

Shadow size

● Draw the figure shown in the illustration on to thin card, making it about 10cm high. Score the base of the figure and bend it at right angles to allow the figure to stand, or use Blu-Tack or Plasticine. Fix

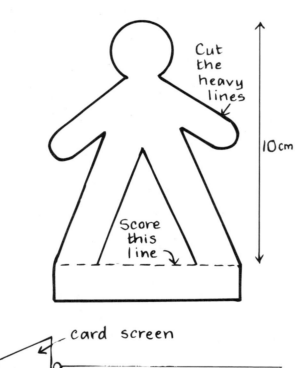

Cut the heavy lines

10cm

Score this line

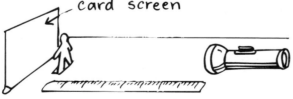

card screen

another sheet of white card, about 50cm x 50cm on to the table to form a screen.

Stand the figure 10cm in front of the screen, and lay a torch with its lens 20cm in front of the figure. Turn on the torch and carefully measure the height of the shadow. Repeat with the torch to a distance of 15cm, 10cm and 5cm. Record the findings on a graph. Put the distance of the figure on the

horizontal axis and the height of the shadow on the vertical axis. What do you notice? (The nearer the light source to the figure, the larger the shadow. This is because the nearer the figure is to the light, the more light it is blotting out.)

● Investigate whether a translucent shape (perhaps made of greaseproof paper) makes a shadow. (It does but the shadow is rather fuzzy because some of the light passes through.) *Does a transparent object make a shadow?*

Mirrors

Safety: Plastic mirrors are safest. If you only have unframed glass mirrors available, tape the edges and stick a cross of tape on the back. That way there is less risk of splinters if the mirror is dropped. Warn the children of the dangers of reflecting the sun, or any other light, into other people's eyes.

Hint: Mirrors often need to be held steady while the hands are used for other purposes. Plasticine is not very effective as it leaves greasy marks. A large bulldog clip attached to the bottom of one side of the mirror makes an effective holder and stand.

● *Why and when do we use mirrors? How are mirrors used for safety and security purposes?* (Driving mirrors, the mirrors used on 'blind' road junctions, and those used in shops and supermarkets, for example.)

Shiny things

Make a collection of shiny objects and materials, including mirrors, metal cutlery, metal cans of different shapes, cooking foil, cake tins, saucepans, milk bottle tops, ornaments, Christmas decorations, a car hub-cap and so on. Examine the shiny parts and highlights of the objects and materials. *Can you make the highlights move? Which objects can you see your face in? Is your face always the same or is there any distortion? Can you find a way of making one of the objects reflect more and better?* (Perhaps by polishing it with a duster or, if it is metal, with a suitable polish). *Can you find a way of making, say, a tin can less shiny?* (Possibly by scratching it or rubbing it with sandpaper). Record the discoveries.

Investigating mirrors

The children have a mirror each (or one between two). *Does your reflection do what you do?* Touch your left eye. Touch your nose. Put your hands on your head. Now use your mirror to look behind you, to look underneath a table, to look at the ceiling, to look round corners. Write your name while looking in the mirror. *What else can you find out about mirrors?* (The children will soon discover that we see a reversed image in a mirror.)

Curved mirrors

The children take it in turns to look at their faces in both sides of a shiny spoon and record what they see. They can use a curved mirror (or a bendy one) to investigate images of themselves and of objects in the classroom. *Can you predict what you will see? Can you work out rules about what kind of reflections things make?* (Concave surfaces – make-up and shaving mirrors – magnify things which are close. With distant objects they produce a tiny inverted image. Convex surfaces, which bend

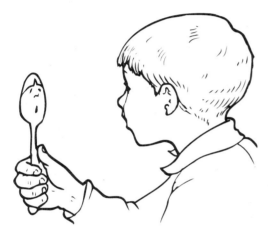

outwards – driving mirrors and security mirrors – make things look smaller, but give a wider view. Teach children the terms 'concave' and 'convex'. To help them remember which is which, tell them that a 'concave' surface bends in like a cave.)

Repeated images

Set up two mirrors facing each other about 20cm apart. Place a toy figure midway between the two mirrors. Peep over the top of one mirror into the other, and see multiple images of both the back and front of the figure.

Hinged mirrors

Hinge two mirrors together with tape. Put a small object, such as a toy figure, between the mirrors. Open and close the mirrors slowly and watch the number of images obtained. *Is there a pattern to this? If another mirror is added to make a triangle and the toy figure is placed in the middle, what effect does this produce?* Drop tiny pieces of tinfoil and coloured sweet wrappers in the triangle of mirrors to demonstrate a kaleidoscope.

How a light beam behaves

Cut a small slit in a piece of black paper and then tape the paper over the glass of a torch so that it makes a narrow beam of light. Reflect this beam from a flat mirror held vertically and watch what happens. Move the torch. *Does the light always travel in straight lines or can you make it move in a curved pathway?* Stand the mirror at the edge of a sheet of squared paper. Lay the torch down so that its beam passes across the paper on to the mirror. Carefully mark on the paper the paths of the beam and of the resulting reflection. Now repeat this with the torch beam in other positions. (There is a regular pattern in the beam and the reflection. When the beam from the torch strikes the mirror at an angle, it is reflected at the same angle.)

Sound

Safety: The ear drum is delicate. Warn the children of the dangers of poking things in their ears and of the damage that can result from persistent exposure to loud sounds.

Feeling vibrations

Feel the vibrations made when an object is producing a sound by touching, for example, chime bars or a handbell.

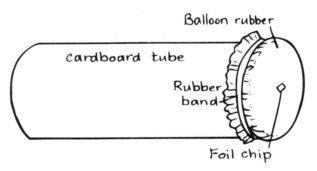

Vibrating radio

To reinforce the connection between sound and vibrations, lay a sheet of tissue paper over the loudspeaker of a transistor radio. Carefully sprinkle sugar or salt on the paper. Turn on the radio and gradually turn up the volume. (The grains of sugar or salt jump up and down in time to the vibrations.)

Make a soundscope

A soundscope makes it possible to enlarge the vibrations of sound so that they can be seen. Use a clean cardboard tube about 25cm long, a large balloon and a rubber band.

Inflate and let down the balloon a few times to stretch it, then cut a big circle out of the stretched rubber. Stretch the rubber over the end of the cardboard tube and hold it in place with the rubber band. Cut out a tiny scrap of smooth kitchen foil and glue it, shiny side up, in the middle of the rubber.

Test the soundscope on a sunny day. Hold the soundscope so that it reflects a small patch of light onto the wall or ceiling. Someone speaks into the open end of the soundscope. Watch what happens to the reflection. *What sort of sounds make the reflection move fastest?* (High notes.) *What sort of sounds make the reflection move the most?* (Loud sounds.) *What sort of sounds make the reflection move least of all?* (Soft sounds.)

Tuning forks

Collect a set of tuning forks. Look at the differences between the tuning forks (length, thickness, weight and material). *How can you make the sound from a tuning fork louder?* (Tap it harder.) *How can you show the tuning fork is vibrating?* (One way is to put the vibrating tuning fork in a bowl of water, when a series of concentric waves on the surface of the water will be seen forming.)

Sound travels

Sound vibrations can travel only if they have a carrier – a solid, liquid or gas that can transmit them. Sound travels at different speeds in different materials. It travels faster through water than through air, and fastest of all through solids such as glass, wood and metal.

There are a number of ways of demonstrating the various ways in which sound travels:

◗ a speaking tube made from a length of garden hose or some other plastic tube with a funnel fitted to each end shows sound passing through air;

◗ placing a ticking clock or watch at one end of a table and putting an ear against the other end of the table shows the transmission of sound through wood;

◗ the transmission of sound through string is shown by the familiar 'telephone' consisting of a length of string stretched between two yoghurt pots;

◗ placing a balloon full of water against one ear and holding a ticking clock or watch against it, will show that sound travels through water.

Rubber bands

Provide some thick and thin rubber bands of the same size. Stretch a thick rubber band between the thumb and first finger and then flick it with one of the fingers of the other hand. *Can you see the rubber band moving? What kind of sound does it make?*

Now put the rubber band around a small box. Flick it. *What kind of sound does it make? Is the sound louder or softer than before?* Put a thin rubber band around the box and flick it. Is the sound higher or lower than it was with the thick rubber band? (In general, the thin rubber band will make a higher note than the thick one, assuming they are both under approximately the same degree of tension. The sound is louder when the rubber bands are stretched around the box than between the fingers. The box vibrates as well as the rubber band, causing larger air movements.)

Vibrating strings

Tie a hook to one end of a piece of thin string. Fasten

the other end of the string to a piece of wood with a nail. Lay the whole apparatus on a table so that the hook hangs over the edge of the table. Lay two pencils a little way apart under the string.

Hang a small weight from the hook. Pluck the string. Notice the pitch of the note produced. Add further weights to the hook. How does the pitch of the note change? Now see what effect varying the distance between the pencils has. (The more the string is stretched, within reason, the higher the note that is produced.) Repeat this activity with fishing line and thin wire stretched taut by the addition of different weights.

Plucking the strings

With a guitar or violin, examine the thickness of the strings and pluck each in turn. (The thicker strings produce lower notes, while the body of the instrument, like the box in the activity on page 84, amplifies the sounds produced.) Experiment with holding the strings down to shorten the length that vibrates and so change the note. Write about what you saw and heard.

Comparing noise levels

⚫ Noise is unwanted sound. It is a form of pollution. This is one way of comparing the noise levels in different parts of the school. It also demonstrates that sounds become fainter as you move further away. (The children work in pairs, and need a battery-powered cassette player, a tape of music or speech, and a long tape measure.) Put the tape in the recorder, and set it to play softly. Holding the tape recorder, one person walks some distance away, while the other (the 'listener') stays still. The person with the tape recorder walks slowly towards the listener, playing the tape. When the listener can just hear the tape, he or she raises one hand. Both mark where they are and then measure and record the distance between them. Record the results on a table consisting of two columns. Label the first 'Where we tested the sound level', and the second 'The distance between us'.

⚫ Repeat the activity, with the tape recording playing at the same volume in other parts of the school – the playground, library, dining hall and so on. Draw a block graph of the results, putting places along the horizontal axis and the distances up the vertical axis. *Where are the noisiest and quietest places?* (Other pairs could carry out this activity at different times of the day and on different days of the week. The children can use a computer to generate the graphs.)

Green plants

Safety: Be careful to ask the children about any allergies they know they have before they are allowed to handle plants. Ensure they wash their hands thoroughly afterwards.

Plants and light

⚫ Leave a potted plant, such as a geranium, near a window and water it as usual. After a day or so, it can be seen that the plant has grown towards the light. If the pot is turned round, the plant soon grows back towards the window again in its search for light.

If the plant is fairly mature, it will simply turn its leaves back towards the light each time it is turned. (It does this because the leaves respond positively to light which the plant needs in order to make food.)

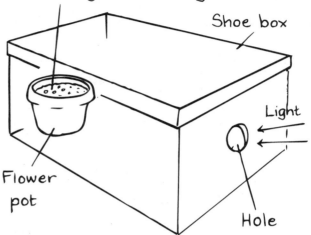

Cress or grass seedlings

Shoe box

Light

Flower pot

Hole

⚫ Put some moist soil or compost in a small flower pot and then sprinkle grass or cress seeds on top. As soon as the seeds start to grow, make a small hole, the size of a 2p coin, in one end of a shoe box. Put the pot of seedlings at the other end of the box and put the lid on. Stand the box so that the hole faces a window. Water the seedlings if the soil begins to dry out, but do not move the pot or box, and always put the lid back on the box. *What happens to the seedlings? Why is this?* (All green plants need light if they are to make their food, and if the light is coming from one direction, they will grow towards it, as these seedlings do.) *Do other seedlings do this?* (Yes.)

Staying green

Plant leaves need light to make the green substance, chlorophyll, which is vital in the manufacture of food for the plant. Investigate what happens to plants in the absence of light by laying a brick, a piece of wood or a tile on a lawn or corner of the playing field for a few days. (When the covering is raised, it will be seen that the grass underneath is a yellow colour. If the cover is removed completely, the grass will quickly resume its normal green colour.) *Can you devise a fair experiment to show what happens when, say, grass or cress seedlings are deprived of light?*

Plants and oxygen

Investigate the oxygen given off by green plants in

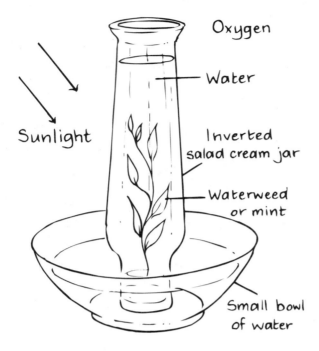

sunlight by putting a piece of waterweed or a sprig of garden mint in a clean salad cream jar completely filled with cold water. Invert the salad cream jar in a

bowl of water, and put the whole apparatus on a sunny windowsill or near to a desk lamp. (Bubbles of oxygen will be seen coming from the plant and these collect at the top – which is really the bottom – of the jar.)

Different kinds of roots

Carefully dig up a small dandelion plant and a small grass plant from the garden or a piece of waste ground. Wash the roots and examine them. *What differences do you see?* (The dandelion has a long taproot, while the grass plant has many small fibrous roots). Often in hot, dry weather the grass on a lawn may start to die, but the dandelions stay fresh

and green. *Why do you think this is?* (The taproots of the dandelions are longer than the grass roots and are able to obtain moisture from deep down in the soil).

Evaporation from a plant

Cover a potted plant with a clear, unperforated plastic bag and tie it around the main stem. Stand the plant in a sunny place. Look at the bag after three or four hours and notice the film of water droplets inside. (The water has been taken up from the soil, transported through the plant, evaporated from the leaves and stems, and finally condenses on the inside of the bag.)

Water loss from a plant

Using sensitive balance or scales, weigh a freshly cut plant. Leave the plant on a sunny windowsill (or near a radiator) until the next day and then weigh it again. *How much does the water in the plant weigh? Where did it come from? Where did it go to? What does water do in plants?* (Keeps the cells of the plant firm, and is used by the plant when it makes its food and is used to transport food.) Introduce the word 'evaporation'.

Plant reproduction

Although they vary considerably in shape and size, the majority of plants begin life as a seed produced by the parent plant. Flowers are the reproductive structures of the flowering plant. If your botany is rusty, find a suitable book to remind you of the processes of plant reproduction. Make a collection of clearly illustrated books about plants for the children to use.

Flowers

● Explore the structure of a typical flower. (A trumpet-shaped daffodil is ideal but buttercups or

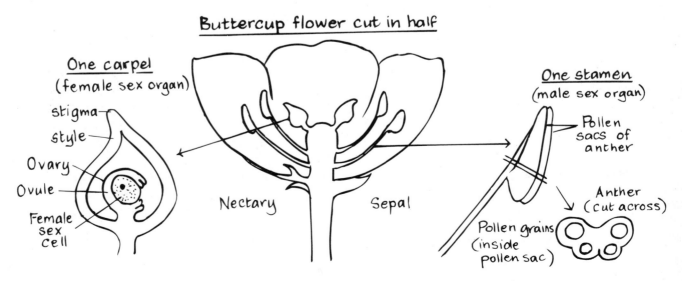

Buttercup flower cut in half

single tulips are also useful.) Dissect the flower carefully and find a diagram in a book to help identify the different parts. Use a hand lens or, even better, a binocular microscope. Cut a flower in half to see the ovary and the ovules (or egg-cells). Draw each part of the flower as accurately as possible.

● Make a collection of flowers from garden plants and the so-called 'weeds'. *How many ways can you find of grouping these flowers based solely on looking at the petals?* (Care is needed with flowers of the Compositae family, dandelions, daisies, thistles and so on, since what appears to be one flower is in fact a collection of many flowers.) *What other ways of grouping the flowers can you suggest?*

Insects and flowers

Observe which plants bees and butterflies prefer (carefully!). Keep a tally record and use graphs and other data-handling techniques to look at the data collected and draw conclusions if possible. *What are the insects doing? Do bees always visit the same coloured flowers? Which plants do they like best?* Make model flowers with coloured tissue paper and thin sticks or drinking straws for stems. *Will bees and butterflies visit them? Are the artificial flowers more attractive to insects if they are given a strong smell (perfume or after-shave) or if they taste sweet (a speck of honey in the centre)?*

Fruit and seed dispersal

Plants need to disperse their seeds and the fruit exists to aid this process. Collect as many fruits as possible and then discuss the ways the plants disperse their seeds. A method of classifying seeds is:

▸ winged – for wind dispersal (sycamore, pine or maple);
▸ fluffy – for wind dispersal (dandelion and thistle);
▸ juicy – dispersed by being eaten by animals and the seed voided (strawberry, apple, plum);
▸ nuts – dispersed by animals burying them as well as falling to the ground (hazelnuts, walnuts);
▸ pods and capsules – burst open (peas, broom, gorse, antirrhinum);
▸ hooked – dispersed by being caught on an animal's fur or human clothes (goosegrass, agrimony, burdock).
Encourage the children to use their own criteria to classify the fruits and seeds initially, rather than providing too much direction.

Dandelions

The large yellow dandelion flower is really a collection of many tiny flowers. When the flowers have died, the white fluffy balls, the dandelion

'clocks', are left. These are really a collection of tiny fruits, each consisting of a seed with its own little parachute of down.

● Study some dandelion clocks. *How many seeds are there in a dandelion clock? Blow another dandelion clock. How many blows do you take to blow away all the seeds? How far do the seeds travel? Can you really tell the time with a dandelion clock?*

● Moisten the parachute of a dandelion seed. *Does it float in the air now? What kind of weather would be best for a dandelion plant to scatter its seeds?* (Dry, windy weather.)

● Plant some dandelion seeds in pots of moist soil or compost. *How many of the seeds germinate? What do the seedlings look like?* Draw one. *Can you grow a dandelion plant from seed and get it to flower?*

Winged fruits

Make a collection of winged fruits from sycamore, maple and ash trees. Drop each fruit in turn from a window or the top of a staircase (carefully!). Aim for the centre of a PE hoop. *How accurate can you make your drops?* Time each drop and keep records. Work out the average time for each fruit. *Are the results any different if part of the wing of each fruit is cut off?*

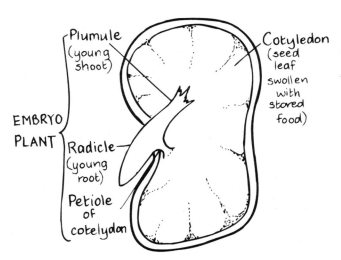

Seed structure

A seed contains a plant in its embryo stage and a store of food. You can see the embryo (a small root, a tiny shoot and either one or two leaves, called cotyledons which contain a store of food) in large seeds, such as broad beans or runner beans. Soak them in cold water overnight and then split them open with the fingernails.

The conditions for germination

Investigate the conditions a seed needs if it is to germinate. Use cress or grass seeds, some small jars and some cotton wool.

● Fill each jar with cotton wool. Take two of these containers and wet the cotton wool in one of them. Sprinkle seeds on the cotton wool in both and stand them on a warm, sunny windowsill. Keep the cotton wool in the first container watered. Look at the seeds every day. *Which of the two lots of seeds grows? Why is this?* (The seeds will not grow without water.)

● Repeat, but water both containers. Put one in a warm cupboard and the other in a refrigerator. *What happens?* (The seeds in the cold will not grow.)

● Repeat with one container in a warm, dark cupboard and the other on a sunny windowsill. *What happens?* (Both lots of seeds will germinate, but those in the light will be a healthy green colour, while those in the dark will be yellow and straggly, since they are not able to form the green pigment, chlorophyll, in the absence of light.)

● Repeat with one batch of seeds on a sunny windowsill and the other lowered into the bottom of a jar of water (ideally water which has been boiled to drive off the dissolved air, and then allowed to cool to room temperature). Stand the jar on the sunny windowsill. *What happens?* (The seeds which do not have air will not grow.)

From these experiments the children should learn that seeds need air, water and warmth if they are to germinate. If the seedlings are to grow healthily, light is also needed.

Swollen peas

Pack pea seeds into a small plastic container with a snap-on lid and add water so that all the seeds are covered. Put the top on the container and leave it overnight. *What happens?* (The peas will lift the lid of the container as they swell with the water they have absorbed.)

Seed sprouts

Sprouting seeds are some of the easiest and quickest vegetable seeds to grow. They can be grown at any time of the year indoors; varieties available include alfalfa, mung beans and fenugreek. They can be eaten raw or fried the Chinese way.

● Put a handful of seeds in a jar and cover the jar with a piece of muslin or J-cloth held in place with a rubber band. Wash the seeds through the cloth under the cold water tap. Shake them around inside the jar and drain them thoroughly. Stand the jar on its side somewhere warm (these seeds do not need sunlight).

Water and drain the seeds every morning and night until the seedlings are ready to draw (or eat). (This takes five to seven days in a warm room. If the seedlings are to be eaten, then the jar and cloth must be kept scrupulously clean.)

Potatoes

● Grow a potato tuber. Fill a large flower pot to within 2 or 3cm of the top with damp sandy soil or potting compost. Plant a small potato, or piece of potato which has an eye, just below the surface of the soil or compost. Stand the pot where it will receive the light and do not let the soil dry out. Record what happens. Re-pot the plant if necessary. Draw or describe the flowers. (If the plant should happen to produce a fruit, remove it and destroy it. The fruits of the potato plant are poisonous!). After the plant has finished flowering, pull it up and see whether it has produced any new potatoes.

● *What is the smallest piece of potato that will grow into a plant? Do potato peelings grow?* (If they are fairly thick and contain a bud or 'eye' they will usually grow.) In the late spring and summer, potato tubers, or pieces of them, can be planted in the school garden.

☀ Ideas bank

A plant diary

Keep a seasonal diary of a tree, shrub or herbaceous (non-woody) plant. Growing interesting species, in tubs or pots if necessary, will improve the appearance of the school grounds and provide inspiration. The children can plant and care for the plants, keeping a diary of growth, sketching and taking photographs as appropriate. Grow house plants, such as cacti, cheese plants and tradescantia, or create an indoor herb garden.

Daisy flowers

Hundreds of years ago the common daisy was called a 'day's eye'. *Can you find out why?* (If the children put a flower pot over a daisy flower for an hour or two, they will discover that the daisy flower closes up when in the dark.) *Can you find any other flowers which do this?*

Bird and mammal food

Try to grow some bird seed or the seeds in hamster food in small pots of moist soil or compost. *How many of the seeds grow? What do they grow into?*

Crease resistance

Devise a fair test to compare the crease resistance of difference fabrics. One method would be to take equal-sized pieces of several different fabrics, to fold them to the same extent, and then to leave them individually under bricks or some other equal weights for the same length of time. Then compare the degree and permanence of the creasing.

Torches

Make a collection of torches. *What do they all have in common? How are they different?* Look at switches, handles, the materials they are made from, how you use them, how wide the beam is. Design and fill in a table to compare the torches, including such headings as 'Colour', 'Main materials', 'Ease of switching', 'Stability', 'Size', 'Width of beam at a distance of 1 metre', and so on.

Candles

Make a collection of candles. Light one of the candles in a sand tray and ask the children to observe the flame. Light the other candles and encourage them to notice similarities and differences. *Does it matter what colour the wax is?* (No). Light a candle in a dark place and ask them to compare it with an identical one in daylight. Ask the children to sort and group the candles in a variety of ways (shape, stability, colour of wax, type of wick, flame size and so on.) Talk about the times people relied on candles as their only source of light after the sun went down.

Mirrors

Devise a 'Hall of Mirrors', like those seen at some fairgrounds. Use mirrors of different sizes, shapes and types at different angles; fix flexible mirrors in different shapes and positions.

Table forks

If you do not have any tuning forks, use old table forks. Tap the prongs of the fork on the table to make a dull sound. The prongs are vibrating although they cannot be seen. Suspend a table tennis ball from a length of thin thread and bring the vibrating fork gently near to the ball. Watch what happens when they touch. Tap the fork again and this time quickly dip it into a bowl of water.

The sounds can be heard better if the fork is tapped and then the handle is quickly placed on the table top or a wooden box. This amplifies the sound. Try using other containers as sounding boards.

Reduce the distance the sounds from the fork have to travel by tapping it and then placing the handle against the side of the head or on the cheek bone. The vibrations are transmitted through the bones straight to the ears.

Assessment

When you have finished your science work with your Year 3 class, you will have a good idea as to whether the children enjoyed the topics and which style of teaching was most effective. You should also be able to judge how much the children have learned. Now is the time to evaluate each topic against the criteria with which you started.

What do they know?

There is no set list of facts they should know, but all the children should have gained something, even if that something varies from child to child. In Year 3, you might expect most seven- to eight-year-olds to know:

- the names of the main parts of a plant and their functions (Sc2);
- the conditions necessary for healthy plant growth, i.e. water, warmth and sunlight (Sc2);
- how to make measurements of plant growth (Sc2);
- the functions of the parts of a flower and their role in a plant's life cycle (Sc2);
- that there is a variety of methods of seed dispersal (Sc2);
- that there are lots of different materials (Sc3);
- how to examine and compare materials (Sc3);

- how to identify the most appropriate materials for a wide range of situations (Sc3);
- how to identify a wide range of sounds and be able to sort them in terms of loud and soft (Sc4);
- how the pitch and volume of a musical instrument can be altered (Sc4);
- how we hear and what factors affect how we hear sounds (Sc4);
- how to recognize and name a wide variety of light sources (Sc4);
- how to sort light sources into luminescent and reflectors (Sc4);
- that light cannot pass through some materials (Sc4);
- how shadows are formed (Sc4);
- that we see because light enters our eyes (Sc4);
- that light travels in straight lines (Sc4);
- how light is reflected (Sc4).

What can they do?

They should be able to:
- describe objects and materials (Sc1);
- describe things that happen (Sc1);
- identify a number of questions which can be investigated, in familiar situations (Sc1);
- recognize the need for a fair test (Sc1);
- change one factor and observe or measure the effect whilst keeping other factors the same and know that this allows a fair test or comparison to be made (Sc1);
- explain what a prediction is and how it differs from a guess (Sc1);
- make a prediction based upon relevant prior knowledge (Sc1);
- suggest what observations should be made and suitable ways of measuring these (Sc1);
- record their predictions and results (Sc1);
- present their findings in a variety of ways, including using ICT (for example, using charts, pictograms and simple bar charts and line graphs) (Sc1);
- provide explanations for observations and, where they occur, for simple patterns in recorded measurements (Sc1);
- begin to relate these observations to scientific knowledge (Sc1);
- review investigations and suggest improvements to them (Sc1).

What have they experienced?

They should have:
- examined a variety of plants;
- studied the reproductive structures and life cycles of a number of flowering plants;
- handled a variety of materials;
- carried out simple experiments under guidance;
- devised their own simple fair experiments under guidance;
- investigated a variety of sources of light and sound.

How have they made their knowledge public?

The children should have discussed their work with others and displayed their work through drawings, models, charts, graphs and tables. They should also have produced short, clear written accounts of their various observations, activities, discoveries and conclusions.

History

The past is a subject of fascination to young junior children. It seems to them to be full of strange people and romantic stories, heroes and heroines. At play, eight-year-olds will often re-enact the stories and events that they have learned about in class because they need to 'work them out' in their imagination. Your Year 3 class will undoubtedly be receptive to history, and ready for a curriculum that is much more specific in content than at Key Stage 1, albeit with the main areas of the subject unaltered.

There are no specific key areas for history at Key Stage 2, however, children's knowledge, skills and understanding are to be developed through these topics:

- Local history study
- British history
- Romans, Anglo-Saxons and Vikings in Britain
- Britain and the wider world in Tudor times
- Victorian Britain or Britain since 1930
- A European history study
- A world history study

As it is generally sensible to do less history in the early years of the primary school and more later, you probably won't want to tackle more than one major history project in Year 3.

Reasonable arguments can be made in defence of teaching the topics in almost any order, but where there is no overwhelming advantage in the alternatives, the majority of schools opt for a chronological route through British history.

Clearly it is impracticable to deal in this chapter with all the possible topics, or combination of topics, that you might be teaching in Year 3, so the activities here relate to the most commonly taught Year 3 topic: Romans, Anglo-Saxons and Vikings in Britain. Even if this is not your allocated period, the ideas and approach will serve as a model for tackling any historical period with your children and, of course, the rest of the material in this chapter will apply whatever the topic. (You can also check whether your particular history unit has been dealt with in one of the other Yearbooks.)

Key elements

When studying any historical topic, children will have to tackle the essential elements of history itself which are usefully defined in the National Curriculum as:

- Chronological understanding
- Knowledge and understanding of events, people and changes in the past
- Historical interpretations
- Historical enquiry
- Organization and communication

You can introduce the children to these through the work on whatever topic you are teaching.

What should they be able to do?

The first year in the juniors is usually associated with one of those upward surges of the maturation curve. This coincides with a move into a phase of education that tends to be more structured. General changes, such as a decrease in the size of handwriting, start to become apparent around the new year and ability in history, including a growing awareness that the subject exists, develops steadily in parallel with children's language skills.

Bearing in mind that individual differences can make a nonsense of statistical generalisations, here is a guide to what most Year 3 children will be able to do and understand in relation to their studies of the past.

Key element: Chronological understanding

Some children will have begun to establish a few landmarks on their own personal time map of the past. These may be single features – the odd date, their own birth, for example – or large blocks of time such as 'World War Two' or 'The Stone Age'. This growth in knowledge and understanding of chronology enables Year 3 children to order historic events and objects with increasing accuracy as they now have more fixed points of reference. They will use words connected with the passing of time with greater understanding than before and will start adding a few period labels to their vocabulary.

Key element: Knowledge and understanding of events, people and changes in the past

A child's personal body of historical knowledge is not wholly, or even mainly, dependent upon what has been taught in school. Much of it is gleaned from the world outside the classroom. Therefore, even before you start teaching history in Year 3, some children will have acquired information about specific periods or individuals from the past.

By the end of the year, most will be able to demonstrate considerable knowledge about the periods they have studied. History catches the imagination of children of this age and there is no greater stimulus to the memory. Their factual knowledge can be quite astonishing and you may well be treated to a detailed lecture by a Year 3 child on a Roman villa or a Viking longboat. They seem to have a particular relish for new and interesting words and will soak up the foreign vocabulary of the past with considerable delight.

Eight-year-olds are much more sensitive to the similarities and differences between past societies and the present than infant children and will readily compare, for example, Roman habits of hygiene with their own.

Key element: Historical interpretation

Although confronted daily with representations and interpretations of the past, most children, like most adults, will not necessarily have identified them as such and generally do not question them. This is the critical skill which, when applied by historians to the writings of other historians, helps to establish the validity of an argument. Does a particular interpretation fit the known facts? Historians also examine the motives behind a representation of the past and the use to which the 'facts' have been put.

Year 3 children are not ready to grapple with ideas such as these at such a high level of complexity and sophistication, but they will begin to consolidate their experiences of, and contact with, an ever-widening range of historical representations. Film, artefacts and, increasingly, museum presentations will become part of their vocabulary. They will be able to recognize these for what they are with considerable confidence.

In order to go beyond this and to question or assess an interpretation, considerable understanding and information is needed. By and large, Year 3 children are insufficiently equipped in this way, although occasionally knowledge on a particular aspect of the past is sufficient to make the more able child question something seen on a film or in a museum because it does not fit what he or she knows.

"They can be considerably affronted when one book says something at odds with another."

Key element: Historical enquiry

For the eight-year-old, history is a story, a story happily accepted and believed. Year 3 children can, however, be trained to question and interrogate the story, asking *How do we know?* They will have been introduced to this notion at KS1 but the topics they are likely to be doing in Year 3 are considerably removed in time and there are no participants to interrogate. They are learning to question, however, and will know an ever-lengthening list of sources of information about the past. They still expect books (and teacher) to be 'correct' and can be considerably affronted when one book says something at odds with another.

Given appropriate training and direction, children will select information from a number of sources to answer simple historical questions *(What was it like to be a soldier in the Roman Army?)*. Their ability to cope with documentary and literary sources is, of course, still extremely limited, so history must be predominantly 'hands-on' and visual. This is definitely the year of the picture.

Key element: Organization and communication

While involved in a history project, the majority of Year 3 children invariably soak up information. Although their ability to recall this information long-term may be questionable, they will be able to select and recall facts and to make presentations at class assemblies or open evenings. Some groups and individuals will be capable of presenting the outcomes of their work in highly competent ways that involve using specialist terminology correctly in context.

This key element is about making public knowledge that children have gained; it involves being able to recall, select and organize that knowledge and being able to use appropriate terminology correctly. Their ability to organize and present information effectively can be considerably improved if teaching places emphasis upon the language element in the work – for example, making lists of specialist words associated with a topic; providing appropriate history books and time to read them properly; giving examples of good ways of presenting information.

Children's ability to communicate the history that they know will depend very largely on their ability in English but, orally at least, they should be beginning to tell a story in which can be identified the beginning, the middle and the end.

Planning

It is a good idea to map out broadly the ground that you hope to cover in history but, whatever the topic you are studying, initially you will almost certainly put too much on your map. This will get you thinking about the topic but is not very effective planning – you won't be able to see the wood for the trees. So take a red pen to your 'map' and cut it until you have reduced it considerably, preferably to a few straightforward questions.

If we take Romans, Anglo-Saxons and Vikings in Britain as our example, it is suggested in the National Curriculum that you should tackle one of these invaders in detail but in the context of all three invading groups. Choosing the Romans as the main focus, the key questions might be:

- *Who were these invaders?*
- *Why and when did they invade?*

Specific further questions on Roman Britain might then be:

- *What happened when the Romans invaded?*
- *What kind of lives did the Romans live in Britain?*
- *What remains of Roman Britain today?*

Of course you can only answer these questions at a certain level of generality and understanding (some archaeologists and historians have spent their entire lives just studying Hadrian's Wall!) but they will help to keep your work on track. You might even use the three questions on Roman Britain to link together the material you choose to display in the classroom.

You will not find a shortage of books or resources on the invaders (unless your school and library are astonishingly short-sighted or totally penniless) and much of it is pitched at the eight-year-old level. In fact, you may well find the material (and helpful advice) a bit overwhelming, which is why you must keep your key questions in the forefront of your mind. You really cannot do everything, so discard or turn a blind eye to material not germane to your main study, however fascinating. It is best to do a little well than a lot badly.

Armed with key questions and the appropriate resources you now have enough for a satisfactory project. However, two other elements, which although not essential are highly desirable, should be considered. These are visits and fiction.

Making visits, reading stories

Try to go somewhere if you possibly can. A historic site or museum brings an element of reality that is hard to generate from books. Don't go too far with children of this age. The worth of the visit decreases with every mile you travel. A few key places are given below as examples.

England: Bath, Roman Baths Museum; Colchester, Castle Museum; Cirencester, Corinium Museum and Chedworth Villa; London, British Museum and the Museum of London; Kent, Lullingstone Villa; Northumberland, Roman Army Museum, Hadrian's Wall, Carvoran, Green Head.

Scotland: Melrose, Trimontium exhibition, Ormiston Institute.

Wales: Caerleon (Isca), baths, amphitheatre and museum.

Good stories to read aloud or for able readers to read to themselves are *Eagle's Honour* by Rosemary Sutcliff and Victor Ambrus (Red Fox), *Word to Caesar* by Geoffrey Teece (Macmillan) and *Legions of the Eagle* by Henry Treece (Puffin).

Practical ideas

Making a start

One advantage in teaching Year 3 is that children come to everything fresh. This is probably their first true history project and even those old tried and tested teaching ideas that may seem rather worn out to you, will be new and exciting to your class. Whatever you choose to do you can be pretty certain that the children will not have done it before!

With you and the class raring to go, it is imperative that you do not start the project by putting dates on the blackboard or colouring in titles on work folders or some other similar busy work. Get straight to the history.

Read Caesar and Pliny

● Read Caesar's account of the invasion of Britain. A good version is to be found in the Cambridge Classics series (CUP). Discuss the account and invite questions from the children. You should be able to make a long list. Involve the children in sifting and sorting the questions and you could end up with an agenda for the entire project. The beauty of this approach is that the agenda will have been set by the class which will give the children considerable ownership of subsequent work.

● Read extracts from Pliny's letters describing the destruction of Pompeii. Show slides of the site. (This is a good way to get children interested in the Romans and to give an indication of how we know what it was like in Roman times, but remember that you will need to switch the focus to Roman Britain quite quickly. You might do this by using maps of the Empire.)

Use a video

Show a video – a period piece or educational broadcast. Give children one question to consider while they watch; it could be a very general one such as *In what period is this story set?* but warn them that you will expect them to give evidence to support their answer. Review and discuss afterwards.

Tell or read a story

Finding time for historical fiction may be difficult, but the eight-year-old imagination craves to be fed, so feed it if you can. Choose a story on its merits as a good story not because of the information it imparts. Alternatively you can use your skill as a storyteller and simply tell stories from the period. You might, for example, tell the story of Boudicca or Caesar, or simplify or adapt a famous tale such as Rosemary Sutcliff's *Eagle of the Ninth* (Puffin) which would otherwise be inaccessible to children of this age.

Use artefacts

Bring in some mystery objects – genuine Roman pottery is easy to obtain and your local museum service will probably lend you some more obviously interesting Roman artefacts. Play guessing games. Pass the objects around – every child has to make one observation.

Make a mosaic

Start by creating Roman mosaics (you can use coloured paper instead of clay). Use pictures of mosaics in books and

examine the different types of geometrical pattern. Children can copy and colour the patterns. This is only a start. Questions come next: *What patterns are these? Who made them? Where were they used?* and so on. A visit might be a useful next step if you have access to a genuine mosaic, although you may prefer to use the visit at the end of the project as a culmination of the work the children have done.

✱ Developing key elements

Visitor from the past

Introduce a visitor from the past. Another member of staff acting 'in role' might enter the class as a Roman slave or legionary. They will, of course, have to dress up in costume. Have a dialogue. Never allow the person to come out of role. (You may be fortunate to be able to use members of an organization such as the Ermine Street Guard (c/o Oakland Farm, Dog Lane, Crickley Hill, Witcombe, Gloucestershire) who can provide a very authentic visitor for you.)

Map the Romans

Make a map of Roman Britain. Find out the Roman and modern names of places. Search for Roman roads on a modern map.

Experts

Set up expert groups. Groups of children are given the task of becoming experts on a very limited Roman topic (mosaics; road building; villas; the army) and are then sent away to research their subject. At the end, you set up expert information desks with displays and pictures, and invite other children to go around asking questions.

Alternatively the groups of children can make a presentation to the class or produce a number of 'hand-outs' in the style used by tourist offices and DIY stores, carefully explaining aspects of their particular subject.

Romans at home

● Research the life of a Roman family living in Britain. Start by deciding what questions you need to find answers about houses, furniture, food, decoration, floors, slaves, animals, heating, lighting and so on. Each child, or group, makes a contribution to the class's Book of Roman Family Life. Every entry should carry a section: 'How we know'.

● Using pictures (unless you can manage reproductions or the real thing!) of domestic Roman objects (a lamp, clay writing tablet, pestle and mortar, for example) get children to sort (then/now) and compare. Notice change and continuity.

● Make rod or shadow puppets and tell the story of a day in the life of a wealthy Roman in a British town (visit the baths, the amphitheatre and so on).

● Using pictorial evidence, make an arcade of Roman shops to run around the classroom. Treat it as a museum display with the children providing captions explaining what everything is.

Roman army

● Make a model of a section of Hadrian's Wall. *Where was it? What was it for?*

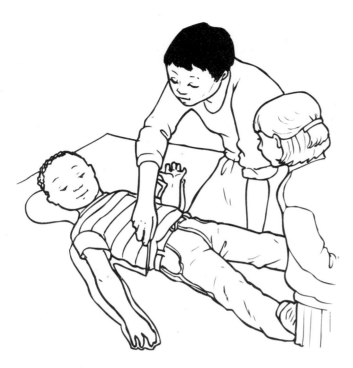

● Put together an infantryman's pack (*Jewish War,* Flavius Josephus (Penguin) gives an excellent description of its contents: a saw, a basket, a shovel and axe, a scythe, a chain and three days' food rations). You might also add his side arms and shield. How were all these things used?

● Get togged up in a toga. Use old curtains or sheets and let the children try to copy the dress of a Roman as illustrated by a statue.

● Create a cohort of soldiers. Practise the fighting tactics used by the Romans, for example, the tortoise.

● Have a taste of Rome. Ideas for simple foods are readily available. (English Heritage, for example, produce a useful booklet, Roman Food and Cooking.)

● A letter home. The more able children will be able to write a letter telling their family about life in Britain. This should be done towards the end of the project. It could be written by a cavalryman from North Africa or an army officer from Rome – perhaps even an educated Greek slave. Choose place, occupation and situation of the fictitious letter writer carefully.

● After finding out about Roman gods, the children might enjoy writing their own curses to be placed upon their enemies (fictitious of course!) in the Roman fashion.

● Do an Invaders assembly. Have a group represent (dressed up is more fun) each wave of invaders. Give each group the main questions (as agreed at the beginning of the project) to answer for their particular invading group. 'I am Tota the Saxon. I came to this land ...' (NB Tota's people settled in Tooting!)

● Somewhat anachronistic but fun, is to make up radio news broadcasts, with reporters on the spot, for some major event like Boudicca's revolt.

● Make a wax writing tablet. (Work from pictures and evidence. Use candle ends melted down and poured into shallow box lids.)

● Compare writing in Roman letters with writing in a modern cursive hand. Which is easier to read/ to write?

● Make large cut-out figures (by drawing round children lying on the paper) then, using pictorial evidence, the children can draw clothes on the figures as accurately as possible to represent the important members of a Roman army (centurion; standard bearer; signifer and so on). Hang the figures from the ceiling.

Leftovers

Make a display of things the Romans left behind. Look at the alphabet, Roman numerals, roads, milestones, language and so on. Get the children to watch out for signs of how the Romans have left their mark in your town. Once they understand what they are looking for they can be very good detectives. They might find, for instance, Roman-style inscriptions on memorials and buildings, architecture of banks and town halls which echoes the Roman style, Latin writing, Roman numerals.

Hot-seat

After finding out about Roman Britons (again towards the end of the project is best – this can be used for assessment purposes) children are placed in a 'hot-seat' where they are interrogated by the rest of the class. They are designated as say 'a slave in a villa' and questioned in role. (You might insist that the questioners know the answers to the questions that they ask!)

✴ Ideas bank

● Make a giant comic strip of the main events of the Roman conquest.

Assessment

Apart from records that you will need to send to the next teacher, you will need to be able to report to parents on the child's progress in the subject. There are no SATs in history or formal assessments but the expectations given at the start of this chapter can be used as a measure against which to assess the child's general progress.

What do they know?

For this topic you might check children's knowledge of:
- the main events and dates. Can they place the various invasions in order? Do they know any key dates? Caesar's invasion (55 and 54 BC)? The conquest of Claudius (43 AD)? The sacking of Lindisfarne (793)?
- major historical figures (Boudicca, Caesar, Alfred the Great, Bede).

What can they do?

Most Year 3 children should be able to:
- explain simply the reasons why some key events happened (why the Romans left Britain; why their invasion was successful);
- recognize stereotypical period images and artefacts correctly (identify a Roman woman, a drawing of a villa, or Roman mosaic).

What have they experienced ?

They should have:
- examined a range of evidence, especially pictures;
- experienced some simulations of period life (eaten food to a Roman recipe; made a mosaic in Roman style; tried wearing a toga).

Geography

During Key Stage 2 the children continue to learn about places, including the local area around their school. They compare this with contrasting localities of a similar size, which might be within or beyond the UK, perhaps in Europe. They also learn about more distant localities in less developed countries.

Key Stage 2 children will investigate aspects of their immediate and wider environment, including settlement, rivers, weather and environmental change, or other themes particularly appropriate to their school. These studies are about real places, near and far, large and small.

Within these place and thematic studies, the children extend their geographical skills, particularly by using maps and pictures in context and by collecting and handling data, and develop their research skills using relevant geographical information from sources including books and ICT.

Your school will have chosen the places and themes and decided when they will be studied during Key Stage 2. Your geography curriculum model needs to provide opportunities for children to 'revisit' themes and localities, perhaps in mini-topics, to reinforce and extend their geographical knowledge and understanding.

Whichever model your school has chosen, there are four fundamental key areas of geography in which the children should be progressing:

- Ability to undertake geographical enquiry and use geographical skills.
- Knowledge and understanding of places.
- Knowledge and understanding of patterns and processes.
- Knowledge and understanding of environmental change and sustainable development.

What should they be able to do?

In Year 3, the children should make progress in these four key areas of geography. Therefore you should provide spatial experiences and opportunities for them to observe, describe and compare physical and human geographical features; explain and identify patterns, processes and relationships; and investigate issues with a geographical dimension, in a variety of locations. This may be in designated geography lessons or in topic or thematic work in which the geography is explicitly identified and planned.

Key element: Geographical enquiry and skills

Children should develop and extend their ability to:

- understand and use appropriate geographical vocabulary;
- respond to geographical questions about places and environmental topics on the basis of information you provide;
- make, record, communicate and compare their own observations about places and environments from first-hand experience, practical activities and secondary sources such as photographs, videos and CD-ROMs;
- collect, record and represent information or measurements pictorially and graphically, and begin to analyse or explain it;
- carry out simple enquiries set by you, by undertaking fieldwork tasks and activities using simple equipment (for example, measuring tapes) and other resources (maps, diagrams, photographs, for instance) which you provide.

Key element: Places: features, characteristics, contrasts and relationships

Children should begin to recognize, describe, compare, record and express views about:
● the main physical (landscape, weather, vegetation) and human (industries, transport networks) features of their local area and other localities studied, using appropriate geographical terminology; (the suggestions given in brackets here, and below, are examples only);
● how the human and physical features give a place its character (a seaside resort, a high rise estate);
● how places change on a range of time scales (traffic densities, people move in and out);
● how buildings and land are used for a variety of purposes (housing, agriculture);
● the significance of location, why features are where they are, why things happen when they do (the provision and location of car parks);
● similarities and differences between the places they visit and study (comparing their local area with a contrasted locality).

Key element: Patterns and processes

Children should make observations and respond to questions about:
● where things are (hotels along a sea-front);
● physical (natural) and human processes; begin to explain why things are like they are (colder on the north side of the school playground);
● the pattern of where things are (shops in the town centre, distribution of old/new houses).

Key element: Environmental relationships and issues

Children should begin to:
● express and explain their own views about physical and/or human features of their environment, recognizing attractive and unattractive aspects (the new houses have spoilt the view);
● recognize that their environment changes and that people affect it (building on greenfield sites);
● appreciate that the quality of the environment can be improved (by pedestrianising shopping centres) and that environments can be managed sustainably.
These aspects are looked at in more detail in Practical ideas.

Introducing a range of localities and themes

There is choice here and your school may have allocated particular geography topics to particular years, but it is not practical to cover here all the possible topics you have been allocated for Year 3 so the following content structure has been adopted. The ideas and approaches provide a model for tackling any topic.

Year 3:   *Place:* Local enquiry
          Theme: Settlement (major), River (minor)
Year 4:   *Place:* Contrast (UK), Less developed country (urban) enquiry
          Theme: River (major), Weather (minor)
Year 5:   *Place:* Contrast (EU), Less developed country (rural) enquiry
          Theme: Weather (major), Environmental change (minor)
Year 6:   *Place:* Local land use enquiry (revisit), Less developed country (contrast)
          Theme: Environmental change (major), Settlement (minor)

Practical ideas

✲ Developing key elements
Geographical vocabulary

Practise and extend children's vocabulary for direction, location, scale and distance, quality and aesthetics and for geographical features, patterns and processes in natural and built environments. Do not be afraid to introduce specialist terminology and 'big' words. Children should learn classifications (for example, that farms, fields, crops, barns and so on are associated with agriculture) and hierarchies (village, town, city).

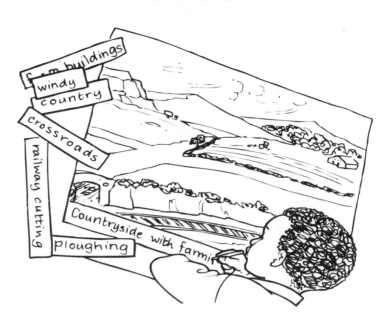

Word lists
Make word lists from pictures

Use pictures that are topical, interesting or specific to place and thematic studies, to extend geographical vocabulary. List the features, including buildings, weather, landscape, activities, land use.

From the lists, make labels for children to use with the pictures. Also ask the children to give each picture a title, to encourage generalisation and looking at the picture as a whole, as well as at its parts.

Make alphabetical word lists

Select a theme (such as Towns) and encourage the children to find the name of one for each letter of the alphabet – in the UK: Aberdeen, Belfast, Canterbury and so on, or global: Amsterdam, Budapest, Chicago and so on, and find them in an atlas and mark them on a wall map. This extends children's geographical general knowledge in an entertaining way.

Photographs

Field sketching is an important geographical skill which can be learned in the classroom before being used outdoors. Make 'field' sketches from photographs.

● To introduce this, make a tracing of the key features in a photograph, omitting small detail. Make photocopies of the 'field' sketch for the children to label; colour each according to a particular code (for example, features such as roads, houses, schools, shops, fields each in a different colour); make a key (with the explicit purpose of remembering what the colours represent). With experience, the children can make their own 'field' sketches.

● Make traced 'field' sketches of several similar

photographs (streets in their local area for example), photocopy them and ask the children to match photograph to sketch. This enhances observation skills. Then proceed with labelling and colouring as in the activity above.

Geographical I-spy

● Play geographical I-spy with pictures, reinforcing vocabulary already listed and introducing classification words illustrated by the picture.

● Play alphabet I-spy seeing how far you can get: *in this picture I-spy an a..., In this picture I-spy an a... and a b..., in this picture I-spy an a... and a b... and a c...,* with each child in the group repeating the list and adding one more letter. Alternatively choose one letter: *in this picture I spy a b..., in this picture, I spy a b... and a b...,* with each I-spy beginning with b.

Questioning pictures

● Encourage children to ask geographical questions about a picture, especially one with people in. *What would you like to ask the children in this picture? What would you like to know about this view? What would you like to find out about this place? What would you like to ask this farmer about his work?*

● When looking at photographs, ask the children different types of question – concrete (*What can you see?*); descriptive (*What are the people doing?*); speculative (*What would they do if it started to rain?*); reasoning (*Why aren't the people wearing jumpers?*); evaluative (*Is this a good place to shop?*); problem solving (*How, or where could all these people do their shopping?*).

Oblique aerial photographs

Use the activities described above and, in addition, match ground-level photographs to features in the aerial photograph, especially of the local area; match an aerial photograph to an appropriate map, orientating the latter appropriately; on the aerial photograph, identify landmarks and plan a route to visit them.

Making maps

● Provide opportunities for groups of children to make large-scale maps or representations, and for individual children to draw freehand maps or representations of the following:

▶ the classroom and the school building;

▶ short walks undertaken in the local area;

▶ areas in stories they are reading (to help them to visualize the location of a story).

● Ask them to make a plan of the classroom and its furniture to an appropriate scale (10 centimetres represents 1 metre, for example), and use it to debate the arrangement of furniture.

Using maps

● Use a wide range of plans, maps, atlases and globes (for example, sketch maps, pictorial maps, different scales, road and world atlases, political and physical globes) whenever appropriate, to locate places:

▶ being studied (introduce 'nesting' – county, city or town, district, neighbourhood); in the news (have a topical event map on the wall, with newspaper cuttings and photographs);

▶ to be visited or that have been visited (colour the route on a photocopy to identify 'shape', distance, direction relative to school); and

▶ to relate to photographs of places;

▶ to help answer questions (especially in local place study): *How will/could/did we get to X? How many different ways could we get from A to B?*;

▶ to carry out enquiries around the school and the local area.

● Use atlases to develop research skills (for example, using the index), and globes to recognize continents, northern and southern hemispheres, the equator, the north and south poles, and also to explain day and night.

Points of the compass

Introduce the four points of the compass (N, E, S, W): in PE play games in which the four walls or corners of the gym are labelled N, E, S and W; in the playground carry out simple orienteering activities, including using compasses to find direction. (See also the mathematics and PE chapters.)

Topical geography

Each week find an item in the national or local press that has a geographical flavour, such as a volcanic eruption, flood or sporting event. Use it as text for the Literacy Hour, for discussion to develop geographical general knowledge, interest and understanding. If appropriate, use it for a small-scale geographical enquiry. (It doesn't need to be a half-term's topic!)

Geographical facts

Give the children some new geographical facts each week – names of high mountains, long rivers, 'nestings' (such as Bangalore is a city, in the state of Karnataka, in the country of India, in the Indian sub-continent). You could develop this into your own version of Geographical Trivial Pursuit.

ICT

Use appropriate software, including *My World; Make a Town; Weather Mapper.*

Developing key elements
Local area enquiry

● Children observe and describe their own locality every day. It is important that you now exploit this and provide opportunities for them to identify similarities and differences between their own environment and others; that is, to compare places. Obviously they can only do this if they learn about more than one locality. You may consider that it is more important to study aspects of your locality and to compare it with aspects of another than to carry out an encyclopaedic study of one place. The former encourages more in-depth geographical thinking and learning.

● Consider both cognitive aspects (human and physical features, routeways and landmarks,

'Use local issues for small-scale role play.' (See page 106.)

'Observe, record and talk about the movement of rainwater on and around the school.' (See page 107.)

morphology, function, aspects of character) which will be the same for each person, and affective aspects ('feel', preferences, experiences, memories) which will be different for each person; these collectively contribute to a child's 'sense of place'.

● Pose geographical questions about the places (and themes) that you study, but, increasingly, encourage the children to ask, and seek answers to, their own geographical questions. In the study, extending the children's geographical thinking beyond 'observe and describe', to encourage them to compare, recognizing similarities and differences, and to explain their observations.

● Before you begin a place study, ask the children: *What do you already know about this place?* And *What are you interested in finding out about it?* Respecting and using their answers to the latter question, could give both structure to your study and extra motivation to the children. With your help they will consider how they can find out, and how to set up an enquiry (see the table opposite).

The questions in the table should form the framework for any study. They are challenging questions, but Year 3 children are not too young to

meet them. They make cognitive and affective demands on the children, who will be learning about the morphology (the features, shape, form, structure) of the place, and also developing a 'sense of place'. This is about their own, unique experience of a place. They will be learning that everyone experiences, and thinks about, a place differently – there is not one 'right' answer or opinion. This will be reinforced as you introduce children to controversial geographical issues. (Later they will learn about consensus and decision-making processes.)

● Another model you might choose to use is familiar from science: hypothesis testing. Children make observations in their local area, suggest explanations for them and, with your help, set up an investigation to test their ideas. (See the Rivers study, page 107.)

● If, as a school, you have chosen to 'revisit' the local area in other years, you have probably selected a focus for each study (such as economic activity, communications, settlement, land use). These will give depth, rather than breadth, and enable you to reinforce geographical skills and enquiry in different contexts.

Local enquiry area

In studying the local area (and other places) you could use the following question framework:

Question and skill or concept	Response
What is it? What is it like? Observation, description.	Identify the main human and physical features that characterise the local area. Describe the morphology of the local area.
Where is it? Location, distance, direction.	Name the 'address' of the local area; its links with other places; and the position of the human and physical features in it.
What sort of place is it? Categorisation, classification.	Understand how the features within a place give it a specific identity as, for example, a residential area or suburb.
Is it like any other places you know? Comparison, similarity and difference.	Self-explanatory.
How can/did/will we get there? Communications, time, cost.	Find and describe (using maps, pictures and words) routes to features in the local area, including those to be visited for fieldwork.
Why is it like it is? Hypothesis, speculation.	Begin to consider how and why a place develops in a certain way, for example, as a mining village.
Is this place changing? How? Continuity and change, dynamics, time, spatial process, development.	Recognize that places change, that they are dynamic, and study recent or proposed changes (for example, looking in the local press).
Why do you think it is changing? Cause and consequence, power (economic, social, political) in the sense of who or what has the power to sanction or cause change.	Begin to look for explanations, for example, why more houses are being built locally.

As the local area is a place the children know and in which they will carry out fieldwork, you could also ask the following questions:

What do you feel about it? *Do you like it?* Opinions, values, attitude.	Recognize particular likes and dislikes, and give reasons for these preferences.
What is it like to live/work here? Empathy.	Give opinions and justify them.
What gives this place its character? Generalisation.	Begin to consider that places have a character of their own, and what that character is for their own area.

If there is a problem, issue or something about the place the children don't like.

What is the issue or problem? *Why is it a problem/issue?* Opinion, explanation.	Identify matters of local concern. Give personal opinion.
Is there anything you can do about it? Action.	Begin to consider individual and community responsibility for action.

Geographical patterns and processes

At this stage, when children have observed, described, recorded and begun to explain their observations, introduce them to the idea of geographical pattern and process. From fieldwork and information that they have recorded in pictures and on maps, encourage them to recognize associations between human and physical features, such as: patterns in the distribution of housing types, amenities, recreational facilities; street patterns in housing areas; a concentration of significant buildings in urban centres; the relationship between the school's location and their homes; patterns of land use in the local area; the daily tide and 28-day lunar and seasonal weather patterns.

Environmental relationships and issues

● Developing from their study of the local area, at this stage encourage children to investigate some of the changes they observed. They will: make a list of changes; sort them into 'improvements' (likes) and 'detractions' (dislikes); identify responsibility for the changes: *Who or what caused the change?*

● Using local newspapers, identify local environmental issues. Use these issues for discussion, and to develop small-scale, informed role play.

● Identify global environmental issues using the national press, television and the Internet. Use these issues for discussion and investigation, leading to informed role play.

Settlements study

● The Settlements study, which will be linked with the local area study, could either precede or follow it. In their local area study, children investigate their local area as a 'place' (see page 103). In this study they investigate the nature of the settlement of which their local area is part. In doing this, they use their full repertoire of geographical skills, notably graphicacy (maps and pictures), enquiry and investigation.

● The children will know whether their school is in a village, town or city. If it is in a city, town or large village you should provide resources (maps, pictures, aerial photographs, videos) for them to discover where and how the school fits into the large settlement, including its location, direction and distance from the centre. The children will use geographical language (words, maps, aerial photographs and diagrams) to describe its relationships. Wherever the school, from city to small village, provide information and opportunities for the children to describe the settlement's characteristics: its form (shape); location with reference to major transport routes; landscape features (such as hills, rivers, coast); other nearby settlements (villages, towns and cities); main

economic activities. The children will investigate why, when and how journeys are made both within and between settlements. They will begin to get an understanding of 'urban' and 'rural', 'residential', 'commercial', 'industrial' and 'agricultural'. They will use aerial photographs, maps and census data (this also provides an opportunity to use large numbers, and look for information on the Internet), to begin to develop an idea of settlement size, and to compare settlements of different sizes.

● You could set up an ICT database to facilitate comparison of settlements, for use by the children throughout KS2.

● Initially children will learn about the cities, towns and villages nearest to home, sorting the settlement names into categories, and associating them with, and listing, specific characteristics: buildings, function, size (spatial), population, facilities and amenities, economic activities, transport links. Encourage them to widen their horizons by including other settlements they know about (for example familial, holidays, topical or TV locations), in the UK, EU and the wider world.

Rivers study

● Before children carry out their major Rivers study:
   a) introduce or reinforce the appropriate vocabulary; and
   b) check their conceptual understanding of the movement of water in the environment.

● To do a), visit examples of water in the local environment (streams, rivers, ponds, lakes, canals, reservoirs), and use photographs, videos and stories about rivers.
   For b), the children will observe, record and talk about the movement of rainwater on and around the school and local area.
   This movement models a river system, with the roofs representing the mountains or hills defining a catchment area – water flows downhill (down the roof or playground slopes); moves material (soil, stones on the school field or playground); flows along and makes channels (gutters, drains, gulleys); collects in the lowest points (puddles); drains from a wide area into a channel (from whole roof area into gutter); flows in different directions from the highest 'ground' (flows from opposite sides of the rooftop into different gutters); behaves differently on different surfaces (rests on tarmac, percolates into grassy areas); infiltrates at different rates (compare flower beds with trodden mud paths).

Assessment

In Year 3 keep a simple record of the progress children are making, against the expectations..

What do they know?

Evidence will include their accurate use of geographical vocabulary to talk about the places and themes studied and their understanding of maps and geographical pictures.

What can they do?

Evidence will include their use of geographical skills, their ability to ask and respond to geographical questions, and the resources they can use to find information, give opinions, make comparisons and offer explanations.

What have they experienced?

This will include place and thematic studies, the geographical skills introduced, activities, and fieldwork (experiences outside the classroom).

How have they demonstrated their knowledge?

Evidence will include talk, drawing, map-making and using, writing, practical activities.

What are they working towards?

What is the next conceptual, skills or enquiry stage?

Music

At the beginning of Year 3, you should establish just how much or how little the children in your class have already experienced. Most children will have come from Year 2 in the same school, but others may have joined from other schools and there could be a wide range of experiences and abilities. Look at the National Curriculum requirements for Key Stage 1 and see how they compare with your children's skills and experience. You may need to do some revision to create a sound base on which to build Key Stage 2 work. Then it will be time to explore the musical elements in more depth (gradations of pitch, groups of beats, different levels of volume, different speeds, different qualities of sounds, different ways of putting the sounds together and new ways of structuring pieces of music) and this should form the core of the work for this year.

Alongside this work, the children will be recording their music through graphic notation and some very simple traditional notation. Pieces should also be tape-recorded when appropriate.

The numbers of children having specialist music lessons (piano, violin, guitar, recorder, brass or woodwind) is likely to increase greatly at this stage. Encourage these children at all times to take part in classroom as well as whole-school activities.

Also encourage any peripatetic teachers to come into the classroom and take part in the music-making activities, and any willing players among parents and friends.

At all levels, music should be seen as part of the whole curriculum, integrated with any project work the class is involved in, while keeping an identity of its own.

Key skills: Listening, composing, performing, appraising

A curriculum for music-making will always ask for sounds to be explored through listening, composing, performing and appraising and at times it is useful to look at the areas separately. However, in a successful music session, all four areas are in action at the same time. A music-maker will listen to sounds, discuss them, choose appropriate ones to place together in some order, move them around and then will perform them. This is as true at Year 3 as it is at university and should be encouraged at all times. These skills are involved in all the activities suggested here.

The activities explore all the elements of music: pitch, duration, dynamics, tempo, timbre, texture and structure.

What should they be able to do?
Key element: Pitch

You may find it necessary to begin the work on pitch by exploring sounds high and low (in the environment, vocal sounds, instrumental sounds) before moving on to gradations of pitch. The children will need to have explored the sounds thoroughly before they can use them effectively, especially when they come to use tuned percussion instruments.

They will need access to instruments that can play sounds that move up and down (glockenspiels, xylophones, chime bars, metallaphones) as well as untuned percussion instruments. In their explorations, the children should recognize where on the instrument the high sounds come from (short notes) and where the low sounds come from (longer notes). Use high/low sounds as a basis for creative work in small groups of four or five children working together as a team. By the end of the year, they should have explored and used sounds that slide and sounds that move in steps. It should be possible also for most children to invent their own graphic notation to show these changes in sound. They should also use the letter names, which are printed on the notes of each instrument, to keep a record of simple tunes they have composed. If you enjoy and understand tonic sol-fa (see pages 115 and 116), then introduce some singing games using Soh (G) and Meh (E). You can also introduce the pentatonic scale (a five-note scale C D E G A) at this stage in starter activities, as a preparation for later compositions.

It is always important to encourage the children to discuss their work with you and with each other, to improve it and to listen to the work of others.

Key element: Duration

Children on reaching Year 3 should know the difference between a long or a short sound and now is the time to encourage them to use these sounds in a more organized way. Recapitulate on the work done in Year 2 by finding the regular beats/pulse of a known piece of music and then introducing the idea of a different rhythm in the tune. The children should be used to using body percussion (using the body as an instrument) to clap/stamp/slap/click the beat while singing different rhythmic tunes with their voice. We all foot-tap the beat when we listen to certain pieces of music (dance music/jazz/some popular songs). Encourage the children to do this too. They should be beginning to recognize the feel of the differences in time (waltz time or a march time) even if they are not yet able to understand the time signatures at the beginning of the music (3/4 or 4/4). However, by the end of the year most children should be able to group their own music in 2s, 3s or 4s.

Key element: Dynamics

By Year 3, the children should be in some control of the dynamics of their pieces (soft and loud). They will be aware that famous composers, as well as themselves, can make effective use of dynamics since they will have listened for the changes in well-known recorded music. The majority of children should by now be well acquainted with some of the dynamic symbols (*p f pp ff < >*) and by the end of the year should know their musical names.

Much work should have been done in the previous year in the use of these dynamics in their own compositions, and these ideas can be developed even further. Where a composer gives a specific symbol in a known song or piece to play, then the majority of children should recognize and respond to this. They should be able to discuss, using the correct terms, the dynamics of their own pieces and those of others.

Key element: Tempo

During Key Stage 1, the children will have explored fast and slow sounds both in a whole-class situation as well as in small groups and will have listened to how some composers make effective use of tempo. This work should be revised with an emphasis on control of the speed.

The role of the conductor becomes important here and everyone should have the opportunity to direct the class and experience their response to a variety of speeds. Some will have a natural instinct for tempo, others will have to learn it. A slow piece (the tortoise) should be played with care and as much control as a fast piece (the hare). The children should also have experimented in their creative work with music that changes speed from slow to fast or fast to slow. They should also be able to respond to the mood of pieces of music by known composers written in differing tempos (lively, calm).

Key element: Timbre

All children can listen. However, to listen attentively for certain sounds and for subtle changes of sound is not easy – but it can be encouraged. 'Timbre' means the special sound that each voice or instrument has. It is special to one particular person or group of instruments. The National Curriculum calls this 'the different qualities of sounds' and gives the examples 'harsh, mellow, hollow, bright'. The various classroom instrument sounds should have been identified by the end of this year so that a child can recognize the differences in sounds. The majority of children should be able to use to good effect the different qualities of sound in their creative pieces.

Key element: Texture

The National Curriculum definition of texture at Key Stage 2 is 'the different ways sounds are put together'. The children will already have experienced the texture of sounds through the different combinations they have been exposed to in previous music sessions. One texture is the sound of voices all singing the same thing together in unison, another would be the sound of voices in a round. A different texture would be the sound of untuned instruments accompanying voices or a simple ostinato (a repeated tune) played on an instrument to accompany a solo voice. These are all different textures and the aim during this third year will be to create other opportunities for combinations of different sounds.

Many published songs have suggestions for creating a variety of textures with the very simple accompaniments given. The children will also be able to explore different textures in their own creative work. Encourage them to listen for different combinations of sound in recorded music and begin to form their own opinions.

Ask those children who have instrumental lessons either in or outside the school to play any accompaniments within their ability range, to create more interesting textures.

Key element: Structure

All musical compositions need a definite structure and the more the children learn about the elements of music, which are the tools of the trade, the better will their creative work be. The idea of using repetition or patterns in music making should be reiterated, with the children using this form in some of their group work. Many famous composers have used this very satisfying structure (Ravel in his 'Bolero', Holst in 'Mars' from the *Planets* suite).

Just as in a successful story one needs a beginning, a middle and an end, so music can follow that form. The simplest form of this is the sandwich, which asks children to create a tune, add another one and then return to the first one (A B A). During Year 3, many children should have experimented with this form.

Another easy-to-follow structure is the question and answer, with one child acting musically as the questioner and a partner giving a different answer (A B).

A round is an interesting structure used often in the classroom, where one tune begins and the same tune follows later.

All these elements, either on their own or in different combinations, can be used in all of these musical patterns and, by the end of the year, most children should be beginning both to recognize and to use them.

Practical ideas

Music-making can often look and sound very disorganized. In fact, the best results will always come from very careful organization, even if the preparation is very noisy. Decide what it is you would like to achieve in a session, or group of sessions, and make a plan of linked starting activities and main group activities, always giving time at the end for performances to one another. Some music-making will be in small groups so plan your space well. Check on the availability of instruments, that they are complete and have beaters. If you are expecting the children to record their music, have paper available for both graphic and traditional notation as well as a tape recorder for the final results. Time your sessions and keep stopping and starting small-group work, inviting children to perform. Ask How much have you done? to check that some progress is being made. Visit the groups, giving a helping hand when required, but generally stand back and watch as leaders emerge, instruments are chosen and creations develop. Encourage the children to discover for themselves, to make decisions, to create, to work in a team and then to perform.

Making a start

Copy the leader

● Clap an easy-to-remember rhythm. Ask the children to copy you like an echo. Repeat until everyone feels comfortable and then change the rhythm. Invite a child to become the leader and make their own rhythm for everyone to copy.

● Play follow-my-leader fast and slow. Begin by asking the children to follow the conductor's hand beating 1-2-3-4. Ask them to clap in time, then click in time. The conductor might get faster or slower. Can everyone keep together? On another occasion, play follow-my-leader using instruments.

Sing together

● Sing lots of simple rounds, for example, 'London's Burning'. There are many to choose from in *Flying a Round* (A & C Black). Make sure everyone knows the tune before dividing the group into two parts. An easy way to learn a round and to give an instant performance is to give each group only one line to

sing over and over again. Place enthusiastic singers next to shy singers to give them confidence.

● Sing a well-known song. Encourage the children to tap their foot to the beat, not the rhythm of the song, in just the same way that we can often be found tapping our feet to dance music and popular music.

Pass the rhythm

Play a short rhythm on a tambour (small hand drum). Pass it to the next person who plays your rhythm and adds a bit more. Keep passing and adding until someone forgets the rhythm, then begin a new one.

Introducing key elements

Body percussion

● Make up patterns using body percussion. Clap, clap, stamp, stamp, click, click, slap, would be a good starter. Ask the children to copy you, then change the pattern. The children will enjoy being more adventurous in their patterns.

● Clap two, think two, clap two, think two. Keep this pattern going until everyone is in time with you. Now ask the children to add names that will fit the thinking time: Clap clap *Jo-seph*, clap clap *Am-rit*, clap clap *Ra-chel*, clap clap *Hea-ther*, clap clap ...). Change it to three claps and three beats thinking time. Add names that fit into the space of three (*Jo-se-phine, Jon-a-than, Par-am-jit*). Can you think of any four-beat names? (*Gab-ri-ell-a.*)

● *Whose name has one beat? Two beats? Three beats? Four beats?* Ask the children to get into name groups: one, two, three, four beats. Ask one child to be the conductor and to point at random to a whole group who should be able to respond at once and clap their name pattern. The conductor should move quite quickly from one to the other to keep the pattern going.

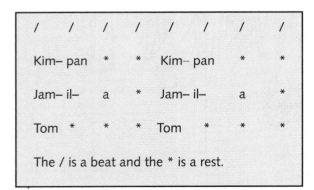

/	/	/	/	/	/	/	/
Kim– pan	*	*	Kim– pan	*	*		
Jam– il–	a	*	Jam– il–	a	*		
Tom	*	*	*	Tom	*	*	*

The / is a beat and the * is a rest.

● Make a name score with a small group of children and see if they can use it correctly. It might look like this.

Ask the children to make up name scores of their own and to say them, reading from left to right.

Ostinato

Introduce the idea of an ostinato (a short repeating phrase). Use 'Frère Jacques' to show how an ostinato can accompany a song. One group sings the first line, repeating it until the song has ended. The rest of the singers sing the whole song. The first line is the ostinato. Some children might be able to do this on tuned instruments using this easy-to-learn tune.

Timbre

Divide the untuned percussion instruments into four timbre groups: tapping, shaking, scraping, ringing. Take a well-known rhyme with four lines. Each group of children practises the rhythm of only one line on their instruments. *Can you play the rhythms in the correct order?* What would it sound like if they jumbled the order in response to a conductor's direction?

Dynamic symbols

● Review any work done previously on the dynamic symbols (*p f pp ff < >*). Make flash cards of each symbol. Teach the correct musical name for each: *p* – piano, soft; *f* – forte, loud; *pp* – pianissimo, very quiet; *ff* – fortissimo, very loud; *<* – crescendo, get louder; *>* – diminuendo, get softer.

● Put the flash cards of the dynamic symbols on the floor in the centre of a circle of children. Put a variety of instruments next to them. A child is chosen to go to the centre, pick up a flash card, say the correct name, choose an instrument appropriate to play the symbol, play, then take the next flash card to a new person in the circle. The game continues until all the flash cards have been played.

● Give each person in the class or group an instrument and one dynamic flash card. Ask them to try to create a short piece using their symbol. It might help them to have a title (*p* – Baby sleeping; *f* – Thunder; *pp* – Raindrops; *ff* – The explosion; *<* – Train arriving; *>* – Footsteps going away).

Opposites

With the children, think of as many opposites as you can before you play the game. Clap two, say a word (*tall*), clap two, a child says the opposite (*short*), clap two, say a different word (*nice*), clap two, the next child says the opposite (*nasty*). How

long can we keep the beat going until we run out of opposites? You can tie this in with Literacy Hour by pointing out that the opposites are all adjectives. (Another time you could use adverbs.)

Long and short

Use a stop watch to measure the vibrations of an instrument. *For how long does the sound carry on? Which instruments can play the longest sounds? Which ones can only play very short sounds?*

Losing one

Give five children a different instrument each. Ask them to decide who will only mime playing their instrument. Ask them to begin playing very quietly, and then gradually get louder in response to your hand signal and then to get quieter and stop. Can the rest of the class hear which instrumental sound was not there? (If the players find it hard to mime convincingly, you can position them behind a screen so that only you can see them.)

Louder and softer

Encourage everyone in the class to sing any note at random in response to an open hand signal from you. They should stop when you close your hand. Repeat this many times until everyone is working with you. When you move your open hand up, the children should sing a higher random note and when you move your hand down, they sing a lower random note. They will be surprised how effective this can sound.

Developing key elements

Up and down

Discuss with the class sounds they know that move up and down (a fire engine siren, for example). Give small groups of children each a title which relates to things that go up and down (steps and slides). Some titles might be The swing boats, Swimming pool flume, See-saw, Over the bridges. Ask them to decide on a simple pattern to follow, which could be repetition or beginning/middle/end, and to create a short piece of music to describe their title, remembering the up/down theme. Make sure each

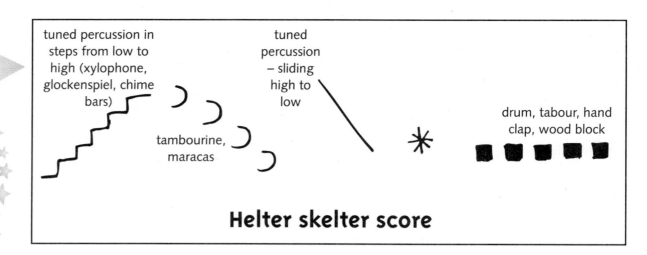

tuned percussion in steps from low to high (xylophone, glockenspiel, chime bars)

tuned percussion – sliding high to low

tambourine, maracas

drum, tabour, hand clap, wood block

Helter skelter score

group performs to the other groups. Can they notate their music using these symbols?

Rhythm

Choose some phrases linked with work in other subjects. For example, if you are working on weather they might be 'wet and windy', 'cold, damp'. 'misty, moisty morning', 'hot, baking sun'. *Which words am I clapping?* Divide the class into teams of six or eight children. One person taps a chosen rhythm on the shoulder of another who passes it on. *Can the last person recognize the rhythm?*

Dynamic symbols

● With the whole class, look at any piece of music to find some dynamic symbols (*p f < >*). It could be a song sheet or a hymn book. Sing a well-known song responding to these signs.

● Listen to Ravel's 'Bolero' as an example of much repetition. Can you hear which dynamic sign is also suggested? Do you think the composer has used the sign well? Can you make up a piece with friends to show both repetition and the sign *p <*?

Timbre

● Play four of the pieces of music from *Carnival of the Animals* by Saint Saens to identify different timbres (donkey, fossils, swan and pianists). *Can you say which sound is harsh, mellow, bright, hollow?*

● Divide the class into four groups and give each group one of the different timbres to work with. Can they create a cameo of music to explore this sound? Again titles will help. They might be: harsh – an argument; mellow – a sunrise/sunset; bright – morning dew/raindrops; hollow – the cave.

● Introduce the sounds of paper as a new timbre. With the children's help, make a collection of many

kinds of paper objects (foil, cardboard tubes and boxes, tissues, cling film, magazines and newspapers). In small groups, how many different sounds can they discover? Can they make up a piece of music using these sounds based on a soft/loud/soft pattern?

Instruments

● Pass one instrument around a circle with each child in turn saying, and showing, *I can play the —— like this.* Some instruments can be played in many, many ways. When the children have exhausted the possibilities and begin to repeat themselves, change the instrument.

● Some children may be learning to play recorders, maybe violins, piano, and possibly woodwind and brass. If so, encourage them to take part, on their instruments, in classroom music-making and school assemblies. Listen to the special sounds these instruments make. Look for songs that have simple accompaniments (A & C Black have a wide range of these) or work out a simple ostinato (repeating tune) for them to play.

● Make a collection of different-sounding drums. Conventional ones and tambours can be used alongside upturned buckets and cardboard boxes. Ask the children, working in pairs, to speak to each other, using the drum sounds for their questions and answers.

● Invite instrument players to talk about their written music, how they use it as well as why they need it.

Music from other cultures

● Look at the traditions of other countries and their festivals. Encourage anyone from a culture other than British to talk about their traditions and their music. Where possible, invite friends, neighbours and peripatetic teachers into the classroom to share their knowledge with the class.

● Listen to some appropriate recorded music. Espana by Chabrier gives the flavour of Spain, Ravi Shankar's music will bring India into the classroom.

Tonic sol-fa

● If you understand the tonic sol-fa signs (see page 116), use Soh and Meh to encourage children to sing 'Good morning' (s m m), 'How are you today?' (s s s s m), 'What is your name' (s s s m), 'Where do you live?' (s   s   s m).

Ask the children to reply using just two notes and their hand signs. (Soh could be G on a xylophone and Meh could be E.)

● Ask the children to close their eyes. Play or sing either Soh or Me. *Can you hear which is the higher and which is the lower?*

Musical vocabulary

Make sure you use the correct names for the instruments to help the children build up a musical

vocabulary. Shakers should become maracas, clickers are castanets, scrapers are guiros. There are many books with good illustrations, such as *A Primary Teacher's Handbook*, D Tipton (Folens).

Pentatonic scale

Introduce the idea of a pentatonic scale for question-and-answer rhythm games and copy-me activities. This simply means a five-note scale which can be C D E G A. The joy of using this scale is that at all times it is pleasant to listen to, even when a whole class uses it at the same time.

☀ Ideas bank

● Collect a variety of containers (yoghurt pots, tubes, opaque plastic bottles, small cardboard boxes) and number them. Glue them to a base board and, using seeds, paper, rice and sand and so on, fill some of them full, some partly full and leave some empty. Number them, cover them and give beaters and a sheet of paper to a group of children. *Can you decide, by tapping the containers, which are full, which are part full and which are empty? Record your results.* Let a second group try and compare and discuss their results.

● Make some flash cards which represent opposite sounds (high/low, long/short and so on). With the children in a place where they can easily see the cards, play them, but make some mistakes. *Who can hear when I make a mistake?* Then ask a child to be the player.

● Together with the children, collect some long words or phrases. 'Combine harvester' would be a good starter. *How many different ways can it be said by putting the accent in a different place?*

● Make a collection of found objects (stones, string, boxes, pots, wood). *How many of them can be played as an instrument? Can you use these sounds in your music-making?*

● Play 'Copycat' with you as the leader, playing an instrument and making the tune move in steps. You will need to use a tuned percussion instrument. *Can someone copy me? Can someone play the opposite sounds to me?* If you have enough instruments, divide the class into pairs and let them try.

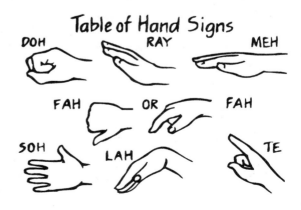

Table of Hand Signs

Assessment

The most important outcome of music making with all children is that they should have enjoyed it. If this is the case, it should be extremely obvious at the end of a session since the children will be animated about what they have been doing as they move on to their next activity.

However, there are many other observations to be made to help in your evaluation of the work they have done.

The most important things for you to do at all levels in music-making are to:
- involve the children;
- encourage them to listen to sounds around them and the sounds they and others make on the instruments;
- let them perform as often as possible;
- ask for their opinion on all the music they hear;
- give them many opportunities to be creative in their music-making.

What can they do?

Most Year 3 children should be able to:
- listen attentively to sounds;
- collect sounds;
- recognize some differences in sounds;
- recreate sounds;
- use sounds in a more structured way;
- respond through dance/drama and movement to sounds;
- discuss sounds;
- sing a wide variety of songs;
- play simple pieces on tuned and untuned instruments;
- use found objects as instruments;
- play simple accompaniments;
- have an awareness of pulse/beat;
- move/dance in response to music;
- listen to longer pieces of music;
- use simple music terms in their discussions;
- use a form of graphic notation;
- use the letter names of notes to record and remember accompaniments;
- use a pentatonic scale in musical games;
- work in a small group, sometimes leading;
- discuss with some musical confidence;
- use their new musical language.

Can they perform?

The music-making should be shared as much as possible with other children in the school, parents and friends. Everyone, not just the specialist performer, should be given a chance to perform. Look for abilities rather than disabilities – everyone can do something. Encourage those children who are having specialist lessons to demonstrate their skills to others by joining in whenever it is appropriate. School assemblies and school concerts should become a place for sharing successful activities.

Art and Design

This year you build on the things which the children explored and experienced in Year 2. Their experiences should cover the development of visual perception and the skills that are needed for investigation and making. The children will reflect on and adapt work, and will:

- record what they have experienced and imagined, expressing their ideas with increasing confidence and representing chosen features of the world around them with developing accuracy;
- gather and use resources and materials and experiment with ideas in response to these;
- experiment showing increasing control using a range of tools, materials and techniques.

Children will also be introduced to a range of work by artists, designers and craftspeople, and will:

- begin to recognize the work of artists, craftspeople and designers;
- begin to look at the intention and purpose behind works of art;
- begin to understand the historical and cultural context of works of art;
- respond to and evaluate their own art, craft and design and that of others.

What should they be able to do?

Most Year 3 children will be familiar with a range of materials and techniques and will have a developing ability to control them. Most children should have:

- had experience of a range of graphic materials and thick paint and watercolour;
- made prints using found objects and possibly experienced other methods;
- been introduced to collage;
- modelled and constructed with materials in three dimensions;
- been introduced to the work of a number of artists, craftspeople and designers.

There is still a need to experiment with any new or unfamiliar tools and materials and you should enable children to make connections between this exploratory work and the finished product.

From Year 3, children show a preference for creating a likeness and working representationally. This sometimes results in a lack of confidence if a likeness is not achieved. You should provide support and encouragement and show a range of examples of non-representational art.

By the end of Year 3, children will have:

- developed their experience in the use of familiar tools and materials, and been introduced to new or more complex ways of working (including work in three dimensions);
- continued work in the use of the visual elements which are the building blocks of art: pattern, texture, colour, line, tone, shape, form, space;
- communicated and expressed their own ideas visually and worked from their imagination and memory – stimulated by visits, events, stories, music and so on;
- developed skills in drawing, painting, printing, collage, fabric work and digital media;
- been introduced to imaginative and abstract images in the work of other artists, craftspeople and designers including at least one example from a non-Western culture;
- had opportunity to develop an art vocabulary by discussing their own work and that of others.

Practical ideas

Working through the senses, particularly sight and touch, is of vital importance at all stages. You can develop the children's visual and tactile skills by giving them increased opportunities to work from observation of real and interesting things brought into the classroom or through taking them outside to experience a place of visual or historical interest locally or further afield. Ask open-ended questions: *Who can tell me about the colours/shapes/textures …? What materials would you choose to make the smooth/shiny/fluffy surfaces? How could you develop some of your sketches into pictures?* Discuss what they have seen and discovered to stimulate interest and provide ideas and starting points.

Give them opportunities and strategies for researching images and ideas from related books, videos and the computer so that they are informed and made aware through a variety of resources.

Encourage them to suggest starting points – triggered, perhaps, by a favourite story or character, an exciting object, an important family event or happening. Give them the opportunity to work freely from their own ideas and imagination. In addition to working as a whole class, they should also sometimes work in pairs, collaboratively or individually.

The knowledge and experience which they gained at Key Stage 1 should enable the children to make choices and decisions about materials and the way in which they will work on two- or three-dimensional tasks.

If they have not already used simple graphics and painting software as another means of drawing, creating and changing patterns and exploring alternative combinations of colour, now is the time to introduce it. *Paintbrush*, RM *Colour Magic* and *Splosh* are all suitable software programmes for Year 3 children.

Making a start
The learning environment

The whole classroom environment, from the pictures on the walls to the way in which the tools and materials are arranged and cared for, is part of the display and so is a statement about the way in which children's work is viewed and valued. This, in fact, is a significant part of the teaching and in Year 3 children should begin to assume responsibility for

organizing and maintaining the materials for art, craft and design.

A lively and rich learning environment, with collections of visually exciting and tactile objects brought in by you and the children, will stimulate their curiosity and encourage an interest in, and response to, the world around. Accompany the displays with written comments and try to present these in the form of a task or challenge. Don't forget to include displays of work in three dimensions. For

example, a theme of Colour lends itself to collections of coloured fabric and artefacts. The class could be divided into colour groups with a different group responsible for the colour display each week. These displays can then be used as a starting point for exploring aspects of colour such as 'hue' (which in simple terms means a 'family' of colour) 'hot' and 'cold' colours, complimentary colours.

Tools and materials

Provide good quality tools and materials and remind children of the need to care for them .

Brushes should be washed and stored with the bristles uppermost. Glue spreaders should only be used for glue and stored away from the brushes. Put water in shallow containers which are not easily knocked over. Paint, especially in readymix pots, can be an attractive feature in the classroom if the jars are kept clean and stored tidily. Plastic sweetjars make good storage for coloured threads and small collage materials. These can also look attractive if the threads are sorted into colour families. Involve the children in sorting the threads and in sorting fabrics into small open plastic storage trays for future use in collage work or stitching activities. Flat trays also make good storage for watercolour boxes, packets of crayons or oil pastels.

Images and artefacts as sources of ideas

As far as possible, encourage the children to bring interesting objects and artefacts into the classroom as this gives them a feeling of ownership. You can also borrow collections of interesting items and artefacts from museums. These may relate specifically to a topic or theme and can be useful for extending children's experience. Use discussion and open-ended questions to help the children to discover the potential of images and artefacts and collections as a source of ideas for their own work. If it is a picture, discuss the colours, the way the artist has worked, the mood and what is happening. If it is an artefact, ask the children to look at the

shape, colour and pattern. If the object is not valuable, allow them to handle it and encourage them to describe its texture.

The children can record their initial responses in a sketchbook using words and drawings and then follow this up by making a painting, drawing, print or collage, or by making something similar using clay or junk materials. For example, items related to the world of work can be brought in from a building site or from a museum such as a mining museum. The children can use these objects for a variety of purposes, including observational drawing.

Themes

Things relating to people and the world around them are of interest to Year 3 children. People and their differences can be a good starting point as it encourages children to be appreciative of art from different cultures. This is an area where factual and creative writing, prose and poetry, drama, movement can all play a role. Other theme suggestions offering potential for this age group could be Colour and Working.

Colour

Look at the paintings of, for example, Henri Matisse (*Lady in Blue*), Robert Delaunay (*The Window*), André Derain (*Westminster Bridge*) Piet Mondrian (*Composition in Red, Yellow and Blue*), Franz Marc (*Blue Horses*), Wassily Kandinsky (*Composition No. 2*), Alexei Von Jawlensky (*Still Life*), Guiseppe Santomaso (*Red and Yellow of Harvest Time*). There are many other examples which you could use, but all of these paintings can be found in *A Concise History of Modern Painting* by H Read (Thames & Hudson).

The Fauves and Expressionists are movements in art which provide other useful examples.

A good book for this theme is *The Elements of Colour* by Johannes Itten (Chapman and Hall).

Working

The world of work has often been depicted by artists and children can see the way in which working life has changed over time by studying pictures such as those by the Limbourg Brothers, *The Haymakers* (an early fifteenth-century illumination), *The Gleaners* by Millet (see *Art Book*, Phaidon, among others) and many pictures by Peter Breughel, the sixteenth-century Flemish painter who painted peasants feasting and working. You could use his *A Country Wedding*, which shows people at work. A coloured illustration which focuses on this can be found in *The Story of Art* by E H Gombrich (Phaidon).

✦ Introducing key elements
Investigating and making

Give your Year 3 children opportunities for expressive work based in real or imagined experiences and encourage them to work from memory as well as their imagination. Stories, music and drama are all good starting points – encourage individual responses and ideas which can then be shared. Introduce observational work from both natural and made forms, for example, pebbles, shells, feathers and so on, or a collection tools of or machine parts – perhaps car parts from a breaker's yard.

An essential part of the art experience at all stages in children's development is exploring to find out what art tools and materials will do. This can sometimes be through trial and error, and sometimes through guided discovery. Recognize and accept that combining materials and overlaying them is part of this process. You will also need to teach specific techniques.

Techniques
Drawing

● In Year 2, most children should have had experience of the range of marks that can be made with soft drawing pencils and charcoal. In Year 3, you can introduce chalk pastels. Provide a range of colours and encourage children to experiment in

their sketchbooks to see what marks they can make. Show them how to use the side of the chalk as well as the end.

Linked to the theme of Colour, ask the children to make a small patch of colour using a primary colour of their choice and then to make another small patch next to it using one of the other primary colours. *What happens if you blend the two colours together? What happens if you use one colour directly on top of the other? Try red over yellow. Is there any difference if yellow is used first? What happens if thin stripes of alternate red and yellow are held at a distance? What happens if they are rubbed together? Try blue and yellow, blue and red.* Immediately after the experimentation, ask the children to do a drawing which gives them an opportunity to use some of the effects which they have explored. For example, you could set up a still life of fruit and colourful material for them to work from.

● Look at a painting by Breughel of people working (such as *A Country Wedding*). You could invite a child or adult to pose as one of the workers in the painting for the class to draw. Keep the poses short so that the person posing does not find it an uncomfortable experience. Encourage the children to work quickly by talking to them as they work about looking carefully. *Look at the way his left leg is bending as he leans forward. Can you make this leg look as though it is taking lots of weight? Do you think you need dark thick marks or thin light marks for this?* Try drawing alongside them, talking about the way you are looking carefully as you draw and the things you are looking for.

● In *Drawings* by Van der Wolk (Arnoldo Mondadori Arte) you will find reproductions of the drawings that Van Gogh made of workers. For example, there is one called *A Digger* which is ink, black ink, chalk and watercolour. The children can achieve similar effects if they use charcoal and chalk for their drawings. Van Gogh's series of drawings of peasants working are in charcoal and chalk and show a range of interesting working poses which could also form the basis for a movement lesson based on working. The children could draw each other in the lesson, half the class posing or moving and the other half drawing. Sketchbooks and pencils would be suitable materials for this.

Painting
Colour

● Children should have experienced general colour mixing in Key Stage 1. Linked to the theme of colour, this can be developed in a more structured way by offering the children one colour and black and white so that they can begin to explore tone.

● Colour poems could also be a starting point for a painting. Encourage children to use and control different consistencies of paint, for example mixing from thick (impasto) to thin washes.

Work theme

The theme of work can be linked to a visit to a farm or a factory. On a farm visit, the children can do drawings in a sketchbook which can then be used as reference in the classroom to develop into a painting. Show them a reproduction of Millet's *The Gleaners*. Involve them in discussion about the painting. Ask them to look for tone (light and dark colours) and discuss what colours they might choose for their picture. *Will you choose the same sort of colours as Millet used, or not? Why?* They can use their sketchbooks to experiment with different colours. Spend some time talking about their final pictures. These could form part of a display which could include photographs of the children at the farm, and a reproduction of Millet's picture.

Printing

● Introduce press print using small rectangular pieces of polystyrene. (The small polystyrene trays found in supermarkets are not suitable as the surface is usually sealed for hygienic reasons and this resists the paint. The type used for printing can be obtained from County Supplies. It comes in square sheets which can easily be cut on the Rotatrim.)

Print-making can be a messy process unless it is done in a methodical way:

▶ Cover a table with paper. Keep clean things on one end of the table (paper for printing on and a clean roller) and use the other end for the 'messy' equipment (ink, inking plate, roller and polystyrene block).

▶ Draw round the pieces of equipment when they are first in position and then ask the children to replace them in the drawn spaces. This prevents ink, particularly from the roller, from getting everywhere.

▶ Tear some rectangles of newspaper larger than the printing block and always place the block on the newspaper when inking up. The newspaper can then be thrown away leaving a clean space.

▶ Take a rectangle of perspex about A4 size and squeeze a small amount of white waterbased printing ink at the top. Using the roller, spread the ink up and down and from side to side. It should be thinly spread and have a suede-like appearance. Transfer the ink to the printing block using the roller.

▶ Pick up the inked block and place it ink side down on to the first section on the paper. Use the clean roller to roll on the back. Gently remove the block. Repeat this process for all sections. Yellow ink can also be used effectively on black paper. Bright colours or black can be used on white paper.

▶ If you are using the theme of Work, the children can cut the polystyrene with scissors into the shape of cogs and wheels or they can work with a small rectangular piece of it which can be drawn into using a pencil or ball point pen. They should press quite hard to make an indented mark but should not press right through.

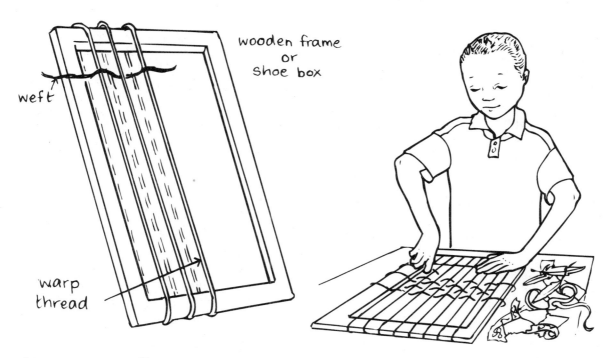

weft

warp thread

wooden frame or shoe box

Tissue paper collage

▶ Cover the tables with newspaper.

▶ Provide paper, scissors, glue and spreaders and a selection of pieces of tissue paper of varying colours.

▶ Encourage the children to experiment with overlaying the tissue paper to produce another colour.

▶ Spread glue on the supporting paper rather than on to the back of the tissue paper which tears easily. Use PVA glue as it dries transparent. Small folds can be produced, which are darker in colour, by pushing the wet tissue paper about.

Modelling

Build on previous experiences of working with clay or other malleable materials.

● Challenge the children to model a figure from one piece of clay. They could use their drawings of workers as a starting point.

Weaving

Weaving can be introduced at any time but is particularly useful as a technique if children are beginning to be frustrated by not being able to achieve a likeness.

● Show the children examples of weaving from artists in this country and from other cultures. Use the words *weft*, *warp* and *shuttle*.

● They can make a simple loom from stiff card with corresponding serrations at each end, or a more sophisticated loom can be made from a wooden frame with pins for attaching the warp threads.

● Give the children a selection of coloured and textured threads to choose from for the weft. Their choice could be based on observations of colour in a shell or stone, the sky, or even a painting. It is useful to keep a 'bit box' with random things as children often enjoy choosing and using unconventional things to weave with.

Sculpture

Look at examples of sculpture, preferably the real thing.

▶ Discuss shape, form, space and texture.

▶ Talk about the variety of materials for three dimensional work – clay, plaster, wire, papier mâché, fibres, plastic, metal, timber and so on.

Sketchbooks

Year 3 is an ideal time to introduce working with sketchbooks (as recommended in the National Curriculum). This is the place to experiment with different tools and materials, to record observations, and to develop ideas or designs.

For more information about how to make sketchbooks and use them effectively as a tool for learning, see *Sketchbooks Explore and Store* by G Robinson (Hodder & Stoughton).

The elements of art

Provide opportunities for experimentation with the elements of art: line, colour, shape, pattern, texture, form. It is seldom that a work of art has only one element in its make up and children will usually be involved in working with several of the elements in one challenge or project. For example, in connection with the theme of Colour you could introduce the

Art and Design

children to the work of the modern Russian artist Wassily Kandinsky who used colours and shapes in an abstract way, often related to sounds. You could involve the children in:

◗ expressive use of line working in a less structured and more uninhibited way – making marks in response to music and sound;

◗ using their sketchbooks to try out various ways of combining marks and textures;

◗ selecting abstract shapes used by Wassily Kandinsky in his work; each shape can be filled with a different pattern or texture;

◗ wool winding or weaving to explore the colours in a Kandinsky painting;

◗ a final painting or collage.

This is a useful activity for introducing abstract or non-representational imagery.

Vocabulary

Discuss the words 'art', 'craft' and 'design' with the children. It is important for them to understand words and concepts from earlier experience, for example *explore, observe, imagine*.

Introduce the vocabulary relating to a range of art and design forms, for example *sculpture, construction, modelling, collage, weaving*. Identify, in the school and the locality, the materials and methods used by artists, craftspeople and designers. This will generate opportunities to discuss both two-dimensional and three-dimensional work. Encourage the children to make links between the art forms around them and their own work and talk about the ways in which works of art differ according to time, place and purpose.

Reviewing

Spend time sitting alongside children so that they can talk to you about their work and evaluate it, finding something positive to say about it. From opportunities to discuss their work children will learn to reflect on their work, to modify it and suggest new ideas. It is also an opportunity to reinforce vocabulary related for example to new experiences, elements, tools or techniques.

Knowledge and understanding

● In addition to books about individual artists the following are helpful as a general reference to get some idea of the range of artists' work available: *The Art Book*, *The Modern Art Book* and *The Pop Art Book* (all published by Phaidon; *The Art Book* is now available cheaply in a small format volume.)

● The education departments of the main galleries in London are also very helpful if you are planning a visit or want information about artists relating to a specific theme. You can introduce children to a range of different artists and to three-dimensional forms through reproductions on postcards, old greetings cards and so on, which can be collected in a photograph album and kept in the book corner. Parents and friends may be able to add to the collection.

● If you know a lively local artist who would be willing to come into the classroom, this would be a great stimulus.

● Encourage children to describe a variety of images and artefacts, to voice likes and dislikes and make choices about which they like best. This can take place in whole-class discussions, group work or spontaneously on an individual basis. They can learn to recognize the elements of art in the work of other artists, craftspeople and designers and apply this knowledge to their own, looking at colour and line in artists' work and responding by using it vigorously in their own work to express feelings, for example. In Year 3, they can begin to analyse aspects of the artists' work, comparing and contrasting materials, techniques and imagery.

Developing key elements

Recording from experience, observation and imagination

● Gather together a collection of tools. You can bring in some yourself or invite the children to bring in an item which is used by someone in the world of work: a hammer or a safety helmet for example. Use this collection as a starting point for observational drawings or painting.

● Suggest different approaches: working with the whole collection, focusing on one item, or drawing an area selected by looking through a card 'window'. Later, using a paper or card viewfinder placed over the drawing, children can select an area to develop into an abstract image.

● The children can make a large-scale, close-up study of a colourful flower (for example, a large sunflower, a hollyhock or a cyclamen) using a range of materials to achieve a colour match. They could

try working into a painting with oil pastels. This could be combined with a visit to a garden or garden centre to observe and record in sketchbooks the range of colours and textures to be found in flowers and plants. Further exotic plants and flowers in an imaginary environment can then be painted. This could generate work for a large display.

Look for:
▶ the ability to concentrate and observe carefully;
▶ the ability to select and develop an aspect of their drawing;
▶ the development of observational work into abstract or imaginative images;
▶ an awareness of the difference between art which represents something and art which has abstract qualities.

Images and artefacts as sources of ideas

Remember that the intention here is not for children to make an exact copy but to look intently and notice things which they had not noticed before. Some of these things they will be able to apply to their own work.

● Provide a collection of objects for the children to draw from. Once again, you could focus on tools. Try to include a range of forms and textures. Pass round the objects and ask questions such as *Can you tell me what it is? What is it used for? Can you describe the texture?*

Then ask them to explore in their sketchbooks ways in which they can use pencil/chalk and charcoal to suggest a textured surface. They can make drawings using soft pencils or charcoal and chalk, and simplify the drawings and make repetitions.

● Ask them to design a tool or machine for a special job. (Edward de Bono's book *The Dog Walking Machine* (Penguin) is a useful starting point for ideas.)

● Bring in some ceramic objects/pots with a textured surface. The children can use clay to make shapes or pots with rough and smooth surfaces. Clay can be removed by scraping or incising and it can also be added to the surface again as long as it is pushed and blended in so that it is secure.

Look for:
▶ interest and motivation;
▶ a personal response;
▶ visual and tactile awareness;
▶ the ability to use descriptive vocabulary;
▶ inventiveness;
▶ the ability to use initial stimulus to generate ideas.

Tools, materials, techniques and the visual elements

● Place a group of objects against a background and use a light source to emphasize tone. Talk about light, medium and dark tone. The children experiment making tonal marks using charcoal and chalk and then attempt a drawing on a large scale (A2 size or above).

● Encourage the children to experiment with mixing colours to camouflage an object. Use 'mixed media', for example, oil pastels over paint, paint over collage, watercolour and ink.

● They can make a textured printing block using scored pieces of card, threads, string, sand, rice and so on pressed on to a piece of card covered with PVA glue. The things on the surface, although different textures, should be the same height. The block can be used for taking rubbings; alternatively it can be inked up and used as a printing block. The resulting print is called a 'collagraph'.

● Challenge the children to design and make their own brush. Provide a range of materials: thick string, dried reeds, cotton wool for the bristles; sticks or dowelling for the handle; tape for the ferrule.
Look for:
▶ a willingness to try new tools and techniques;
▶ a personal response and use of imagination;
▶ an ability to build on previous experience of colour mixing;
▶ involvement and concentration;
▶ manual dexterity in the manipulation of materials;
▶ the use of appropriate descriptive vocabulary.

Artists, craftspeople and designers

● Bring in examples or reproductions of a range of art relating to the theme of colour. You could use *Yellow Chair with Pipe* (Van Gogh), *Blue Horses* (Franz Marc), *The Dinner Table (Harmony in Red)* (Henri Matisse), pictures from Picasso's Blue and Rose periods.

Ask the children *What main colour can you see? Can you see different hues of the same colour? Can you suggest names for them? Why do you think the artist used so much of one colour in this picture? How does it make you feel? What would happen if you changed the colour? What colour would you choose?*

● Look at colour in art from another culture, for example, Aboriginal paintings.

Discuss the way these colours are produced. *What natural materials could you use to make your own colours?*

Look for:
▶ an ability to choose colour to express or evoke feeling and emotion;
▶ awareness of the range of 'hues' in one colour;
▶ experimentation;
▶ an ability to make links between their own work and that of appropriate artists and craftspeople.

Responding and describing

● Bring in artefacts from a museum, for example, tools used by craftspeople in the past or in another culture.

● Invite a local potter or other craftsperson to talk about their job. Children can make quick drawings and notes in their sketchbook to be developed later.

● Look at and discuss the use of colour on non-European artefacts, for example masks, body painting, textiles, ornaments. You could use Chinese tribal masks or African masks and body painting. The Museum of Mankind in London is a useful resource.

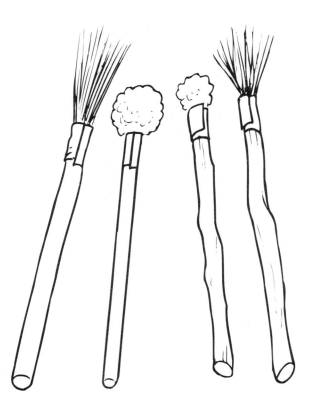

The children should demonstrate:

- observational skills;
- communication skills and art vocabulary;
- an ability to understand the purpose of a mask or other personal adornment as personal expression or part of tribal or cultural tradition;
- personal motivation and response;
- independent thinking.

Special occasions
Decorations
The 'unit' approach

Each child makes or paints an object or image which is a unit for a large wall display. For example, you could make textured panels by sticking objects and natural materials to card using PVA glue. The surface can be left as it is, sprayed, varnished or painted or covered with glue and metallic foil laid over it and pressed around the shapes.

The children's units should be of their own devising – it could either be a direct response to the materials provided or be based on a theme.

Greeting cards

- The children can choose from a limited range of white and coloured card.
- You might need to restrict the size.
- Suggest to the children that they choose their subjects and ideas.
- Give them a choice of tools and materials from a range which you have selected.
- Sometimes choose to restrict the colours used, for example, at Christmas.

- Use collage, painting, drawing, print.
- An image stitched from an observational drawing, mounted on a piece of card with a message underneath, is something a little different.
- Encourage the children to write their own messages. This could be a short poem.
- Try using coloured pens or crayons for the wording in the card.
- Try something three-dimensional, for example a textured clay tile.
- The children can also print their own wrapping paper and design gift tags.

Display

Display is one of the ways in which we evaluate children's work.

- Try to involve the children as much as possible in making decisions about the way in which their work is displayed. They can use the computer to make simple labels for the display.
- Encourage the children to mount their own work.
- Try to include everybody's work in the display.
- Sometimes a 'pavement show', laying out the work on the hall floor, for example, or pinning it up quickly so that it can be celebrated and talked about immediately, is a valuable way of building on the children's experiences and making teaching points while the experience is still fresh in their minds.

Involve the children in making positive observations about each other's work at this time. This helps the children to identify developing skills and to use art-based vocabulary to describe these skills.

Assessment

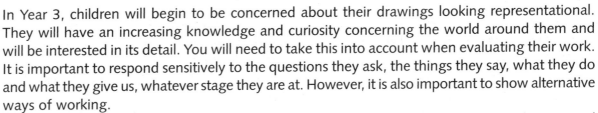

In Year 3, children will begin to be concerned about their drawings looking representational. They will have an increasing knowledge and curiosity concerning the world around them and will be interested in its detail. You will need to take this into account when evaluating their work. It is important to respond sensitively to the questions they ask, the things they say, what they do and what they give us, whatever stage they are at. However, it is also important to show alternative ways of working.

A vital consideration in any evaluation of outcomes in art and design is respect for personal and cultural identity, particularly as art should be instrumental in developing self-confidence. It is also important to develop positive attitudes to art through praise, help and encouragement. The beginnings of peer group evaluation are to be encouraged with an emphasis on the importance of positive comments. For example: 'I like the way Hannah has experimented using charcoal and chalk together.'

You should evaluate some of the following aspects of the children's art endeavours at this stage:

- How have they used what we have given them?
- What have they done and what are they trying to do?
- What evidence do we see of independent thinking and personal ideas?
- Have they been willing to experiment?
- Are they developing an increasing knowledge of how tools and materials behave?
- Have the materials been used in an imaginative way?
- Have they built on previous experience of colour mixing?
- Have they learned a new skill/technique?
- Are they becoming more aware of art, artists, galleries?
- Have they learned about art from another country/culture/period?
- Are they growing more confident?
- Can they make a personal response?
- Are they motivated and involved?
- Can they work independently/co-operatively?
- Can they talk about their own and each other's work, using appropriate vocabulary?

Physical Education

Children in Year 3 need a wide variety of movement experiences on a regular basis to develop and enjoy their rapidly growing movement confidence and competence. In most schools, PE is timetabled only two or three times a week so you will need to decide when the six activity areas of PE are taught and for how long. You should ensure that you teach a balance of the three core activities of gymnastics, games and dance throughout the year. The length of each PE lesson may vary, but normally teachers have a minimum of 30 minutes' activity for each session. For the purposes of this chapter, it is assumed that one unit of work (for approximately half a term) for athletics and outdoor and adventurous activities will be included in Year 3, although swimming may also be one of the activities which are included for your class.

Whatever their previous experience of PE the majority of children will be keen and eager to please, and you should provide a consistent, firm but supportive environment so that they can use their energies in purposeful and positive ways. You will need to explain and establish your own special routine and arrangements for this area of the curriculum, (changing, lining up and going to the hall or playground). Some mention in the school brochure and a notice on the classroom door will help to remind your class and their carers of what clothes to bring and when. You will find many opportunities to develop other aspects of children's learning (language, mathematics, personal and social experiences) within, through or related to the practical physical activities that follow.

Because many general expectations apply to all areas of activity, some of these are included before focusing on expectations for specific activities.

What should they be able to do ?

There will be vast differences in experience, interest, physique, temperament, attitude and effort between the children who come into your class. Whatever the experiences they have had outside school or in their first years of schooling, they will still need reminders to move safely with others in a large space, with equipment or on apparatus, although they can be expected to be more aware and independent than in their first years of schooling. They should be encouraged to discuss the reasons for changing into suitable clothing for each activity and be expected to get ready quickly and independently and to help others prepare for activity.

Throughout the year, the children will show increasing control and awareness when performing basic actions in the different areas of activity. Many will be agile and energetic and have a wide range of actions which they can perform successfully. Most children will enjoy the challenge of learning new skills, but some will be able to manage their bodies more easily and with greater control than others. By the end of the year, the majority of children should be developing their ability to clarify or refine their own actions (for example, make a shape clearer, use their whole body) when asked to do so, or when working with a partner. Watch for some children who may need particular encouragement or those who need additional challenges. Many children will be able to combine actions (for example, run and jump; bounce a ball and move sideways; creep and turn), some more fluently and easily than others.

Although the sequence of progression through the stages of motor development is similar for most children, they do not progress at the same rate or at an even rate and so there will always be a wide range of differences in the ways children in your class achieve various actions/ movements. This is natural as every child is unique. Sometimes in sheer excitement or the demands of the situation a child will use inconsistent or less advanced movements but, by the end of Year 3, most children's responses should be more consistent. Observe and enjoy the actions of each child, continue to create an atmosphere of success, fun and satisfaction, and support, watch and enjoy their rapid progress.

Key element: Dance

Depending on their previous experiences and their practice during the year, most children will show increasing sensitivity in their movements and be able to explore contrasts in movement, enriching their movements by varying shape, size, direction, level and speed. They will be able to use different body parts to gesture, travel, support their body weight or to lead movement as they explore different shapes and body positions. With practice and encouragement, the majority will be able to do this in time with different forms of accompaniment (sounds, music) and will begin to recognize and respond to changes in rhythm and phrasing and adjust their movements accordingly. As you would expect, there will be great variations in the ways that they do this, some being more aware of differences than others.

Most children will enjoy dancing and will be able to move confidently with increasing co-ordination, while some will still need encouragement to create and clarify motifs or phrases of movement and to link them into a short sequence, whether individually, with a partner or in a small group. Many will be keen to use their imagination when given a clear stimulus or framework but, without some directions, some will feel uncertain or insecure and may find it difficult to be creative. Watch for their ideas, develop and use some of them to feed in new suggestions to others in the class.

By the end of the year, most children will show an increasing ability to observe and repeat short phrases of movement with varying degrees of accuracy and fluency, and contribute ideas of their own. They will be showing increased body awareness when performing the key actions of dance (travelling, turning, jumping, making a shape, gesturing and stillness) and should be able to include other actions like slithering, drifting or soaring as their movement vocabulary increases. Encourage them to side-step and skip, or make up their own step patterns; most of them will be beginning to do this rhythmically and continuously in time to music. As a group in a large space they should be developing their ability to use the space thoughtfully and well, using interesting and varied pathways (figure of eight, curving, straight, zig-zag). They should be increasingly able to describe their actions to others and begin to explain what they liked about the movements of others. Encourage your class to express their own ideas in response to the tasks set and enjoy watching them move and expand their vocabulary of movement ideas.

Key element: Gymnastics

Most children will be agile and adventurous, although some may still need lots of encouragement to participate fully and others may need reminders to be more cautious and aware of others. Give them plenty of time to try out and practise their gymnastic actions (jumping, rolling, moving on hands and feet and climbing) in the context of different themes on the floor and then on different parts of the large apparatus.

They will be able to use a variety of jumping, hopping and stepping patterns in their travelling and you can encourage them to practise these in the warm-up part of the lesson (from one foot to two feet, two feet to two feet). Ask them to work on the quality of these actions, to practise their leaping and to try different patterns of jumps and hops. Most children will be able to move about the floor and apparatus in a variety of ways using their feet, hands and feet and other body parts. Throughout the year, help and expect them to show increasing control and awareness of their actions. Encourage them to be inventive and imaginative in response to tasks and suggestions. They should be able to balance with increasing confidence and control in a variety of positions: holding still, in clear shapes (wide, thin, tucked, twisted), on large and small parts of their bodies (sides, tummy, shoulders, seat, one foot, or head, hand and foot).

If you give the children opportunities in nearly every lesson to take their weight on their hands (all fours, two hands and one foot, bunny jump) they will begin to develop strength in their upper bodies. Check that hands are flat on the floor and arms are straight (as they hold still shapes or move on their hands and feet while bunny jumping or walking on all fours). They will also use their hands to hold on to, climb, hang and pull themselves along on the apparatus.

Most children will be able to share the space and apparatus with others in the group considerately, but some will still need help and reminders to do so, particularly where there is some favourite apparatus. Many will use the large apparatus confidently but should be encouraged to clarify their actions while answering the movement tasks set. Help them to develop a greater awareness of what they are doing and to improve their own performance through observation, demonstration, review and practice. By the end of the year, they will be able to link two or more actions into a short sequence and add starting and finishing positions.

Check that all children have the opportunity to use all pieces of apparatus over a series of lessons and that they share the responsibility of setting it out and putting it away. Teach them to lift and carry equipment efficiently and safely.

Key element: Games

Most children will be energetic and keen to participate in games. They should be more aware of the space and others as they play, but they will still need reminders to use the space well, particularly when using games equipment. Running, chasing and dodging games will provide opportunities for them to practise and improve their ability to stop, start and change direction quickly and nimbly.

They should be able to roll, tap, bounce, throw, or kick a ball with increasing accuracy towards a large, still target (between skittles, into a hoop, to a partner, or between markings on the floor or wall). Many will be able to do this (or can be challenged to try) in more difficult circumstances (to a smaller target, from further away, with less preparation time). They should be able to pass a ball accurately to a partner using hands and feet (stationary and on the move). By the end of the year, the children should be able to receive a thrown ball (or quoit or beanbag) with their hands in different ways (two hands, one hand; high, low). Most of them will also be able to bounce a ball (large, medium or small) and dribble it with one or both hands while moving in different directions. Many will enjoy using a bat (or their hands) to tap up or bounce a ball with increasing success, and count the number of times they can do so.

The children should be given lots of opportunities to co-operate in small groups (pairs, threes or fours) to make up their own games. As they do so, they will show an increasing ability to negotiate, plan and discuss ideas and tactics with others. By the end of the year they should be able to invent simple rules to make their games fair (take turns to start the game, three goes each, pass to each person) if helped to do so.

Encourage your class to take responsibility for looking after the equipment, putting it out and away. (It is helpful if this is colour coded so that each colour group can check the contents of their own baskets.)

Practical ideas

Making a start

Dance

● Try different ways to start dance lessons:

❱ moving, shaking, stretching different parts of the body (raising awareness of the different ways this can be done);

❱ developing and practising travelling actions (skipping, side-stepping, creeping, striding) with various forms of accompaniment (percussion, music or voice);

❱ using phrases of beats to encourage the use of space and movement in different directions (eight beats one way, eight beats another). Try variations in the action (striding forwards, tip-toeing backwards), encouraging response to the rhythm and gradually raising the heart beat. Children will enjoy doing this to popular tunes or music such as the *Blue Peter* theme.

● Explore the essential qualities in a variety of action words (*jerk*, *sag*, *slither*) to enhance both the children's language and dance experiences. Use percussion instruments or words as the accompaniment. It helps if you say the words in ways which enhance the actions (*crumple*, *shiver*, *glide*) and in phrases to allow the children time to respond.

● Work on levels (high, medium, low) by choosing contrasting action words (soar/roll; fly/sprawl; slide/jump) and encourage different directions (forwards, sideways, backwards, up and down) and pathways (straight, curving, round-a-bout, zig-zag).

● Gradually build phrases of movement (for example, leap, leap, leap and collapse … roll, roll, roll and slither away). Encourage children to do this individually and to vary the level at which they are moving or to choose their own starting point.

● Encourage relaxation and a cool down by using music for slow walking or stretching or a short piece of calm music to sit or lie and listen to at the end of every lesson.

Gymnastics

Encourage and help children to think carefully about their actions by selecting a focus or theme for their attention, (for example, lifting feet high). Try out ideas in the floorwork part of the lesson and then try them on the apparatus.

Organization of apparatus

Whatever the theme, teach the children to handle and use the apparatus carefully, emphasizing the safety factors.

❱ Divide the class into five or six groups (to ensure all children have a range of experiences and to help spacing).

❱ Each group should be responsible for handling the *same* apparatus each lesson. (Change over each term.)

❱ Make a plan of the apparatus to be used, which will support the theme (for example, more flat and separate surfaces for balancing).

❱ Establish a fair and logical pattern of rotation of groups (zig-zag, clockwise, or straight swap if there are groups with similar apparatus) so that over a period of several lessons, the children can explore fully each group of apparatus in turn. (Have a maximum of two apparatus changes in one lesson.)

❱ Teach each group how to get out their apparatus

(positioning to carry apparatus, bending knees not back, all looking in direction of travel) and where to put it. (Use chalk marks initially to help indicate positioning of apparatus.)

▶ Check apparatus fixings and placement before it is used.

▶ Establish rules (working quietly and considerately, making use of the spaces).

▶ Insist on a quiet working atmosphere, but discuss why.

▶ Encourage and help children to share space and equipment (using the floor space around the apparatus), particularly when there is limited apparatus.

▶ Establish a consistent routine for stopping, coming down and sitting away from the apparatus.

Children will enjoy the responsibility of lifting and carrying the apparatus and co-operating with their group to make sure it is carefully and safely placed and checked by you and them.

Games

● Use a variety of travelling actions (walk, jog, run, hop, jump, gallop, skip, stride) to practise starting, stopping and changing direction. Start on the spot or moving slowly and gradually speed up the changes so that children develop the ability to respond quickly. As the activity increases, so does the pulse rate. Encourage the children to try to sustain activity for longer periods each time. There will be great variations in their ability to do this.

● Use a range of class games to start and/or finish the lesson. Start with those with which some children are familiar like Chase and Change (*in pairs: A chases B until teacher shouts 'change', when B chases A. If B is touched before 'change' is shouted, then B becomes chaser*) or Tag games, and gradually introduce new ones like Catch the Tail. (In pairs, A tucks a band in the back of his/her shorts. B starts facing A and then tries, by dodging from side to side, to catch the tail. They change over when the tail is caught or when you say so.) This will encourage listening and quick responses to your stop and start commands, and will give children the opportunity to become more aware of the space and others as they dodge and move quickly around.

● Children will be familiar with a variety of equipment, but they will still need lots of practice in using different ways of manipulating it. Select from rolling, stopping, collecting, aiming, catching, throwing, kicking or passing, or give a choice of activity with specified apparatus (hoop, rope, ball, quoit).

● Introduce individual challenges within a chosen or specified activity. *How many? Can you beat your own record?*

● Develop shared, co-operative challenges (in pairs, *How many?*). Provide opportunities for made-up games in pairs or threes using a specified action (throwing, catching or bouncing).

This will allow children to be inventive, use their initiative, share ideas as they discuss and negotiate with a partner or small group, and practise and consolidate their selected actions. By doing so they will become more aware of some of the fundamentals of games play in a situation in which they are in control, and not made to feel inadequate as they may do when they are trying ideas which are imposed upon them. These challenges and made-up games are the best form of simple competitive games for children of this age.

● Establish safe and careful use of equipment by teaching the children to take responsibility for putting it out and putting it away. If the apparatus is colour coded, each group can easily check that it has all been neatly returned to the baskets and counted (if appropriate) to ensure that it is not left about or lost. When they are playing in pairs or groups check that spare equipment has been returned to the baskets.

Developing key elements

Dance

Continue to encourage the children to try a range of rhythmic movements and travelling actions to different forms of accompaniment to start the lessons.

Provide a wide range of experiences to stimulate dance. Use classroom topics or themes (see suggestions below) or simple movement ideas to use as starting points for a few or several lessons.

(How long will depend on the topic and the experience and interest of the class.) Use language and imagery to help focus on the particular movement qualities of the chosen stimulus. For example, don't say 'be a cat', but talk of *creeping*, *pouncing*, *curling*, *stretching* and *arching*.

Circus

Introduce the theme with, for example, funny faces, happy faces, sad faces, a circus parade and march. Then, using actions – walk, balance and fall – explore and develop movement phrases for each of the following:

◗ clowns (funny walks and still shapes, nearly falling over);

◗ tightrope walkers (balancing along the rope, jumping and turning on the rope, nearly falling off);

◗ jugglers (balancing plates and catching balls with several parts of the body, travelling and turning too);

◗ strong people (still poses, strong steps and lifts);

◗ acrobats (rolling, jumping and balancing, nearly falling over).

End the theme with, for example, a parade and bowing and curtsying in character (such as clown stretching braces, making funny shapes).

In the snow

Use a simple narrative based on snow (preferably when real snow has just fallen): waking up (several slow stretches), excitedly jumping up and looking out of window; getting dressed (pulling on warm clothing and boots, wrapping scarf around); treading in the deep snow; making one large snowball and a snowman, snowman melting; skating and pushing or pulling a toboggan; shivering; curling up in thick blanket. Exaggerate and repeat motifs and phrases of movement. For example, trudge, trudge, trudge and shiver (knees), trudge, trudge, trudge and shiver (shoulders).

Stories/events as a basis for dance

Select suitable key aspects of a story and carefully emphasize chosen qualities. For example: *Dinosaurs and All That Rubbish*, M Forman (Puffin) – pollution/environmental theme. There could be four parts to this dance.

◗ 'Building a rocket to go to the stars': cutting down trees, digging coal, sawing logs and so on. Focus on strong working actions (hammering, pushing, pulling) and rhythm. Use sawing and hammering sound effects or percussion.

◗ 'Searching on a star': explore the idea of weightlessness – jumping, turning, leaping, stepping and searching (high and low). (Music: 'The Snowman Theme'.)

▶ 'Dancing dinosaurs broke up the roads': waking, heaving, stretching, then develop step patterns (stamp and stamp and stamp and hop). (Music: 'Elephant' from *Carnival of the Animals*.)

▶ 'The earth belongs to everyone': create a happy dance when everyone dances together, skipping, clapping, turning . (Music: 'Circassian Circle' or 'Lord of the Dance'.)

Moods and feelings

Select key feelings of characters such as Mr Angry, Miss Happy, Master Grumpy and so on, to help children experience the actions and qualities of each mood.

▶ Angry: stamping, jumping, punching, strong still shapes, clenching fists.

▶ Happy: light skipping, clapping, jumping, turning and waving gestures.

▶ Grumpy: slow shuffle, jerky moves changing direction, shrugging shoulders.

▶ Proud: nose high, superior strut, tall, erect stance, shoulder turn.

▶ Frightened: cowering, creeping, moving backwards, turning and looking around.

Try each of the five dance actions (travel, jump, turn, gesture and stillness), exaggerating those features. Develop phrases for each, concentrating on one or two contrasting moods each lesson.

Gymnastics

Themes

Use a focus or theme as the main objective of the lesson(s) to help the children to develop their ability to think about their movements and to become more aware of the different ways they can use their bodies.

Lifting feet high

With this activity, children will, over several lessons, become more aware of the shape of their bodies and the position of the feet in relation to other parts. They will be able to practise both travelling and balancing actions which they have experienced previously. Encourage them to raise their feet higher in hops, skips, jumps or balances on feet; while balancing or travelling on hands and feet (hops or bunny jumps) and while balancing (shoulder balance, seat balance) or moving on tummies, backs or sides. Ideas can then be tried on the apparatus. Encourage holding onto planks, poles or ladders or with part of the body on the floor so that the feet can be the highest part of them.

Push, pull and hold

This focus raises children's awareness of pushing, pulling and balancing actions. Using muscles to:

▶ hold a still shape or to balance;

▶ push up in the air (jumps);

▶ absorb forces slowly (squashy safe landings);

▶ push along (forwards, backwards, sideways);

▶ pull along up or away from parts of the apparatus.

Rocking and rolling

● Explore rocking actions on backs, fronts and from hands to feet (bunny jump). Practise different ways of rolling sideways. Teach teddy bear rolls (sitting with legs wide apart, tip over onto one side of the back, roll across on to one side of the back, roll across shoulders and down the other side of the back to finish facing in the other direction) and introduce half rolls (rocking to stand – keeping feet close to seat – and rocking to tucked shoulder stand). You can then develop these in stages to enable the more formal teaching of forward and/or backward rolls.

● On the apparatus, encourage rolling around the bars/poles, turnovers on the ropes, rolling along the mats or benches and so on.

Bridges – raising and lowering

Focus on thinking of ways of making bridges with the body, using different parts to rest on. Think of different aspects of stability and the span or height of bridges. Encourage the children to hold bridges (balances) for a count of three. Explore different ways of pushing up into a bridge or lowering the bridge and travelling to a new space to make another bridge – this can begin to help control and continuity.

Games

Do not play full-sided games.

Developing ball skills
Passing

With the children in pairs, encourage them co-operatively to practise rolling, bouncing, underarm throwing, tapping or kicking the ball to a partner when stationary and on the move. Encourage the use of two hands, one hand and the non-dominant hand or foot. When passing, stress the need of sympathetic passes and the foot or fingers finishing in the desired direction of the pass. Consolidate the different passes explored at KS1: chest pass, underarm pass and bounce pass, and practise the two-handed, over-head pass and shoulder pass.

Receiving

Stress keeping eyes on the ball, being ready to receive, reaching to gather and bringing the ball into the body. Gradually introduce small-sided games 1v1, 2v1, 2v2 using a variety of passes, such as the bounce, chest and foot passes. Sometimes use conditioned games when only one type of pass is allowed for a specified time.

Aiming

Practise rolling, throwing, kicking the ball at targets (for example, marks on the wall, hoops on the ground, skittles, a partner or other targets devised by the children) or to rebound against a wall.
▶ Tower ball: 3v1, pass the ball around the three players to aim at skittle guarded by one player.
▶ Skittle ball: 2v2 or 3v3, pass the ball, aiming at skittles (use a sixth of netball court).
▶ Bounce ball: 1v1, bounce the ball over a line or low net, using small area (like mini tennis). Emphasize holding the ball for less time, and making the partner move from side to side.

Bat and ball skills

This provides a basis for striking and fielding games.
Start by asking the children to use their hand as a bat, moving the ball along the ground, in different directions, stopping and starting, changing direction and making patterns on the floor. In pairs, they can aim at their partner's bat/hand first when stationary and then with some side-to-side movement.
● Retrieving, fielding: practise different ways of stopping the ball and collecting the ball. Encourage being alert and prepared to move in any direction, trying to put hands and body behind the ball.

● Throwing: suggest throwing a beanbag hard into a hoop only a few metres away. *Can you feel the follow-through action?*

● Made-up games: using a variety of equipment – beanbags, quoits, balls – ask children to make up games in 2s, 3s and 4s. Emphasize using different skills in different games (a bouncing game, an aiming game and so on).

● Games making: focus on passing and receiving in twos, threes or fours.

Physical education

☆Introducing new key elements

Athletics

Athletics can be introduced either as part of games (jumping and skipping) or as a unit of work (problem solving: for example, jumping for height and throwing).

Jumping and skipping

● Explore and practise a range of jumping games. For example, running and jumping over lines; Stepping Stones (to get across to the other side, using either all the stones, the fewest stones, timing groups or individuals, or using only even or odd numbers); hopscotch; Widening River (jumping over a v-shaped rope, starting at the narrow end and progressing to the wide end); making patterns of jumps in a hoop or a rope shape (you could ask the children to repeat their pattern twice or four times, and/or to teach it to their partner).

● Teach skipping – establish the rhythm of jumping backwards and forwards over lines in and out of hoops or rope shapes (a good cardio-respiratory exercise); skipping with a hoop; walking and turning a rope; making a pattern of steps and turns. Share and practise skipping rhymes and actions. (Some children may know French skipping – with a loop of elastic.) Use a longer rope for group skipping. (See the *Ladybird Book of Skipping Rhymes* or the British Heart Foundation's *Jump Rope for Heart*.) If boys see skipping as a girls' activity, emphasize that boxers and footballers skip for fitness.

Problem solving: high jump

Encourage the children to try a standing jump over the cane or rope from different positions:
▶ sideways/facing/at an angle;
▶ close to/far away;
▶ taking off with two feet together/one foot then the other.

Encourage them to have lots of attempts. *With which type of jump can you jump the highest?* Suggest other tasks such as *Can you jump as high as the skittle/a cricket stump/Martin's waist?*

Problem solving: throwing

Safety: Throwing can be a hazardous activity so devise a safety code with the children before starting; for example, *look before you throw; look before you collect.*

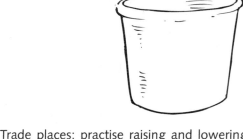

● Design and make a target – or use a box, bucket, hoop, quoit, or chalk marks to practise rolling or throwing for accuracy (start with a large target and gradually reduce the size; gradually move further away; devise a scoring system).

● Throwing hard into a hoop or other target, *How many different ways can you throw a beanbag or soft ball?* Different positions are:

❱ facing the target – overarm, underarm, sideways, squatting, standing; using two hands, one hand;

❱ with backs to the target – kneeling, standing, through the legs.

Outdoor and adventurous activities

There is no one way to teach outdoor and adventurous activities (OAA). Some schools may take children for an activity week which may incorporate some OAA. Other schools may take children on day visits to an environmental or activity centre. Here, some activities are suggested which can be done within the school grounds either as a unit of work, a short series of lessons or as part of geography, mathematics or PSHE assignments.

Parachute games

This is an exciting, different activity which encourages trust and co-operation.

❱ Parachute pass: start with everyone holding on to the parachute standing still, with feet apart and keeping one hand on the parachute at all times. Pass the parachute around faster and faster. Try clockwise and anticlockwise.

❱ Trade places: practise raising and lowering the parachute together, then call names of two children to run under the parachute and change places before the parachute touches them.

❱ Ball surfing: roll the ball around the edge of the parachute.

❱ Bouncing the ball: use the parachute to bounce the ball, keeping it on the parachute. Try bouncing it to a named person.

❱ Parachute golf: use four balls of different colours and divide the class into four colour groups who try to get their ball down the hole in the middle of the parachute.

❱ Sharks: one player (the shark or catcher) moves under the parachute and touches someone's feet. That player is pulled under and becomes the shark and the catcher takes the player's place. (There can be more than one shark.)

Navigation

● Children draw a plan of the classroom (and later the hall or playground) and identify features (door, tables, windows). They mark possible routes from one place to another, then lead a blindfolded partner around their route, holding their hand/arm or giving them verbal instructions only.

● Mark features and landmarks identified by letters on a map of the school grounds. Give pairs of children a map and a set of letter cards (in different orders) and ask them to go to landmarks shown on the cards.

You can ask them to do a number of tasks: pace out the distance between landmarks; record the time taken to visit each landmark, punch the control and return to the start and so on.

Swimming

Swimming is important for safety, survival, confidence, fitness and recreation, but it is unlikely (unless the school has its own pool) that classes will be taken swimming for more than a short time during their primary schooling. Arrangements for swimming, therefore, are unique to each school and very dependent upon facilities, staffing and expertise available, authority guidelines, previous experience of the children, timetabling, transport, funds and many other factors. Your school will need to decide how the swimming requirements are met and so only limited guidelines are offered here.

Note the general requirements which apply particularly to swimming: hygiene, being mindful of others and the environment, responding readily to instructions and following the relevant rules and safety procedures.

● Prepare the children well *before* the lessons take place: what to expect, what to bring, how to take care of dry clothes (use of lockers, for instance). Some children will be confident and competent swimmers while others may be quite fearful of the water and find the pool a worrying or frightening experience. Grouping will need to be considered carefully by or with the instructor. Alert the instructor to any medical conditions (such as ear infections and asthma) and discuss any special arrangements.

● Help to familiarize your class with the environment (depth of water, changing rooms and toilets, fire exit) and discuss water safety principles in the classroom beforehand, including the pool code of practice (walk, don't run; no shouting, jumping or pushing). Consider hygiene requirements (visiting toilets; blowing noses, foot check and bath).

● Insist that children listen and watch and establish a routine for waiting and sitting, before being told to get into the pool. Check the procedure for stopping the class (a whistle, voice or hand signal) and make sure everyone knows it. Be in a position where you can see *all* the children and observe their efforts and responses. Encourage and support them with your interest in their progress.

Ideas bank

● Listen to tapes of dance broadcasts, use them as an accompaniment and develop the ideas in your own way with your own class rather than the voice on the tape.

● Explore ways of encouraging skipping and traditional ball and other games at playtime.

● Mathematics: use the physical activities to engage children in practical timing, measuring and recording. For example: *How many hops in 5 seconds?* Count hops in 10 metres, practise and try to use fewer hops, repeat using other foot. *How far with six strides?*

● Set up a 'Matching symbols treasure hunt' in the school playground, or a treasure hunt for any other things you want children to remember: countries and capitals, number bonds and answers, multiplication tables and so on.

Assessment

Detailed observation of a class of children constantly on the move is difficult. However it is a good idea for you to get a general impression or overall feel for the class response before looking more specifically at the movement of individual children. Ask yourself questions like:

- How do the children respond to/listen to my instructions/suggestions?
- How well do they think for themselves/follow others/do a bit of both/use the space? (Then think how could they be encouraged to use it better.)
- Are they able to use different directions? Are they aware of others when they do so?
- What could I say that might help them?
- How well do they sustain energetic activity?
- Are there other observations I need to make?

Then try to watch how individual children respond and move. Continual review of the class with a focus on a few children at a time is recommended. There will also be times when you note achievement which is particularly significant for a child or the class, or look for specific actions or responses.

- Do they use the whole of the body when required?
- Which parts could they make more use of?
- How controlled are their movements?
- In which ways could they refine their movements? (the fluency of the action – is it easy or awkward?)
- Can they notice, talk about and discuss their ideas and actions in PE?

Dance

- How well do they respond to my voice, the rhythm, sounds or music?
- How imaginative/creative are they?
- Are they achieving the qualities required? When? If not, why not? What might help?
- How well can they isolate and use individual body parts? Do they use some parts more fully?

Gymnastics

- How well do they use the apparatus? Are there pieces of apparatus which I need to encourage them to use more?
- How inventive are their actions?
- Can they hold still shapes on large and small parts of their bodies for the count of three?
- How confidently can they take their weight on their hands (on all fours, bunny jumps)?
- Can they choose, repeat and refine their favourite movements and select appropriate actions?
- Can they select, and perform fluently, two or three appropriate actions with a starting and finishing position, including variations in level and speed?

Games

- How well do they move about the space in different directions and in different ways?
- Can they stop, start and weave in and out of each other?
- Can they use the equipment imaginatively and confidently in a variety of ways?
- How accurately can they roll or throw?
- Can they make up and play a variety of simple games?

Take care to stress the positive aspects of each child's movement and to enjoy and encourage their attempts. There will be as many different responses as there are children.

Information and Communication Technology

In Year 3 you will be building upon the range of skills which children will, by now, have developed. They should generally be happy with the mechanics of loading, saving, printing and inputting information using a mouse and a concept (or traditional) keyboard. Opportunities to practise and develop these skills in interesting and relevant contexts within the classroom need to be given. As Key Stage 2 progresses, they will become more independent in their use of the computer, identifying programs and situations where an ICT solution may be preferable to a non-ICT one.

What should they be able to do?

The emphasis and groupings of the Key elements have changed in the new National Curriculum, although much of the previous coverage remains. The two new Key elements 'Finding things out' and 'Exchanging and sharing information' cover much of the previous Key area 'Communicating and handling information', while the new Key element 'Developing ideas and making things happen' replaces the old Key area 'Controlling, monitoring and modelling'. In addition, there is a new Key element, 'Reviewing, modifying and evaluating work as it progresses', which stresses the need for children to review their work, describe and discuss its effectiveness and talk about how they could improve future work.

Most children should already be familiar with word processing packages and their everyday applications, such as letter writing, and of both the advantages and disadvantages over, say, a pen and paper. Simple terminology such as 'font' and 'word wrap' should be understood. They should be beginning to write straight onto the computer, using its power to help them draft and redraft. Teach them to cut, copy and paste and to consider the finished look of their work. They should know how to change fonts, the size and alignment of text and page orientation.

They will already have used art packages, but should be made aware of the differences between Draw and Paint programs. By this stage, they should be aware of the use of similar commands in different computer packages and be beginning to realize that, once they are familiar with one computer program, the toolbars on others are likely to work in very similar ways. The idea of a database for storing and retrieving information should be understood; encourage them to use this as a method of collecting and analysing information from many areas of the curriculum. Most children should be able to collect information for at least one record and enter it into a database. They should also be able to undertake a search to answer simple questions, be capable of sorting lists of data, both numerically and alphabetically, and to present the information in a graphical form, such as a simple pie chart. They should also be able to search for information on specific topics using CD-ROM databases, such as *Encarta*.

Year 3 children should be familiar with spreadsheets. The use of the *What if I changed this?* type of question can emphasize powerfully how a spreadsheet can model a real-life situation. Finally, children should already have worked with programs such as LOGO and be familiar with programming structures such as REPEAT. The majority should now be building upon this experience to produce more sophisticated routines either on screen or by using a floor turtle.

Practical ideas

Information and Communication Technology

☆ Making a start

Using a CD-ROM encyclopaedia

Give the children a list of rivers in the world (or some other similar list connected with a current topic) and ask them particular questions about the rivers, such as *How long are they? In which country are they?* and *Which towns and cities have grown up on their banks?* The children should find the answers in the encyclopaedia and put them into a table. You can give them a basic table template to fill in, or they can produce their own table within a word processing package. A search for specific information is a more focused task than merely asking them to find out about rivers. If you have a range of books and encyclopaedias available, you can get another group to do the same activity with print-based resources. *Which method do you think is the quickest/most efficient/most enjoyable/teaches you most?*

☆ Introducing key elements

Planning a party

This activity can involve children in planning a simple class party or even something a little bigger. As a group, get them to think of all the things that they may want at a party. They should then find out the costs of all the items – food, drinks, entertainer, paper cups and plates and so on. In groups they should begin to produce a spreadsheet with Items, Quantity, Cost and Total as the headings.

In the Total column put a formula that will multiply the quantity (Column B; Row 2) by the cost (Column C; Row 2) to give you a total cost for all the paper plates. You can then get the children to copy the formula in Column D; Row 2 into all the remaining rows in Column D. This will then multiply all the costs by the quantity of each item required. At the bottom of Column D put a formula to add up the whole row. This will be the total cost of the party. Divide this by the number of people going to the party, and this will give you how much everyone will need to pay. If you decide that they cannot afford that much, they can start changing the figures in the spreadsheet to see where they could save money. *What if we only had one sausage each, rather than two?*, *What would happen if we bought things from a cheaper shop?* and *How much money would we save if we did not have a proper disco, but did it ourselves?* are the kind of questions which the children could investigate.

Initials in LOGO

Children can build upon their existing knowledge of LOGO to produce letters. Start by talking about the types of letters you get on electronic displays in microwaves and CD players. These are 7-segment displays (see diagram below). The children should draw the letters of their own initials, using straight lines where possible. Then they should try to replicate the shapes using LOGO procedures. Some letters are obviously quite easy (L and C) whereas others will need considerably more work requiring PENUP and PENDOWN commands (A and R). Once children are familiar with what is required, they could build up a series of procedures to write words. Here they would need to ensure that, after each letter is drawn, the cursor always finishes in the same place

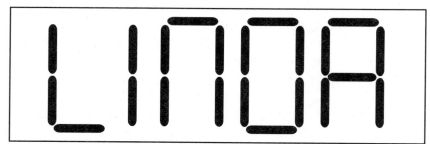

Items	Quantity	Cost	Total
Paper Plates	24	£0.12	=(B2)*(C2)
Orange Squash	2	£1.56	
Sausages	24	£0.22	

and pointing in the same direction, no matter which letter is being drawn.

Shops in the local area

Discuss the local shops with the children and suggest creating a database about them. (This can be part of geography work.) *What do we need to know for the database?* (The names of the shops, what they sell, opening hours, days on which they are closed, location and so on.) Talk, as a group, about the fieldnames and the nature of the data that will be included in the database. This is particularly important in the 'What they sell' field. If children just put in this field a list of items on sale in the shop, it will make the structure of the database very unwieldy and difficult to analyse. A single word such as 'newsagent' or 'butcher' will make the database much more useful. Children should be encouraged to think of questions which the database would help to answer. Easy questions such as *Which shops open at 9 o'clock?* and *How many newsagents are there in the area?* can be followed by more complex ones such as *Which shops stay open the longest?* and *Is there a link between the shop's location and whether it stays open on Sundays?*

Developing key elements

Design a logo

The children can design a logo for a product which they are making, or perhaps for a sporting team. They should use a draw package for this activity, and should also be encouraged to import appropriate clip-art into the package and to combine it with their own ideas. Introduce the lesson with a discussion about what a logo is, ideally by looking at a wide selection of existing logos.

Writing poetry

When the children are writing a poem, let them use a word processor to help them make the words produce a picture. This should provide an opportunity to talk about *tab* keys and aligning text using *left align*, *centred*, *right align* or *justified*. The use of the *enter* key for forcing a new line can also be discussed compared with the normal procedure of leaving it to the computer to decide when a new line should be started. Another useful point to discuss here is to avoid using blank spaces when aligning text. This is because a blank space does not take up a fixed amount of space – it varies depending on how many other letters there are in the line. If you do put in a lot of spaces this makes it very difficult to line up words in columns.

It
was
the
night
before
Christmas
when all through
the house, not a creature
was stirring not even a mouse.
The stockings were hung from the
chimney with care in the hope that
St. Nicholas soon would be there.
S
A
N
T
A
CLAUS

Ideas bank

Taking a line for a walk

Using a paint package, the children can draw a continuous line all over the screen using a *pencil* tool. This will create lots of enclosed shapes on the screen. Then ask them to colour in the shapes using the *fill* tool. The challenge is to make sure that no

two adjacent shapes have the same colour. This activity will give children an opportunity to practise using some of the basic techniques of paint packages, particularly exploring the range of colours which they have available.

Making music

The children can use some music software (such as *Music Explorer*) to make up short musical phrases that sound happy, sad, frightening and so on. These short phrases can be saved and played back later when the class can decide which phrases to use and put together to create a longer piece of music - which might be an accompaniment to a story.

Finding information

In order to use information in a database effectively, children need to know how to use the appropriate search criteria. For example, if they were asked *Which of the animals in this database are yellow?* they would need to look in the 'field name' which identifies the animals' colour and see which 'records' contain the colour yellow. This could be written in a form such as 'colour field = yellow' Children need to understand that questions have to be written in particular ways if they are to obtain information easily from a database. This activity gives them practice in this kind of translation work.

Nice one

Create a piece of word-processed text including many adjectives - and use 'nice' for each one. Individual children then edit the text and change all the 'nice's for other adjectives. Introduce them to the thesaurus in the word processing package to help them with this activity.

Assessment

By the end of Year 3, you would expect the majority of children to:
● use ICT as part of their work in a number of curriculum areas;
● retrieve information from a CD-ROM;
● produce and refine word-processed text;
● draft and redraft simple sentences, saving these between sessions;
● insert and delete characters, words and phrases;
● import, move, resize and edit images;
● save onto hard or floppy disk, and print independently;
● add and edit data in a simple database;
● check accuracy of data entry and results;
● interrogate a database to find the answers to simple questions and question these results;
● produce some artwork using an art package, making use of the mouse;
● paint pictures with straight lines and appropriate regular shapes, saving and loading between sessions;
● use a spreadsheet to answer *What if …?* type questions;
● make a screen robot trace out simple regular shapes;
● use PENUP, PENDOWN, change line colour and use the REPEAT command to build up complex sequences of instructions.

Design and Technology

Designing and making need to be practised in Year 3 in a variety of contexts and with a range of materials. The aim is to develop design and technology capability as a combination of know-how and know-what. The National Curriculum specifies some areas of knowledge and understanding but design and technology draws on others, such as scientific and mathematical concepts . Examples you might use with Year 3 children are described below. You can use them directly, adapt them or use them as models for activities which suit your particular needs.

Design and technology activities in Year 3 develop knowledge, skills and understanding. For instance, by studying a solution to a practical problem children can extend their knowledge of control and structures. They can examine it, mentally disassemble it, name its parts and explain their function. Another activity might be to develop and practise a skill or way of doing something. A focused practical task often serves this purpose. The task can be used to develop either a designing skill, such as considering the practical feasibility of an idea, or a making skill, such as working an unfamiliar, mouldable material into shape.

By themselves, these tasks are unlikely to provide sufficient opportunity for Year 3 children to develop and show their designing and making capabilities. A simple, practical problem which requires some independent designing and making is better suited to this. In Year 3, you can limit materials to those that are likely to be useful and hence provide clues to ensure a successful start.

It is important that there is the opportunity for progression in design and technology capability. In Year 3, existing designing and making skills are to be consolidated and extended. Some simple 'standard' ways of solving certain practical problems can be added to technological knowledge (for example, the push-pull rod, the return mechanism and the use of tubes instead of solid columns for providing support). Materials may require more shaping than in earlier years. Introduce alternative ways of joining and fastening some materials and expect a higher quality of finish. At the same time, your support will often be less immediate.

Children of different capabilities may attempt the same task. In essence, this is differentiation by outcome. You can tune a task to particular children's capabilities by the amount of support you provide and the reserve you show in intervening. Nevertheless, some children who find it difficult to draw or use tools, or to communicate their ideas verbally, may need tasks which offer practice in these skills specifically.

Year 3 children should develop some skill and confidence in using hand tools. They may lack some fine motor skills and act without forethought. Plan for safe working. Consider the safety of the child using the tool, the safety of others and also of yourself. Check tools regularly and withdraw from use any that could be unsafe and repair or replace them. Store them securely. The place where the children use the tools should be in view. Expect Year 3 children to take some responsibility for safe practices and for organizing their workspace. They should recognize some potential hazards in their work and suggest ways of avoiding them.

What should they be able to do?

When they begin Year 3, children should already have experienced some simple designing and making opportunities. This is to be consolidated in Year 3 by:
- continuing to extend their awareness of the manufactured world;

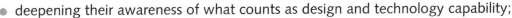

- deepening their awareness of what counts as design and technology capability;
- continuing to extend the range of contexts experienced;
- developing and consolidating designing and making skills;
- increasing technological knowledge and understanding.

Contexts

Design and technology activities drawn from either your broader or subject-specific topics can help to make learning meaningful. However, these may not cover all the aspects of design and technology required by the National Curriculum and sometimes you might organize a separate design and technology activity. In Year 3, such contexts and activities will tend to relate to practical problems encountered in the home, the school and the immediate locality.

Designing skills

Ideas have to be generated by children but vague designing, omitting details of key parts, often leads to failure in making. For instance, children may be unsure how they will contain a push-pull rod. They should practise generating and clarifying ideas and choosing what is likely to succeed. Their technological knowledge may be developed, perhaps by letting them examine a bolt to see the way it is held in place. Children should show a concern for the appearance of their product. Ways of communicating ideas need to be extended and practised (for example, as well as talking and writing, using simple, labelled diagrams, a design for a new playground might be shown by a montage of cut-out trees and play equipment and a structure might be modelled using small boxes). You will have to teach some technological knowledge and know-how directly (for example, the purpose and action of a simple return mechanism).

Making skills and evaluation

The children should be able to suggest alternative ways of working to maintain progress when they meet difficulties. Avoid responding too quickly in such situations. Ask them for suggestions first. Year 3 children should:
- learn to construct a simple plan of action for realizing their designs;
- learn which tools to use for working a range of common materials, like paper, card, plastic sheet materials, wood strip, clay, food, textiles;
- practise measuring and marking out what they need, avoiding waste;
- learn how to shape, join and combine a range of common materials;
- be able to choose, justify and apply some finishes (for example, claddings such as pictures, patterned paper and fabrics);
- practise simple evaluations of their products which tests them, and identifies their strengths and alternative materials and ways of working which might have been used.

Knowledge, skills and understanding
Materials and components

On some occasions, the children should only use familiar materials to consolidate their working skills. When you are offering a wide range of materials (for example, paper, card, plastics, wood, metal foils) supply them in forms which can be fairly readily manipulated by Year 3 children (1cm-square-section wood strip, 1mm-thick plastic sheet). Components children might use include parts of kits, simple switches, wires and light bulbs. Children should explore and apply knowledge of the properties of materials in their products, including the responses of some materials to different ways of working (for example, wood cut across and along the grain).

Mechanisms and control

In Year 3, children should develop a knowledge of the crank handle, push-pull rod (for example, a door bolt), return mechanism (an elastic band to make a push-pull rod return to its starting place), a variety of ways of enabling vehicle motion (table-tennis balls placed under a shallow, upturned box to act in place of wheels), and ways of closing fabric products (using buttons or a drawstring). Energy to make things move will often be provided by muscle power, gravity or a stretched elastic band.

Structures

The children should extend their knowledge of how objects can be supported (by using tubes, for instance) and strengthened (using ribs moulded into plastic boxes). They need to learn that some materials are stronger when loaded in one direction than they are in another (for example, a strip of wood like a ruler may flex and snap readily when bent one way but not in another).

Products and applications

Whenever possible, you should present real products which illustrate the mechanisms and structures the children will make in simpler ways. These are to be at least mentally disassembled. You could extend this into a mini case-study of various versions of a product, highlighting in simple terms how and why different materials and shapes have been used. Children should express their views about what they think is best suited to the need but you may have to guard against a tendency to believe that newer means better. They should also listen to what others prefer and the reasons for their choices.

Quality

You should place an increasing emphasis on the quality of the products that the children make, both in terms of function and appearance. It may be necessary to have a child remake a component rather than use one that was very badly made.

Health and safety

There should be continuing attention given to developing in the children a concern to avoid injury to themselves and others (for example, by having them make and attach warning signs to particular hazards they have identified).

Vocabulary

Knowing the right words helps communication, thinking and learning. The children's vocabulary develops rapidly at this age and their work and case studies provide opportunities for supplementing it with some technological words (*bolt, collar, crank, rigid, flexible* and so on).

Working at higher or lower levels with the key areas

While it is always possible to provide simpler tasks with different contexts, this can make a child's inadequacies, real or otherwise, apparent to all. An alternative is to use a context which allows a variety of possible products or materials (a desk set, say). You can then allocate tasks in a way which ensures that everyone is working at an appropriate level.

Children with well-developed design and technology capabilities can be stretched by offering less help, by expecting more know-how in their products, and by providing practical extension tasks and find-out-about tasks. The latter are activities intended to broaden children's technological knowledge. They are structured research tasks of the kind: *What tools did Stone Age people have? Draw pictures of each one you can find. Think about the tool we use to do the same thing today. Draw it next to your Stone Age picture. Name it.* You will need to make resources available for such tasks.

Practical ideas

Making a start

You may be working on a broad topic such as Moving Around or focusing on a particular area of the curriculum such as Science (Forces and their Effects). These can generate design and technology work on, for instance, simple buggies. Something to catch the children's interest may arise from a recent event in school, a picture, a story or a visit which sets the scene for a problem. Teach the children to clarify their design ideas by responding to *What? Why? How?* questions and by explaining and justifying their intentions. While making, they should be aware of what is and is not working well.

Providing contexts

Children may have some intrinsic interest in solving a problem but they should also see purpose in what they do. The feeling of relevance comes from some obvious need that a task satisfies. Some strategies follow.

Stories

The best stories to use are those which lead up to a need or problem which is then resolved (for example, *Mr Butterby's Amazing Machines* by Pauline Cartwright (Arncliffe). Stop at the point where the need or problem has emerged and discuss how the situation might be resolved. TV stories can be used to set the scene for a problem in the same way.

Visits and visitors

Planned visits which relate to other areas of the curriculum can often have a design and technology element, even on the journey itself. For instance, as the bus passes a bridge, the children's attention may be drawn to tubular supports. You can also use a television programme to provide a 'visit' where it is not otherwise feasible. You might show, for instance, some technological solution to a practical problem (such as a waterwheel) or how something is made (a house being built, perhaps). Often, local people have craft skills which children may not see very often. If you can arrange a visit, structure it so that the children are prepared for it, take part in it and follow up what they have seen.

Challenges

In a sense all design and technology tasks are challenges, but this is when a task is presented explicitly in that form. For example, *Can you think of a way to feed the birds without the cats being able to catch them?*

Supporting designing

Exploring the task

Ensure that the children know what the task means and what it encompasses. Ask questions to stimulate the recall of relevant prior knowledge and check on vocabulary. Supplement this knowledge so that the task is meaningful. Eventually, Year 3 children should begin to contribute to the preparation for a task by using simple sources of information in response to structured questions.

Stimulating ideas and focusing

To help children generate ideas, state the problem and ask for responses to it. Review the suggestions in turn and get the children to consider what is feasible in the classroom and what has most chance of success. Encourage them to be explicit about the vague parts of a design. You might progress to group work in which the children explore the questions *Why? What? How?* together and report back.

Developing new knowledge

It may be necessary to develop additional knowledge at this point. Artefacts can be useful for this purpose, particularly if they are everyday objects in which the parts are visible. The children should examine them and explain how they work or were made. Some things might safely be dismantled and re-assembled. You can use pictures of artefacts in the absence of the real thing.

Supporting making

Choosing materials

Materials come in a variety of forms and sizes. Encourage the children to choose between alternatives and justify their selection. They should do some simple marking out. Discourage waste by, for example, giving them some material that has to be divided between them fairly precisely if they are to have a suitable piece each.

Modelling

Younger children are sometimes so eager to make something that they fix things together and find afterwards that other components no longer fit or function. Discuss the need to try things loosely before fixing them permanently. Have children check that they can fit the final items. Your aim is to develop a consistently mindful approach.

Quality

The purpose of the exercise is not simply to make a product which works or satisfies a need. You should remind the children of what counts as quality and how something which has been well made looks and performs. You might illustrate this with a well-made and a badly-made toy.

Introducing new ideas

In these examples, the first paragraph sets the scene, the second is a focused practical task, and the third is a designing and making task. The ideas may be used as they are, adapted, or serve as models for other activities.

The well (crank mechanism)

● Ask the children how people got water for cooking, washing and drinking in the past. Show a picture of a well. Ask the children to suggest how it was used. Name the crank handle.

● Show the children how to make a model well. A simple well may be made from a square or hexagonal topped paper handkerchief box. Bend a strip of relatively stout card to make a U-shape. Invert it and glue it over the box to provide support for the winding mechanism. Use wire to span the support and bend it to make a crank handle. Fix thread to the wire so it hangs in the hole of the box. A bottle top glued to the thread serves as a bucket. At each stage, ask the children for ideas on how to proceed.

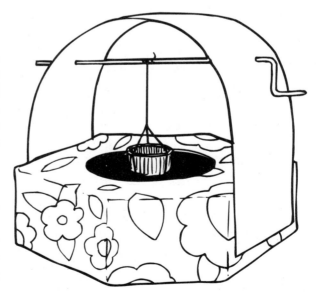

● After making a well, the children might attempt a crane but with less teacher support. This could be applied in solving the problem of letting a dangerous animal, like a bull, out of a pen so that the person who does it is reasonably safe. A large cardboard

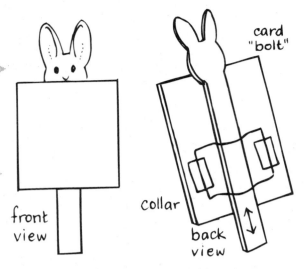
box serves as the pen and the children devise a way of lifting a flap at one end from a safe distance.

Push-pull greetings card

● The children may have made a celebration or greetings card incorporating a simple lever at Key Stage 1. (If so, recall that experience. If not, you could start by making such a card first.) For the push-pull card, show a door bolt and discuss how it works. Name the bolt and collars which hold it in place. Cut out an outline of a face. Attach it to the end of the bolt. Fix the bolt to some stout card using adhesive tape in such a way that, when slid through its collars, the face appears above the edge of the card.

● Discuss how 'bolts' may be made from card. Ask the children to make a pop-up figure using a card 'bolt'.

● This is extended to the use of flat strips of card which can be pulled to and fro through slits in a sheet of card. For instance, if a face is drawn on the card, the strip can have eyes drawn on it so that when it is pulled, the face's eyes move.

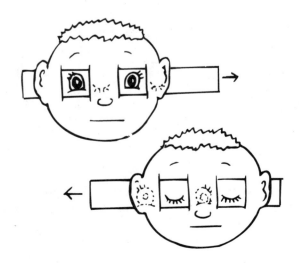

Bags (seams and closures)

● Introduce children to the function of seams and the right and wrong side of the work. They can take old garments to pieces (these may be arranged to make a wall display). Turn a cloth bag inside out and ask the children how it was made.

● To consolidate and apply this knowledge, guide the children in making a small cloth bag for pot pourri. Various ways of closing it may be considered (for example, a button, Velcro, drawstrings, elastic).

● The children design and make a drawstring bag for PE items.

Pecking bird (return mechanism)

● Examine products which have moving parts that return to their original position when released (door handle, press-top pen, clothes peg, stapler, hole punch). These often use springy pieces of steel or coiled springs. Ask the children, *What else could we use to make things go back to their proper places?*

● The pecking bird uses an elastic band as a return mechanism. The children can cut the bird from stout

block of wood

nail (bird free to move on nail)

staple

elastic band

card, using a template if they want. If its foot is nailed loosely to a block of wood and an elastic band stapled to its beak and to the block, it can be made to look as though it is pulling a reluctant worm from the ground. (As the bird is rotated backwards on the nail, the band stretches then pulls the bird forward when it is released.) Finish by painting the bird and cladding the base with carpet or cloth which looks like grass.

● The children look for other examples of return mechanisms amongst the things around them (for example, keys on the computer keyboard, the bulldog clip).

Case study: pegs (product design)

There are a variety of solutions to the problem of attaching clothes to a line. Some pegs depend on the springiness of the material to maintain their grip. Others use a spring (another example of a return mechanism). Give children a number of different kinds of peg to examine and, where possible, disassemble. *What are the materials that they are made from? How do they work? Which is best? What do other people think?*

Ideas bank

A well from strip wood

A simple well may be made using strip wood to make a framework in place of the U-shape of card mentioned above. Card axle supports, glued to the sides of the frame, serve to carry the wire winder. Alternatively, the wire winder may be replaced with a length of wooden dowel. This allows the children to extend their experience of working with strip wood.

Desk set

Using recycled materials, the children might design and make a desk set (for example, a tray with compartments). Ideas may be generated by the materials available and by showing examples of desk sets. The children can finish their products by applying an initial coat of paint, letting it dry, then spattering it with a stiff brush using a different colour. The whole can then be painted with a thin coat of PVA glue to give it a gloss.

Bridges and tubular structures

Card tubes can be used as supports for a bridge and the deck may be made from paper, appropriately stiffened. The problem is to apply what they know, and find a way of making the paper deck stiff enough to take a toy car. Skeletons may also be made from card tubes using free joints. A model tepee may be made from art straws and fabric.

Snow pusher

This needs an opportune occasion when paths are covered with snow and children can be asked how they might clear the snow. A snow pusher can be made by nailing a sheet of wood to a handle (a length of square section wood).

Buggies without wheels

Steel balls and marbles roll easily. This makes them useful for reducing friction and can be illustrated by placing some marbles in a shallow box, inverting it so that the balls rest on a table, and pushing the box. This can be applied in making a 'wheel-less' buggy which can go in any direction. A ball-point pen rolls on its point in this way and steel balls are similarly used to reduce friction around bicycle and car axles.

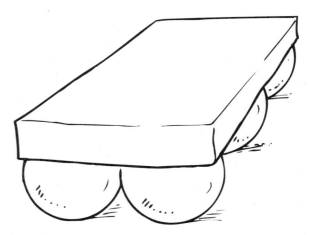

Weaving with wool

The concept of 'weaving' can be introduced using circular cards with radial slits. Wool is woven in and out of the slits to make, for example, a tea-pot stand or table mat to satisfy a practical need. *What have they to do? Why do they work?*

Bird scarer

Sometimes the birds eat the seeds we plant and the fruit we grow. Have the children design and make something which stops them doing this and does not injure the birds.

Case study: footwear

An old, stitched sandal may be taken to pieces and set out to show its parts. The function and properties of each part should be discussed. Compare it with a child's moulded, one-piece plastic sandal.

Case study: key rings

Provide various kinds of key ring for the children to examine and compare for effectiveness. Children discuss their preferences, and make a presentation of their findings.

Boxed scenes

Scraps of wood need not be discarded. Store them in a 'scraps' box. When the box contains a substantial amount of discarded wood, the children can cut and shape the scraps to make a scene – a classroom, for instance. The exercise provides practice in cutting, shaping and fixing wood and some manipulative skills. Mounting the scene in a small box to frame it makes a good display item.

Assessment

In design and technology, both knowledge and skills are assessed. While a product can provide some evidence of skills, it cannot tell you everything. You need to know about designing and making skills which may not show themselves in a product. For instance, were the children able to develop a clear idea of what was to be done? Did they show signs of beginning to think ahead? This means that you need to observe them as they work.

What do they know?

By the end of Year 3, children should know:
● about some simple mechanisms, like a simple push-pull device, a return mechanism and a crank handle, and about electrical circuits;
● about forces and the effect of these on various materials of different shapes;
● how an increasing number of everyday objects function;
● the tools to use to cut and shape the materials they have chosen.
They should have extended their vocabulary so they can discuss tools, materials, and technological matters relating to the products they have made and disassembled.

What can they do?

They should:
● generate some ideas relevant to the task in hand;
● be able to produce a labelled drawing as a design of what they will make, and use alternatives to supplement the drawing (perhaps a loose assembly of materials);
● be able to consider an alternative solution as a possible course of action;
● assess and test their product at various stages;
● make realistic suggestions about how to proceed and accept compromise solutions;
● begin to avoid difficulties by ordering the way they will work and drawing on their knowledge of the properties of materials;
● choose materials, tools and techniques purposefully;
● use tools with some accuracy, measuring, cutting and shaping materials with sufficient precision for assembling the product;
● be able to choose and apply a particular finish.
Products should be perceptibly similar to intentions and children should be able to identify and justify changes during supported evaluation.

Religious Education

RE, unlike other subjects, has to be planned from a local rather than a national document. Agreed Syllabuses differ in the way they present the programme of study but are remarkably similar in what they expect children to do in RE. It is very likely that your Agreed Syllabus expects children to develop a knowledge and understanding of religious traditions, explore fundamental questions arising out of people's experience of life and develop their own ideas and values arising partly out of what they learn in RE. In terms of continuity and progression in RE we should be helping our children to develop a systematic knowledge and understanding of some religions as well as developing their thinking about religious issues and their understanding of common themes across religions, which will contribute to their understanding of religion in general.

In these yearbooks, RE is approached in either of two ways. Some themes are human experience themes. These themes focus on an important question or issue about life such as, *Who is my neighbour?* or *How and why do people celebrate?* This second question underpins the structure for the theme in this book where the children are encouraged to consider important questions about the symbol of light in religious celebrations. The symbolism of light and the human need to use it as a focus for celebration are then explored by looking at a number of examples from the religious traditions.

While children in Key Stage 1 will often learn about religion within the context of human experience themes such as Caring for Others or The World Around Us, children in Key Stage 2 can be introduced to religion in a more systematic way. There are two important aspects of this. The first is that Key Stage 2 children can learn more specific information about religions. The second is the importance of introducing them to some aspects of what it means to think about religion in general. This second aspect, which involves focusing on some basic generic concepts, is the one that informs this chapter. The theme of Celebrating with Light introduces the children to thinking and expressing things symbolically. It also includes the important human experience element of celebration.

What should they be able to do?

You can introduce Year 3 children to more information about religions. They now have the capacity to begin to learn about people, practices and events that are unfamiliar to them. A popular way to introduce children to religions is through festivals. However, merely informing children about a variety of festivals is not an effective way to help them to explore the relationship between learning about religion and learning from it. A mass of information that they cannot process in terms of the key elements of RE has been rightly criticized for confusing children.

The beginning of Key Stage 2 offers you a good opportunity to start to develop children's ability to think intelligently about the meanings around religion, rather than merely gather disjointed bits of information. The theme of Celebrating with Light allows the children to explore the notion of special times when routine and daily round are suspended. They can be encouraged to ponder on the questions of why and what people celebrate and the ways in which they celebrate. The theme of light also gives them the opportunity to begin to understand something of the nature of religious language and communication. All religions communicate essential truths in non-literal ways. In Year 3, most children should be able to begin to understand how people use symbols to express things that are difficult to express in other ways. Only if they are sensitively introduced to such concepts can they develop their thinking about religion as they progress through the Key Stage.

Key area: Knowledge and understanding of religions

Although children at this age will continue to develop their knowledge and understanding through direct contact with people, concrete situations and stories, they can begin to learn about people and practices which are unfamiliar to them. The theme of Celebrating with Light forms the conceptual structure for exploring some key ideas from religious traditions about the relationship between the human need to celebrate and a particular form in which celebration takes place.

Concept development is an essential component of RE teaching at any level. In this key area the range of concepts which can be explored is drawn from the study of religion in general. One such concept is symbolism. In this case, we want the children to understand something of the nature of light as a symbol. This will enable you to explore concepts like goodness and evil. It is important to do this before studying the essential elements of the religious festivals of light.

There are a number of key conceptual ideas in individual religions. For example, in Diwali it is important to understand Rama as an *avatara* (divine incarnation). In the Christian celebrations of Advent and Christmas the key ideas are Jesus as *light of the world* and *incarnation*. While the Jewish festival of Hanukkah is, in one sense, about goodness overcoming evil, the word itself means 'dedication'. This refers to the dedication of the temple by the Maccabees after it had been desecrated by the Syrians.

The best way to introduce the children to such concepts is through the use of artefacts, pictures, video and visits. In this way they can explore the main features of each festival and the way that people celebrate them. Stories can introduce them to the background of the festivals.

Key area: Exploring human experience

The children can investigate the concepts of special time and celebration at the level of their own experiences in their family and community. For the more able children, this would naturally link such times to calendars which are based on the cycle of the year found in the religions.

Encourage children to think about, and respond to questions such as *Why do people celebrate? What do people celebrate? Who do people celebrate with? Why is it important for people to celebrate? What things in life are good and bad? Why is light such an important symbol?*

Questions like these are not only important in themselves but they form a basis on which the children can approach the first key area: Knowledge and understanding of religions.

Key area: Responding to religion and human experience

Responding to questions plays an essential role in this area. The children should be encouraged to respond personally to the type of questions outlined in the first two key areas. You can help them learn how to answer such questions with statements like *I think …* or *I believe …* This helps them to appreciate that people can respond to important questions in their own way which will help them develop important attitudes such as respect for another person's point of view. If you give children this opportunity, some of them may begin to be able to make connections between their own feelings about what is important in their life and how others celebrate what is important in theirs. It should also encourage them to learn to respect the lifestyles and concerns of people who are different from them. Such positive attitudes are essential if the children are to understand the concepts explored in the first two key areas.

Most children should be able to express their responses to what they have learned by drawing pictures, making up poems and writing simple prayers and stories.

Practical ideas

✱ Making a start

Artefacts

You will need the following: an advent candle, hanukkiah, diva lamp.

Wrap or conceal each artefact. Sit the children in a circle and place a candle in the middle. Pass each artefact around asking them to feel it all over and

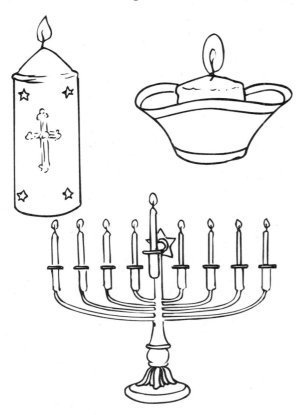

then pass it on. Tell them to remember what it feels like. When each artefact has been passed around, ask the children for descriptions and guesses for each object.

Reveal each artefact and ask the children what they think they have in common, what they might be used for and who might use them.

When everybody has contributed, explain what each object is and how it is used, incorporating the children's suggestions where they were relevant. Carefully light the candle in the middle of the circle and either read out some passages about light yourself or give them to children to read. Here are some examples of the kind of thing you might read.

▸ *If they are blind give them your hand. If they are in the dark, give them a candle.*

▸ *It is better to light one candle than curse the darkness.*

▸ *Jesus said, I am the light of the world; anyone who follows me will not walk in darkness, but will have the light of life.*

Discuss candles

As an immediate follow up to the first activity, ask the children why they think candles are used so often by religious people in churches, temples and synagogues and other religious buildings. *Why are there lights at Christmas and Diwali? What do you think the candle light stands for?*

Symbols

Explain what a symbol is; a means of representing something or recalling something. You could first give some examples such as the poppy which recalls all the people who lost their lives in the wars and which was chosen because of the poppies that grew in the battlefields of the First World War. Then ask the children if they can think of any examples of symbols. (Prompt them, if necessary: road signs, washing symbols on clothes, the Macdonalds 'M', the thistle for Scotland, the leek or daffodil for Wales, the harp for Ireland, the maple leaf for Canada, the wheelchair symbol for facilities for the disabled, coloured ribbons, flags, town crests, coats of arms, the panda for the WWF, the symbol (often an animal) used for each child in the reception class to mark his/her peg and so on. Before starting this theme, look out for symbols in your immediate locality so you can remind them of these familiar ones.) You could make a display of symbols, adding to it as children and their families develop the search.

Light as a symbol

Discuss ways in which light is used as a symbol. When we are in the dark and want to see we switch on a light – in the old days people lit a candle – and so we use a candle to mean that light shows us the way and helps us to see; light means happy things and so we use candles and coloured lights on birthdays and at Christmas.

Write a poem

You could write a class poem about light with pictures or get children to write their own. Here is an example of a poem produced by a Year 3 class.

Light is seeing
Light is not being in the dark
Light is happiness
Light is learning
Light is knowing
Light is good things
Light is warm
Light is hope
Light is God.

An alternative to this is to compose a cinquain. This is a five-line poem composed of a one-word title, two adjectives, three verbs, a four-word statement and one noun. With the children, compile a list of adjectives which describe light, then a list of verbs, then some nouns and then a four-word statement to sum up what light means. (This work could form part of Literacy Hour.) Then you select from these lists. The result might read like this.

Light
Clear, bright
Dazzles, warms, guides
Light guides the world
Peace.

Read some myths

Read together some creation stories which, for the people of various cultures, explore the origins of light. Examples can be found in *Creation Stories* by J Mayled (Wayland). Follow this up with paintings of the stories or get the children to write their own story about how they think light came into being.

Science links

Link your discussions about the importance of light with science work. *What happens if you starve some plants of light?* (See page 85.)

Read a story

It is important that children don't get the impression that light always means good (light can be blinding) and darkness always means bad. One way of balancing these symbols is to read a book like *The Owl Who Was Afraid of the Dark* by Jill Tomlinson (Methuen). Here dark is exciting and kind. Too much concentration on this can lead to a lack of focus for the RE work but it could prove a good story to be reading alongside this work.

Greetings cards

Bring in a selection of greetings cards – ask the children if they can bring some too. Use everything from birthday and anniversary cards to religious cards for baptism, Easter, Christmas, Diwali, Eid and Hanukkah. Ask the children why we send such cards. *What is a celebration? What are we celebrating at* birthdays, weddings, anniversaries, Christmas, and so on? Why do you think it is important to celebrate these things? What do you celebrate that is important? How many of the cards show lights as part of the celebration?

Write about celebration

Get the children to write about a particular celebration that they have enjoyed or one that they enjoy regularly.

Introducing new key areas

After exploring light as a symbol often used in celebrations, you can introduce the children to specific religious festivals which are generally regarded as festivals of light. After a general discussion it is best if each festival is studied in turn.

Artefacts and pictures

Look again at the advent candle, diva and Hanukkiah. Ask the children what the light in each might stand for. They may not know much! Explain that you are going to explore what each light means for the people who are Christians, Hindus and Jews as well as details about their festivals of light. Show the children a picture of each festival (good sources are the Westhill photopacks on Christians, Jews and Hindus, Thomas Nelson's *Living Religions* photopacks and Folens photopacks). Discuss the pictures with the help of the information provided with them, but remember this is only an introduction.

Diwali

Diwali is the Hindu festival of lights (there is a Sikh Diwali as well). It is celebrated in October or November according to the Hindu lunar calendar. For many Hindus the story of Rama and Sita forms the focus of celebration. The story celebrates the defeat of Ravana and the victory of good overcoming evil. Diwali also falls at New Year and is associated with Lakshmi, goddess of prosperity and wealth. Diwali is celebrated in the home as well as the temple.

Watch a video

A good introduction to Diwali is the BBC Watch programme, which is now available on a commercial video called *Festivals*. It introduces the story, the making of rangoli patterns and so on as well as a song 'Diwali is Here'. This song can also be found in *The Tinderbox* (A & C Black).

Act the story

If you have been able to show the *Festivals* video you can go straight on to acting the story. If not, read the story together. Suitable examples can be found in *Myths and Religious Stories from Around the World*, retold by Jean Bews (Sherbourne Press), the *Festivals* resource pack by Bill and Lynn Gent (BBC), or the *Ramayana*.

You could make masks for the main characters: Rama, Sita, Ravana (the demon with ten heads) and Hanuman the monkey king. Or make stick puppets and perform a shadow play (templates are available in *Festivals* in the Teacher Timesavers series (Scholastic Ltd).

Make a diva lamp

You can easily make these from Plasticine or clay. Put a night light inside and use them in a crowd scene in your Diwali play.

Look at pictures of Hindu gods

Rama is an avatara (divine incarnation) of God (Vishnu the preserver) and represents great courage and strength of character in overcoming the demon Ravana. It is important to explore with the children the idea that God (who is one) can be imagined in many forms because God is too big an idea for people to understand fully. You can get Hindu pictures very easily from Indian shops or artefact suppliers (see resources list, page 159). Good pictures to look at would be Rama and Sita, Krishna (an avatara representing love and devotion) and Radha, Ganesha, the elephant-headed god who removes obstacles, and Lakshmi, goddess of wealth and posterity. Look at the symbolism in the pictures and discuss their possible meanings. You may need to look at books on Hinduism to help you with this.

Make Diwali cards

Bring in a selection of Diwali cards to look at. (You can get these from Indian shops or artefact

suppliers.) Get the children to design their own cards based on divas or pictures of the gods. Often Diwali cards will feature pictures of the main gods, already discussed. Have them write a greeting inside: Happy Diwali, Happy New Year.

Make Rangoli patterns

These lovely, colourful patterns are made at Diwali to welcome Lakshmi. You will need some black paper, glue and coloured powder. It would be good to look at some designs and books can be bought from Indian shops. Or ask the children's librarian at your local library to help. If you can't find a book, use basic shapes in different colours. Hindus will also use the swastika sign on rangoli. This is an old sign meaning welcome.

Make some Mehndi patterns

Asian girls often celebrate by decorating their hands with these patterns. The children can draw around their hands and decorate the hand outlines, cut them out and make a display.

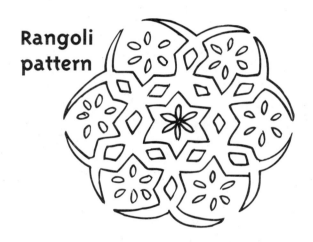

Rangoli pattern

Mehndi patterns

Hold a Diwali assembly

Base an assembly around the Diwali story, perhaps using the play you have acted out. Sing the 'Diwali is Here' song, play some Indian music. There is a special prayer for Diwali:

O Lord, lead me
from darkness to light and
from death to immortality.
Let there be peace on earth
Om Shanti Shanti.

Advent and Christmas
Read the Bible

● Begin by looking at the passage in St John's Gospel (ch 8 v 12): 'I am the light of the world. Whoever follows me will have the light of life and will never walk in darkness.'

Discuss the passage. *What does it tell us about what Christians believe about Jesus?* Do the children know any examples from the life or teaching of Jesus which explain what these beliefs are?

● Look at the Epiphany story in Matthew (ch 2, vv 1–12).

Discuss the idea of God as a guiding light. *How does God guide people? What was so special about Jesus?*

Christian hymns and carols

Small groups can look through hymn books to find carols about light or hymns in which light is a symbol. For example, 'We Three Kings', 'From the Darkness Came Light', 'Light up the Fire', 'Flickering Candles in the Night' (*Come and Praise*, BBC). Ask the children to copy some and illustrate them.

Make an advent crown

You could make an advent crown, an example of how Christians use light as a symbol. It has four candles in a circle of evergreen with a fifth candle in the middle to be lit on Christmas day. Each child could make a small one using birthday candles.

Each child could also make a Christingle. It is derived from the Moravian Church and is now popular in this country. An orange represents the world, a candle as Jesus as light of the world, a red ribbon represents the blood of Jesus, 4 cocktail sticks with fruit on them represent the four seasons and the fruits of the earth.

Make Christmas cards

Make Christmas cards that emphasize the symbol of light. The children can draw candles, Christmas tree lights and so on.

Religious education

Compile a Christmas book

Get each child to compile a Christmas book which includes the story of Jesus' birth and the Christian symbols of light. Ask them to draw and write about each symbol.

Hanukkah

Hanukkah is a Jewish festival which lasts for eight days and means 'dedication'. It falls in the third month of the year on 25 Kislev. (This usually means in December according to the Western calendar.) Jews remember the victory of Judah the Maccabee over the Syrians who were oppressing them. Jews believe God helped them overcome the Syrians. The Hanukkiah, which is lit at Hanukkah, is a symbol of victory of justice and good overcoming evil.

Read and act the story

Versions of the story can be found in *Jewish Festivals Omnibus* (RMEP). Information and stories can also be obtained from The Board of Deputies of British Jews, Woburn House, Tavistock Square, London WC1H 0EZ and The Council for Christians and Jews, 1 Dennington Park Road, London NW6 1AX.

Make a Hanukkiah

You can make one from clay, Plasticine or other suitable material. There should be eight branches with a ninth in the middle called the shamash or servant light. This should be higher than the rest of the candles.

On the first evening of Hanukkah, as soon as three stars can be seen in the sky, the first candle is lit using the servant candle. A second candle is lit on the second day and so on – the candles are lit from left to right.

The lights must burn for 30 minutes each night and Jews are not allowed to work or read by the candlelight. The Hanukkiah is placed in the window to remind passers-by that Judah the Maccabee saved the Jewish religion.

Play the dreidel game

At Hanukkah, Jewish children play a special game with a spinning top or dreidel. On each side there is a letter from the Hebrew alphabet which stands for one of the words *Nes Gadol Hayah Sham* which means 'a great miracle happened here'.

You can make a dreidel by using card with a stick through the centre to make it spin. The BBC *Festivals* resource pack by Bill and Lynn Gent shows you how to make one and how to play the game.

Alternatively, you can buy dreidels from artefact suppliers.

Make some latkes

These are a kind of potato cake. Jews also eat doughnuts at Hanukkah. They are both cooked in oil and so remind them of the miracle of the oil. You can make latkes quite easily.

4 potatoes
1 grated onion
4 tablespoons self-raising flour
2 eggs
salt and pepper

Grate the potatoes and drain. Mix with the other ingredients and fry small amounts (one tablespoon of the mixture) in oil, browning on both sides.

Resources

Artefacts and pictures are available from: Articles of Faith, Resource House, Kay Street, Bury, Lancs BL9 6BU, Tel 0161 763 6232 (mail order); Westhill RE Centre, Westhill College, Selly Oak, Birmingham B29 6LL, Tel 0121 415 2258 (mail order); The Jewish Education Bureau, 8 Westcombe Avenue, Leeds LS8 2BS, Tel 0113 293 3523; Folens Publishers, Albert House, Apex Business Centre, Dunstable LU5 4RL, Tel 01582 472788; Gohil Emporium, 381 Stratford Road, Birmingham B11 4JZ, Tel 0121 515 1183 (mail order).

Religious education

Assessment

When you have finished this theme you will have a pretty good idea whether the children have enjoyed it. You should also be able to judge by the outcomes how much they have learned. Evaluation can take the following form.

What do they know?

There is a great deal of information which the children could have picked up. Being selective it is possible to suggest that most children should know:
- the names of the religious festivals of light;
- the main story associated with each festival;
- some of the ways in which people celebrate each festival;
- some of the reasons why people celebrate each festival;
- some of the things for which light is used as a symbol.

What can they do?

Children in a typical Year 3 class can be expected to respond at different levels. In this theme, for example, all or most may be expected to be able to:
- talk about examples of different kinds of lights;
- retell the basic elements of a story;
- express their ideas in written or visual form;
- give some examples of celebrations.

Some children may also be expected to:
- understand and explain the symbolism of light generally;
- understand and explain the meaning of the festival stories;
- give reasons why celebration is important for humans.

What have they experienced?

The children should have:
- listened to stories associated with each festival;
- contributed to discussions;
- learned about the festivals through video and pictures;
- handled artefacts appropriately;
- expressed their ideas in oral, written and visual forms.